Vladimir V. Karacharovskiy, Ovsey I. Shkaratan,
Gordey A. Yastrebov

TOWARDS A NEW RUSSIAN WORK CULTURE

Can Western Companies and Expatriates Change Russian Society?

With a foreword by Elena N. Danilova

ibidem-Verlag
Stuttgart

Bibliografische Information der Deutschen Nationalbibliothek
Die Deutsche Nationalbibliothek verzeichnet diese Publikation in der Deutschen Nationalbibliografie; detaillierte bibliografische Daten sind im Internet über http://dnb.d-nb.de abrufbar.

Bibliographic information published by the Deutsche Nationalbibliothek
Die Deutsche Nationalbibliothek lists this publication in the Deutsche Nationalbibliografie; detailed bibliographic data are available in the Internet at http://dnb.d-nb.de.

Coverpicture: © copyright 2016 by M. Karacharovskya

Translated by Julia Kazantseva

Note: The book relies on the findings of studies supported by the Khamovniki Foundation for Social Research (Project 2013-002, Expatriates in the Russian Labor Market), the Russian Foundation for Humanities (Project 13-03-00493, Russian and Foreign Professionals in the Russian Institutional Environment: Interaction and Transformation of Work Practices), and the Basic Research Program at the National Research University Higher School of Economics

∞

Gedruckt auf alterungsbeständigem, säurefreien Papier
Printed on acid-free paper

ISSN: 1614-3515

ISBN-13: 978-3-8382-0902-9

© *ibidem*-Verlag
Stuttgart 2016

Alle Rechte vorbehalten

Das Werk einschließlich aller seiner Teile ist urheberrechtlich geschützt. Jede Verwertung außerhalb der engen Grenzen des Urheberrechtsgesetzes ist ohne Zustimmung des Verlages unzulässig und strafbar. Dies gilt insbesondere für Vervielfältigungen, Übersetzungen, Mikroverfilmungen und elektronische Speicherformen sowie die Einspeicherung und Verarbeitung in elektronischen Systemen.

All rights reserved. No part of this publication may be reproduced, stored in or introduced into a retrieval system, or transmitted, in any form, or by any means (electronic, mechanical, photocopying, recording or otherwise) without the prior written permission of the publisher. Any person who does any unauthorized act in relation to this publication may be liable to criminal prosecution and civil claims for damages.

Printed in Germany

Soviet and Post-Soviet Politics and Society (SPPS)
ISSN 1614-3515

General Editor: Andreas Umland,
Institute for Euro-Atlantic Cooperation, Kyiv, umland@stanfordalumni.org

Commissioning Editor: Max Jakob Horstmann,
London, mjh@ibidem.eu

EDITORIAL COMMITTEE*

DOMESTIC & COMPARATIVE POLITICS
Prof. **Ellen Bos**, *Andrássy University of Budapest*
Dr. **Ingmar Bredies**, *FH Bund, Brühl*
Dr. **Andrey Kazantsev**, *MGIMO (U) MID RF, Moscow*
Prof. **Heiko Pleines**, *University of Bremen*
Prof. **Richard Sakwa**, *University of Kent at Canterbury*
Dr. **Sarah Whitmore**, *Oxford Brookes University*
Dr. **Harald Wydra**, *University of Cambridge*

SOCIETY, CLASS & ETHNICITY
Col. **David Glantz**, *"Journal of Slavic Military Studies"*
Dr. **Marlène Laruelle**, *George Washington University*
Dr. **Stephen Shulman**, *Southern Illinois University*
Prof. **Stefan Troebst**, *University of Leipzig*

POLITICAL ECONOMY & PUBLIC POLICY
Prof. em. **Marshall Goldman**, *Wellesley College, Mass.*
Dr. **Andreas Goldthau**, *Central European University*
Dr. **Robert Kravchuk**, *University of North Carolina*
Dr. **David Lane**, *University of Cambridge*
Dr. **Carol Leonard**, *Higher School of Economics, Moscow*
Dr. **Maria Popova**, *McGill University, Montreal*

FOREIGN POLICY & INTERNATIONAL AFFAIRS
Dr. **Peter Duncan**, *University College London*
Prof. **Andreas Heinemann-Grüder**, *University of Bonn*
Dr. **Taras Kuzio**, *Johns Hopkins University*
Prof. **Gerhard Mangott**, *University of Innsbruck*
Dr. **Diana Schmidt-Pfister**, *University of Konstanz*
Dr. **Lisbeth Tarlow**, *Harvard University, Cambridge*
Dr. **Christian Wipperfürth**, *N-Ost Network, Berlin*
Dr. **William Zimmerman**, *University of Michigan*

HISTORY, CULTURE & THOUGHT
Dr. **Catherine Andreyev**, *University of Oxford*
Prof. **Mark Bassin**, *Södertörn University*
Prof. **Karsten Brüggemann**, *Tallinn University*
Dr. **Alexander Etkind**, *University of Cambridge*
Dr. **Gasan Gusejnov**, *Moscow State University*
Prof. em. **Walter Laqueur**, *Georgetown University*
Prof. **Leonid Luks**, *Catholic University of Eichstaett*
Dr. **Olga Malinova**, *Russian Academy of Sciences*
Prof. **Andrei Rogatchevski**, *University of Tromsø*
Dr. **Mark Tauger**, *West Virginia University*

ADVISORY BOARD*

Prof. **Dominique Arel**, *University of Ottawa*
Prof. **Jörg Baberowski**, *Humboldt University of Berlin*
Prof. **Margarita Balmaceda**, *Seton Hall University*
Dr. **John Barber**, *University of Cambridge*
Prof. **Timm Beichelt**, *European University Viadrina*
Dr. **Katrin Boeckh**, *University of Munich*
Prof. em. **Archie Brown**, *University of Oxford*
Dr. **Vyacheslav Bryukhovetsky**, *Kyiv-Mohyla Academy*
Prof. **Timothy Colton**, *Harvard University, Cambridge*
Prof. **Paul D'Anieri**, *University of Florida*
Dr. **Heike Dörrenbächer**, *Friedrich Naumann Foundation*
Dr. **John Dunlop**, *Hoover Institution, Stanford, California*
Dr. **Sabine Fischer**, *SWP, Berlin*
Dr. **Geir Flikke**, *NUPI, Oslo*
Prof. **David Galbreath**, *University of Aberdeen*
Prof. **Alexander Galkin**, *Russian Academy of Sciences*
Prof. **Frank Golczewski**, *University of Hamburg*
Dr. **Nikolas Gvosdev**, *Naval War College, Newport, RI*
Prof. **Mark von Hagen**, *Arizona State University*
Dr. **Guido Hausmann**, *University of Munich*
Prof. **Dale Herspring**, *Kansas State University*
Dr. **Stefani Hoffman**, *Hebrew University of Jerusalem*
Prof. **Mikhail Ilyin**, *MGIMO (U) MID RF, Moscow*
Prof. **Vladimir Kantor**, *Higher School of Economics*
Dr. **Ivan Katchanovski**, *University of Ottawa*
Prof. em. **Andrzej Korbonski**, *University of California*
Dr. **Iris Kempe**, *"Caucasus Analytical Digest"*
Prof. **Herbert Küpper**, *Institut für Ostrecht Regensburg*
Dr. **Rainer Lindner**, *CEEER, Berlin*
Dr. **Vladimir Malakhov**, *Russian Academy of Sciences*

Dr. **Luke March**, *University of Edinburgh*
Prof. **Michael McFaul**, *Stanford University, Palo Alto*
Prof. **Birgit Menzel**, *University of Mainz-Germersheim*
Prof. **Valery Mikhailenko**, *The Urals State University*
Prof. **Emil Pain**, *Higher School of Economics, Moscow*
Dr. **Oleg Podvintsev**, *Russian Academy of Sciences*
Prof. **Olga Popova**, *St. Petersburg State University*
Dr. **Alex Pravda**, *University of Oxford*
Dr. **Erik van Ree**, *University of Amsterdam*
Dr. **Joachim Rogall**, *Robert Bosch Foundation Stuttgart*
Prof. **Peter Rutland**, *Wesleyan University, Middletown*
Prof. **Marat Salikov**, *The Urals State Law Academy*
Dr. **Gwendolyn Sasse**, *University of Oxford*
Dr. **Jutta Scherrer**, *EHESS, Paris*
Prof. **Robert Service**, *University of Oxford*
Mr. **James Sherr**, *RIIA Chatham House London*
Dr. **Oxana Shevel**, *Tufts University, Medford*
Prof. **Eberhard Schneider**, *University of Siegen*
Prof. **Olexander Shnyrkov**, *Shevchenko University, Kyiv*
Prof. **Hans-Henning Schröder**, *SWP, Berlin*
Prof. **Yuri Shapoval**, *Ukrainian Academy of Sciences*
Prof. **Viktor Shnirelman**, *Russian Academy of Sciences*
Dr. **Lisa Sundstrom**, *University of British Columbia*
Dr. **Philip Walters**, *"Religion, State and Society", Oxford*
Prof. **Zenon Wasyliw**, *Ithaca College, New York State*
Dr. **Lucan Way**, *University of Toronto*
Dr. **Markus Wehner**, *"Frankfurter Allgemeine Zeitung"*
Dr. **Andrew Wilson**, *University College London*
Prof. **Jan Zielonka**, *University of Oxford*
Prof. **Andrei Zorin**, *University of Oxford*

* While the Editorial Committee and Advisory Board support the General Editor in the choice and improvement of manuscripts for publication, responsibility for remaining errors and misinterpretations in the series' volumes lies with the books' authors.

Soviet and Post-Soviet Politics and Society (SPPS)
ISSN 1614-3515

Founded in 2004 and refereed since 2007, SPPS makes available affordable English-, German-, and Russian-language studies on the history of the countries of the former Soviet bloc from the late Tsarist period to today. It publishes between 5 and 20 volumes per year and focuses on issues in transitions to and from democracy such as economic crisis, identity formation, civil society development, and constitutional reform in CEE and the NIS. SPPS also aims to highlight so far understudied themes in East European studies such as right-wing radicalism, religious life, higher education, or human rights protection. The authors and titles of all previously published volumes are listed at the end of this book. For a full description of the series and reviews of its books, see www.ibidem-verlag.de/red/spps.

Editorial correspondence & manuscripts should be sent to: Dr. Andreas Umland, c/o DAAD, German Embassy, vul. Bohdana Khmelnitskoho 25, UA-01901 Kyiv, Ukraine. e-mail: umland@stanfordalumni.org

Business correspondence & review copy requests should be sent to: *ibidem* Press, Leuschnerstr. 40, 30457 Hannover, Germany; tel.: +49 511 2622200; fax: +49 511 2622201; spps@ibidem.eu.

Authors, reviewers, referees, and editors for (as well as all other persons sympathetic to) SPPS are invited to join its networks at www.facebook.com/group.php?gid=52638198614
www.linkedin.com/groups?about=&gid=103012
www.xing.com/net/spps-ibidem-verlag/

Recent Volumes

149 Alexander Sergunin, Valery Konyshev
Russia in the Arctic
Hard or Soft Power?
ISBN 978-3-8382-0753-7

150 John J. Maresca
Helsinki Revisited
A Key U.S. Negotiator's Memoirs
on the Development of the CSCE into the OSCE
With a foreword by Hafiz Pashayev
ISBN 978-3-8382-0852-7

151 Jardar Østbø
The New Third Rome
Readings of a Russian Nationalist Myth
With a foreword by Pål Kolstø
ISBN 978-3-8382-0870-1

152 Simon Kordonsky
Socio-Economic Foundations of the Russian Post-Soviet Regime
The Resource-Based Economy and Estate-Based Social Structure of Contemporary Russia
With a foreword by Svetlana Barsukova
ISBN 978-3-8382-0775-9

153 Duncan Leitch
Assisting Reform in Post-Communist Ukraine 2000–2012
The Illusions of Donors and the Disillusion of Beneficiaries
With a foreword by Kataryna Wolczuk
ISBN 978-3-8382-0844-2

154 Abel Polese
Limits of a Post-Soviet State
How Informality Replaces, Renegotiates, and Reshapes Governance in Contemporary Ukraine
With a foreword by Colin Williams
ISBN 978-3-8382-0845-9

155 Mikhail Suslov (ed.)
Digital Orthodoxy in the Post-Soviet World
The Russian Orthodox Church and Web 2.0
ISBN 978-3-8382-0871-8

156 Leonid Luks
"Zwei Sonderwege"? Russisch-deutsche Parallelen und Kontraste (1917-2014)
Vergleichende Essays
ISBN 978-3-8382-0823-7

Contents

Foreword to the English edition 7

Introduction 15
    Acknowledgements 21

**Chapter I. Competition of cultures
in the newest international division of labor** 23

**Chapter II. Foreign professionals (expatriates)
in national economies** 39

**Chapter III. External and internal origins
of the Russian work culture** 57

**Chapter IV. The role of foreign and foreigners
in Russian state-building** 85

**Chapter V. Demand of the Russian economy
for foreign human capital** 105

**Chapter VI. Social criteria for evaluating the role
of foreign professionals in Russian society** 127

**Chapter VII. The cultural distance between
Russian and foreign professionals** 143
    Applying quantitative methods
    to measure cultural differences as a research task 143
    "We" and "they" face to face:
    the cultural distance within multinational work teams in Russia 149
    Summary of findings 160

**Chapter VIII. Effectiveness of business
and cultural exchange in the segment of highly skilled labor.** 163

Conclusion 189

Selected bibliography 199

Information about the authors 221

Appendix 1. Qualitative research tools **223**
  1A. Interview guide for interviewing Russian professionals working together with foreign professionals (expatriates) in multinational teams 223
      I.   Introduction Module 223
      II. Socialization Module 223
      III. Business Module 224
      IV. Creativity Module 226
      V. Projections Module 227
  1B. Interview guide for interviewing foreign professionals (expatriates) working together with Russian professionals in multinational teams 228
      I.   Biography and Motivations Module 228
      II. Socialization Module 228
      III. Business Module 230
      IV. Creativity Module 233
      V. Projections Module 233

Appendix 2. CVSCALE methodology in the original and translated into Russian **235**
  2A. Scale items in the original 235
    Power Distance 235
    Uncertainty Avoidance 236
    Collectivism 236
    Masculinity 237
    Long Term Orientation 238
  2B. Russian translation of scale items 239
    Шкала «Дистанция власти» / Power Distance 239
    Шкала «Избегание неопределенности» / Uncertainty Avoidance 240
    Шкала «Коллективизм» / Collectivism 241
    Шкала «Маскулинность» / Masculinity 242
    Шкала «Долгосрочная ориентация» / Long Term Orientation 243

Foreword to the English edition

This book was first published in Russian in 2015, when Russia was already in isolation because of the international political environment and the conflict in Ukraine. The issues raised in the book are more than ever relevant for our country. The authors emphasize the fact that Russian culture has never developed in isolation (even in Soviet times). One cannot but agree with them that "today, when yet again Russia and the West are clashing in competition, the question about the role of foreigners and everything foreign in Russia's civilizational 'leaps' throughout its history up to the technological breakthrough of the twentieth century is once again on the agenda. The path Russia takes in the twenty-first century largely depends on the answer to this question." And Russia is currently facing new challenges triggered by international competition and global processes.

This book is thought-provoking and useful for readers interested in Russia and in cultural and historical studies. I would like to highlight some of its strong points.

The book is implicitly placed in the context of disputes on the national culture, which have been an integral part of the intellectual and spiritual life of the Russian intelligentsia over centuries. Details thereof are provided in different chapters of the book. Debates and reflections on the Russian culture and foreign influence and, accordingly, ways of Russia's development have become a tradition since the times of Peter the Great. Some people suggested limiting foreign influence. For example, in his article *Love for the Motherland and National Pride*, Russian historian Nikolay Karamzin acknowledged the educational role of foreign teachers and tutors, but repeatedly proposed replacing them with Russians. He wrote, "A foreigner will never understand our national character and, consequently, cannot adapt to it in education. Foreigners very rarely do us justice. We treat them kindly and reward them, and they, once having crossed the border to Courland, mock or berate us <...> and publish absurdities about Russians." Karamzin concluded this idea as follows: "A nation, like an individual, initially always imitates, but eventually should become *oneself.*"[1] Many philosophers tried to find an answer to the "eternal" Russian question—to change by directly adopting features of another culture, primarily the Western, more modernized one, or to change remaining oneself? However, what does "remaining oneself" mean? All nations have their own identity, but in Russia it is also a question of how Russia's place is seen in relation to the West and the East. Nikolai Berdyaev, the famous Russian philosopher and publicist of the early twentieth century, believed that "Only recognition of Russia's antinomy, its terrific inconsistency, can help solving the mystery of the Russian soul."[2] In his work *The Fate of Russia* he wrote, "Russia cannot identify itself as the East and oppose itself to the West. Russia must also perceive itself as the West, the East-West, the uniter of the two worlds and not the divider."[3] The authors discourse about the Russian culture more or less in the same spirit.

After the collapse of the Soviet Union, debates about the national work culture are not so much of an existential or cultural nature; rather, they focus on economic performance, thus acquiring a practical aspect. Discussions center on the capacity and features of the work culture that either facilitate or hamper Russia's economic development, and on the possibility of changing them in a market environment. Primarily, this concerns the Soviet legacy. A crisis of the labor activity is assumed to be one of the reasons that necessitated perestroika. Its essence was the alienation of labor, when its sense-making function was lost for the absolute majority of the workforce. Therefore, no radical reform in the country is possible without a change in the attitude to work. The real effectiveness of any economic activity is determined by the way it impacts the attitude to work. The main focus was to be made on eradicating the Soviet legacy in the sphere of labor, namely low motivation and low performance. The reformers pinned their hopes mainly on the American market development model, with Russia often compared to Latin America and the emerging markets of Southeast Asia and China.

---

1   N.M. Karamzin. *Selected Writings in Two Volumes.* Foreword by P. Berkov and G. Makogonenko. M. — L. Khudozhestvennaya Literatura,1964. p. 287.
2   N. Berdyaev. *The Fate of Russia.* M.: Sovetskiy Pisatel'.1990. p. 10.
3   Ibid, p. 28.

Little was said about the Western European models with highly developed social security systems.

According to researchers E. Shershnyova and Yu. Feldhoff,[4] it is insufficient to simply oppose the Soviet system and the market economy in order to understand the behavior and work motivation of an individual in a society undergoing structural reforms. One must be aware of the national culture, historical traditions, and the basic values of Russian mentality. Can we directly adopt the experience of successful organizations that fully belong to other cultures or combine elements of different cultures in companies or firms? These issues are particularly important in modern Russia, at a time when market reforms and restructuring of the economy are under way.

The obvious advantage of the book is the manner of investigating work culture in association with foreign influence. The authors do not limit themselves to comparisons with the Soviet past, but extend their analysis to a broader historical context of Russia's development.

The authors' treatment of the issue and subject matter of work culture is noteworthy. The book is distinguished by its approach at the convergence of the *civilizational and modernization paradigms*. It is important to bear in mind that the modernization approach implying universal linear development culminating in a market economy and liberal democracy has been dominant in Russian sociological and economic literature since the late 1980s. Neoliberal economists were the principal promoters of this approach. For example, such terms as "catch-up modernization" and "delayed modernization" are often used to characterize Russia. The culture of the developed West serves as a model of modernity. Culture is evaluated based on a logical dichotomy—qualities resembling Western ones are labeled as features of modernization, and those differing are considered to be non-modernized. The simplified logic is such: the one with progressive features shall win the competition race; therefore, it is necessary to discard and transform those cultural traits that do not meet the requirements of modern development. The view that the Russian work culture is a factor hampering economic

---

4 E. L. Shershnyova, Yu. Feldhoff, *Kultura Truda v Protsesse Sotsialno-Ekonomicheskikh Preobrazovanii: Opyt Empiricheskogo Issledovaniya na Promyshlennykh Predpriyatiyakh Rossii (Work Culture at the Time of Social and Economic Change: An Attempt of Empirical Research at Russia's Industrial Enterprises)*, St. Petersburg, Petropolis, 1999 (in Russian).

success is quite widespread in domestic literature. However, this book demonstrates that there can be no simple and one-dimensional solutions to the extremely complex issues of extensive social transformations, such as the changes that Russia has been experiencing since the late 1980s. In contrast to the modernization paradigm assuming a universal unilinear path of development, the book proposes a multi-component vision of work culture development. It offers the readers a fresh perspective—how to modernize the work culture within a particular civilizational model, how to enrich it without undermining. The authors consider the national work culture—a basic element of reforms—in two ways: as a phenomenon resistant to external institutional and cultural impact, but at the same time capable of changing under their influence.

Although the authors do not depart from the logic of modernization theories, they rather focus on attempting to identify converging factors, those areas where the cultures can enrich and complement each other within one civilizational model. The authors suggest distinguishing a culture's sustainable characteristics determined by civilizational factors and to regard them as such in order to avoid mistakes "common for reformers when they try to eradicate qualities indigenous for a national culture and introduce instead some 'proper' qualities, generally, of 'western' origin."

Chapter one, *Competition of cultures in the newest international division of labor*, gives an idea about different civilizational models of integrating into the international division of labor. The authors provide historical examples of various countries "dropping out" of the universal path of development, examples of successful economies that combine the advantages of national institutional and cultural foundations with globalization trends.

Chapter two, *Foreign professionals (expatriates) in national economies*, contains a review of the academic literature on the subject. Although it does not exhaust the entire field of research, it gives the readers an understanding of current theories and methodologies and provides an update on studies addressing cross-cultural interaction. The growing rate of cross-cultural exchanges triggered by globalization necessitates a study of the role that foreign professionals (expatriates) play in national economies throughout the world. The authors place emphasis on foreign professionals (expatriates) as a relatively new and understudied driver of sociocultural and socio-economic modernization. The basic premise is the assertion that expatriates are agents of modernization, and, respectively, play a positive role in economic development. Special attention is given to professionals engaged in different sectors of the economy in various countries; the mixed issues of their integration and performance are considered.

Chapter three, *External and internal origins of the Russian work culture*, analyzes the specifics of the Russian work culture. The authors suggest considering culture as a derivative of internal civilizational factors (national geo-cultural/symbolic environment) and the external influences resulting from interaction with social actors of foreign (primarily Western) origin, which the authors believe modernize the work culture. Russia's history knows several periods of so-called modernization leaps. It was then that the role of foreigners was particularly significant.

The role of foreigners in Russia is placed in a historical context. Chapter four, *The role of foreign and foreigners in Russian state-building*, provides a historical background and analyzes the role of expatriates throughout Russia's long history and over the recent decades. It identifies periods when the areas of influence of foreign ideas and foreign specialists (foreigners in government, science, industry, and the army) expanded and contracted. The authors actually formulated their understanding of the mechanisms shaping a culture as "assimilating and digesting" (I would add "in practice"—ED) foreign (mostly "Western") values, which is an integral part of sustainable Russian development.

Chapter five, *Demand of the Russian economy for foreign human capital,* substantiates the need for foreign professionals, which actually always exists everywhere, especially in an increasingly competitive environment during the transition of economies to innovative development. The chapter provides examples of innovative potential and competitiveness of selected Russian companies and firms in the world market. It also estimates the effects of the ongoing "brain drain" in the post-Soviet period. Professionals from Western countries are considered here as bearers of a higher culture of production, technology, and research. However, the authors distinguish various functional tasks that the expatriates perform within the national economy. They note that the expatriate structure, which existed until now, served to control foreign capital invested in Russia rather than promote the modernization of the Russian economy, thus "servicing" the existing economic system. Today, the Russian society needs the expatriates as much as it also requires a change in their functional structure.

The remaining three chapters are devoted to the findings of the empirical research conducted by the authors. These chapters are based on a survey of Russian and foreign employees of companies operating in the Russian market. The authors focused on highly skilled foreign specialists working alongside Russian professionals. They applied various sociological techniques, both quantitative and qualitative. The result is a rather extensive picture of the interaction of Russian and foreign work cultures.

The book stands out from other studies on work culture by its methodological approach, which is especially noteworthy. It attempts to steer the discussion on interpreting work culture towards *disclosing the essence and practices* underlying the so-called cultural values, and this adds methodological value to the study. The applied methodology suggests abandoning cultural stereotypes and stereotypical reactions, and appealing instead to the essence revealed in particular practical situations and circumstances. The authors quite rightly note that "interaction with representatives of other cultures became part of the production process involving specific business practices rather than abstract romanticized values, forcing people to overcome daily their long-term habits and stereotypes, because the company's performance was at stake, and, respectively, the assessment of their own input." This also explains why the authors turn to such an understudied topic as foreign employees (expatriates).

The findings of the research based on in-depth interviews with Russian and foreign professionals are presented in Chapter six, *Social criteria for evaluating the role of foreign professionals in Russian society*. The chapter considers different types of foreign employees in terms of their impact on the development of the national work culture. The authors attempt to identify the ideological principles of the contemporary expatriates' activity in Russia, and to highlight among them groups with a fundamentally different potential impact on the development of Russian companies. Two criteria are used to distinguish different types of foreign professionals with different "utility" for Russian companies. The first criterion is the nature of integration of foreign professionals into the Russian society; the second—their perception of the Russian society.

Chapter seven, *The cultural distance between Russian and foreign professionals,* analyzes cultural differences in groups of jointly working Russian and foreign professionals based on their survey conducted under a formalized program using the CVSCALE international methodology. The authors measure the cultural differences in multinational teams in Russia, and analyze cultural diversity in comparison with the aggregate national cultural profile of both Russians and expatriates.

Chapter eight, *Effectiveness of business and cultural exchange in the segment of highly skilled labor,* presents the nontrivial empirical research findings. The authors identified the qualities that hamper or promote the effective work of the team or the enterprise in general and those qualities that were not common for foreign/Russian professionals but emerged in the process of working alongside Russian/foreign colleagues. They revealed the areas of tension between Russian and foreign professionals, highlighting at the same time that both parties mutually evaluate many of each other's business qualities as positive and worth adopting. The study identified three basic ways in which foreign professionals perceive the Russian society.

As was already mentioned, a sufficient number of studies has appeared where labor values and motivation are generally addressed in the logic of modernization theories and compared directly with western culture values. The "mirror" analysis proposed in the book focuses on the mutual evaluation of each other's business skills by Russian and foreign professionals working in multinational teams, and the cross-cultural adoptions resulting from such joint work. This allows seeing the features of Russian workers as evaluated and perceived by foreigners—as in a mirror. Indeed, as we see from the interviews, expatriates triggered certain important changes at the level of work teams. The interviews demonstrate that "foreigners engaged in different sectors of the Russian labor market helped Russian employees not only find out what 'Western-style' working and thinking means, but also acquire hands-on experience. Some lessons the Russians appreciated, some rejected, and in certain cases the expatriates themselves had something to learn." This method highlights the ambiguity and inconsistency of Russian work culture features (when such features have reverse sides, which can manifest themselves either negatively or positively, depending on the actual circumstances) and allows identifying areas of beneficial adoptions.

Chapter eight also addresses the features of the so-called "invariant core of the Russian business culture." On the basis of empirical and literary evidence, the authors demonstrate the ambivalent nature of the main features that form the core of the Russian work culture. Following Berdyaev's line of thought, the authors conclude, "Duality, the ability to combine polar qualities is, perhaps, an independent and long observed sustainable feature of the Russian culture."

The book is a brilliant example of scientific reflection on the pressing issues of Russia's development. Besides contributing substantially to the knowledge of the Russian work culture, it stimulates the readers to reflect on the issues raised. The book will undoubtedly be useful for researchers, specialists, experts in culture studies, politicians, sociologists, managers, and economists, as well as everyone who is interested in the complex issues of the development of Russia and its work culture in an increasingly competitive environment. The appended research techniques greatly enhance the practical methodological value of the book.

Dr. Elena N. Danilova,
Head of the Center for Theoretical Studies and History of Sociology,
Institute of Sociology, Russian Academy of Sciences
Member of the Executive Committee
of the European Sociological Association

Introduction

"We need Europe for a century or so; then we will turn our back on it,"[5]—this phrase of the first Russian Emperor Peter the Great perfectly expresses the essence of Russia's modernization breakthroughs throughout its history. As Soviet historian Lev Gumilev wrote, Peter was actually wrong: "Russia needed Europe for about 25–30 years, because Russians adopted all European achievements with amazing ease. It became possible to 'turn the back' on Europe already by the middle of the eighteenth century, and that is exactly what Peter's own daughter Elizabeth did in 1741."[6] Peter was also wrong in something else. Seeking "Western" assistance proved to be a recurring rather than a one-time historic event. However, it is also true that every time it took Russia just several years to assimilate the achievements of other civilizations—a process for which the latter had needed decades and centuries.

Assimilating and "digesting" foreign (mostly "Western") values became a sustainable pattern of Russian development. As a result, Russian economic culture was shaped against the backdrop of a continuous competition between national and foreign standards, values, and socio-cultural patterns; and it is sometimes difficult to distinguish clearly what is inherent/traditional and what has been imported, this being typical for frontier civilizations.[7] In one or another historic version, the political and cultural doctrine was born as a result of perpetual struggle between the "Slavophiles" and the "Westerners", with victory continuously dialectically passing from one camp to the other. However, Russia never lost its core, and absorbing Europe's achievements, it remained true to itself.

Herein, we will attempt to consider two constituent elements of the Russian civilizational development—national culture and foreign influences. We believe this topic is especially relevant today, when cultures

---

5 Cit. ex Gumilev L.N. *From Rus' to Russia:* Essays on ethnic history. M.: Ecopros 1994. p. 287.
6 Ibid.
7 See., *e.g.,* Akhiezer A.S. *Russia: A Critique of Historical Experience.* M.: Philosophical Society of the USSR, 1991.

and civilizations compete directly, becoming counterparties in the latest international division of labor.

It was important for us to discuss the role and functions of foreigners and "foreign" in the socio-economic development of Russia in the context of the characteristics and challenges of the current global economy phase—globalization, post-industrialism and informationalism. It was also important to assess the possibility and expediency of foreign influence on the development of Russian culture and the degree to which such influence is productive or, on the contrary, counterproductive.

These issues are at the core of our review of external studies addressing the phenomenon of foreign professionals in national economies (expatriates), historical retrospective of the role foreigners played in Russian state-building, and identification of historically conditioned channels along which imported culture elements influenced Russia's social and economic development.

Foreign influence is a phenomenon, which seamlessly penetrated different areas of Russian life. We should not fail to mention the fact that imported ideas are relevant even for the ethno-religious foundations of Russian society. Indeed, we know that Orthodoxy was initially a phenomenon imported from Byzantium, whereas, for example, the Russian founders of "Spiritual Christian" sects (Doukhobors and Molokans), famous for their economic patterns and more efficient than the Orthodox village, were admirers of European theology.

The "milestones" indicating the dramatic expansion of the foreign specialists' areas of influence (foreigners in government, science, industry, and the army) are clearly traceable in Russian history. This theme is echoed in Russian history—from the legendary "invitation of the Varangians", through its maximum expression in the era of Peter the Great with the tremendous influence of Western experts on the development of national industry and science, through the Elizabethan time and the golden age of the St. Petersburg Academy of Sciences, where our great scientists, such as Mikhail Lomonosov, had the opportunity to work together with invited European scientists, among them world-famous names—Leonhard Euler, brothers Nicolaus and Daniel Bernoulli, Christian Goldbach, Georg Bernhard Bilfinger, Joseph-Nicolas Delisle, and others.

The trend went on until the end of the nineteenth–beginning of the twentieth centuries with Russia's German industrialists and multinational industrial workforce. It was not discontinued even in the twentieth century, when, ironically, the very existence of the "iron curtain" became not so much a demarcation line as a symbol of the "West's" importance at the new stage of Russia's history. This manifested itself both in a fantastic technological rivalry, and in the lives of ordinary people, when sporadic contacts with foreigners and the appearance of West European and American movies, music, and books in the USSR created a romanticized and sustainable image of the Western civilization as a certain idealized reality that one absolutely wanted to be part of.

At the same time, there were always objective factors of civilizational scale, which opposed or distorted the influence of foreign values, adapting it to the realities in which the Russian society was developing. Such factors include geo-climatic (harsh climate and huge distances), geopolitical (close presence of strong opponent countries—in different periods, both from the West and from the East), geo-economic (the proximity of an older and technologically more powerful western civilization forced to resort to the mobilization model of development), etc.

The 1990s became a separate period that renewed the need in the "West"—not just as a dream about beautiful life, but also as a center supplying Russia with new human capital in management, science, and technology. That was a tragic and controversial era marked by a degradation of key sectors of the economy, brain drain, and a growing number of lost technologies; a period of strategic mistakes and irreparable losses that were the logical consequences of policies of the time. At the same time, it was an era of genuine interest in Russia, a period when foreigners started developing the emerging Russian market, its opportunities and resources. From that time on we can speak about the rise of the largest tide of foreign specialists coming back to Russia. That period shaped the domestic professionals who are currently the core of the Russian economy.

In the first decade of the twenty-first century, when Russia's chances to regain its status on the world stage were promising, the Russian economy became extremely appealing for global business, which resulted in an explosive growth of foreign presence. Multinational financial conglomerates, retail chains, assembly plants...—during this period, Russia accumulates a fundamentally different experience of interacting with foreigners.

Due to the increasing presence of multinationals, the interaction of the Russian and foreign cultures moved to the micro level, the level of companies. It became part of the production process involving specific business practices rather than abstract romanticized values, forcing people to overcome their long-term habits and stereotypes on a daily basis, since the company's performance was at stake, and, respectively, the assessment of their own input.

The years 2008 and 2009 became a new turning point, when first the global financial crisis, followed several years later by the current cooling in relations between Russia, on the one side, and the USA and Europe, on the other side, marked the beginning of a reverse trend—reduction of the number of foreign specialists in Russia. The era of expanding spheres of influence of foreigners and foreign yet again started giving way to the era of Russia's "distancing" from the West. Can it be that at the new development stage of the Russian economy and society foreign professionals have already accomplished their mission? Can it be that the Russian culture has already absorbed enough western values, assimilated them, turned into its own, and is ready to go on independently?

As Samuel Huntington wrote in his famous work *The Clash of Civilizations and the Remaking of World Order*, "Initially, Westernization and modernization are closely linked, with the non-Western society absorbing substantial elements of Western culture and making slow progress toward modernization. As the pace of modernization increases, however, the rate of Westernization declines and the indigenous culture goes through a revival."[8] Perhaps, this has already happened?

These processes are particularly interesting in the segment of highly skilled labor. Therefore, this segment became the target of our research. In today's global economy, emphasis is made on social groups with a high human capital—on professionals. Indeed, they drive modernization processes, and the path that modernization takes depends primarily on them. Business practices implemented by representatives

---

8   Huntington, Samuel P. *The Clash of Civilizations and the Remaking of World Order*, New York, Simon & Schuster, 1996. pp.75–76.

of this stratum are more important than their personal attitudes, because they demonstrate to what extent the professionals are able to change the environment and transform institutions.

Close occupational interaction and business communication between professionals from different countries working together in the same companies is a characteristic feature of modern economies. Cultural differences, on the one hand, serve as an educating factor and a kind of collective benchmarking; on the other hand, they can become a barrier to effective professional communication.

What role do highly skilled foreign specialists (expatriates, also referred to as expats) currently play in our economy? Today, this is a strategically important social group in Russian society. Expatriates participate in strategic decision-making in the largest companies operating in Russia, although their ideology and core values may sometimes differ fundamentally. Is it possible to consider expatriates as agents of new Russian modernization? Will Russia need foreign human capital in the near future, or can it develop without it? We propose a typology of foreign highly skilled labor that allows identifying groups of expatriates varying by the intensity and focus of their impact on the development of Russian companies.

Finally, expatriates can serve as a mirror of our culture. Oddly enough, in the judgments of today's expatriates, we suddenly recognize our own features revealed in studies dating back 10–30 years, which the great minds of the past had also depicted. These include the ethics of idleness, indifference to the "middle area of culture"[9] (notion introduced by Russian philosopher Nikolay Lossky to indicate the area between private life and state affairs—authors' note), love of the "strong hand", last minute "all hands on board" manner of work, and the astounding ability to make superhuman efforts, mobilize and break through. That is all about us. Does it mean that we do not change?

---

9 The notion was initially introduced by Russian philosopher Nikolay Lossky to reflect the phenomenon that "people have little interest in material culture", in "facilitating their everyday existence" (see, e.g., his works *Absolute Good* (1944) and *The Character of the Russian People* (1957)). For Russians, the indifference to the "middle area of culture" has traditionally meant, that they attached little importance to the everyday aspects of life that lie in-between personal/private, on the one hand, and state affairs, on the other hand. This includes everything that is no longer important personally and not yet significant nationally.

We are now living in a period, when yet again Russia and the West are clashing in competition. The question about the role of foreigners and everything foreign in Russia's civilizational "leaps" throughout its history up to the technological breakthrough of the twentieth century is once again on the agenda. The path Russia takes in the twenty-first century largely depends on the answer to this question.

The empirical basis of the research underlying the book is as follows:

- Interviews with foreign and Russian professionals working in Russia in multinational teams of Russian companies and in Russian branches of international companies (in-depth interview guides are provided in Appendix 1). We have conducted 166 interviews.
- Survey of foreign and Russian professionals working together in Russia. The survey was conducted under a formalized program using the CVSCALE[10] international methodology, which is an adaption of Geert Hofstede's well-known method for measuring cross-cultural differences and has been designed as a tool, which allows making respective measurements at the individual rather than the group (as in Hofstede's method) level (the methodology is described in Appendix 2). The survey covered 221 respondents.

The majority of our foreign respondents came from EU countries and the USA, which made it possible to focus on the classic "Russia—West" comparative analysis version.

---

10 Boonghee Yoo, Naveen Donthu, Tomasz Lenartowicz. *Measuring Hofstede's Five Dimensions of Cultural Values at the Individual Level: Development and Validation of CVSCALE* // Journal of International Consumer Marketing, 23: pp. 193–210, 2011.

Acknowledgements

We would like to express our sincere gratitude to the Khamovniki Foundation for Social Research and personally to its founder and Chairman of the Board Mr. Alexander Klyachin. Without his support and trust in the success of our research this book would not have been possible.

The Khamovniki Foundation for Social Research was our leading sponsor. It allocated funds for our studies and provided a special grant for the research (Project 2013-002, *Expatriates in the Russian Labor Market)*. The manifold support of the Khamovniki Foundation enabled us to focus on the fieldwork. In addition, the Foundation sponsored the publication of our monograph in Russian and financed its translation and issue in English. Such a helpful and encouraging attitude to our research gave us the opportunity to achieve our goals.

We are deeply grateful to Cholpon Beyshenalieva, Director of the Khamovniki Foundation, for the unique, friendly and pleasant cooperation in the course of implementing the research project and preparing the book for publication.

We would like to extend genuine gratitude to our close colleagues of long standing—Dr. Simon Kordonsky, Chairman of the Khamovniki Foundation Expert Council, Dr. Vladimir Leksin, Dr. Sergei Khaikin, Dr. Elena Danilova, Dr. Juri Plusnin, and Dr. Natalia Guseva for their involvement and valuable comments.

The project would have been impossible without the direct participation of foreign specialists—expatriates—working in Russia and our compatriots—Russian employees of international companies, who agreed to answer our questions and provided invaluable information during interviews. In this respect we would like to emphasize the contribution of John Harrison, the Editor of the *Moscow Expat Life* magazine, his genuine openness, insightful discussion and unique expert judgments.

We would not have managed without the assistance of our colleagues, who undertook the subtle and difficult work of interviewing and conducting surveys. Here we would like to mention the staff of the Laboratory for Comparative Analysis of Development in Post-Socialist Countries at the National Research University Higher School of Economics—Elena Gasyukova, Sergey Korotaev, and Anna Krasilova; our colleagues from other universities and research centers—Dmitry Anisimov (Moscow), Irina Gulyaeva (Saint Petersburg), Larissa Kosygina (Novosibirsk); Oksana Koptyaeva (Nizhny Novgorod); as well as students of the National Research University Higher School of Economics Natalia Kirsanova, Anna Malova, and Alexandra Kramchenkova.

Finally, we would like to heartily thank our translator Julia Kazantseva for her professional, committed work with the text and the attentive, friendly dialogue with us, the authors.

Chapter I.
Competition of cultures in the newest international division of labor

Participating in the newest international division of labor is key to the emergence and development of promising segments of the national economy. In today's world, any country is doomed to lag behind if it is excluded from the global circulation of capital, goods, and technology. Introducing new production and organizational technologies and applying the achievements of the post-industrial stage of development in business and everyday life is the most important factor of this kind of economic restructuring.

Manuel Castells, one of the most influential social thinkers of our time, has shown that the principal distinction of the current [information technology] era from its historical predecessors consists in the fact that if previous technological revolutions remained for long in a relatively limited geographic area, information technologies have spread throughout the globe with lightning speed. This means "the immediate application to its own development of technologies it [the technological revolution] generates, connecting the world through information technology. To be sure, there are large areas of the world, and considerable segments of the population, switched off from the new technological system... Furthermore, the speed of technological diffusion is selective, both socially and functionally. Differential timing in access to the power of technology for people, countries, and regions is a critical source of inequality in our society."[11] Such inequality, according to Castells, poses the threat of entire national and even continental economies being excluded from the international division of labor.

Compression of the global economic space and tremendous acceleration in the movement not only of capital, but also of knowledge, values, and socio-cultural interaction and activity patterns *make culture, which determines the ability of nations to absorb new knowledge, val-*

---

11 Castells M. (1996, reprinted 1997) *The Information Age: Economy, Society and Culture. Volume 1. The Rise of the Network Society.* Malden, MA; Oxford, UK: Blackwell Publishers Ltd. p. 34.

ues, and approaches to work, as well as generate new global values, an extremely important driver of economic development.

This is also relevant for the future of Russia. Our task is to verify the impact of national culture on the restructuring of the Russian economy and its incorporation into the process of globalization not only as a resource-based, but also as a technological economy.

Different requirements for individual stages of the manufacturing process have resulted in its spatial division and global cooperation. Thus, American companies prefer to keep first-stage production facilities—R&D (high-skilled intellectual labor and pilot production) at home in the USA; to move the second stage—manufacturing of components requiring skilled manual labor—to regions with high technical culture and established traditions of skilled industrial labor (to Scotland, for example); and to locate the third stage of the production cycle, which requires routine, labor-intensive, and low-skilled work (assembly, manufacturing of components for electronic products, etc.)—in countries such as Hong Kong, the Philippines, and Indonesia.

There is evidence that currently the global divide lies primarily not between countries with advanced technology and those with unskilled assembly, but between countries integrated into the information economy and those excluded from it (that do not have the minimum conditions for introducing advanced technologies). Here, however, it is important not to land at the "tail-end" of somebody's chain, thus remaining a cultural isolate excluded from the global business community.

The "new international division of labor" of the 1970s was driven by low production costs, which gave investment advantages. Currently, it is more important for major companies to penetrate a local market, which requires an enhanced technical infrastructure, developed means of communication, a particular quality of technical labor, a general educational level of the population, and a competitive culture.

But has Russia so far not participated in the international division of labor? Of course it has, but in the most primitive form—exchange of goods. Moreover, exports of raw materials and imports of finished goods (with the exception of armaments, where Russia retains the position of a leading exporter) continue to dominate Russia's foreign trade. At present, the international division of labor in the form of foreign trade in finished goods gives way to another form—cooperation between suppliers of intermediate products representing manufacturing enterprises from different countries. In developed economies, the share of such enterprises in the manufacturing sector's total output has been long ranging from one-third to a half.[12]

Such a division of labor has two important effects: an intensive exchange of state-of-the-art production and organizational technologies and an increase of foreign investment in the economy of the host country. The cost of labor, availability and infrastructure of free economic zones, the political situation in the host country, the national legal system, including legislative acts regulating labor relations, the length of the working week, and other factors play an important role in such investment decisions. An essential item of this list are the qualitative characteristics of the host country's workforce.

Measuring the quality of workforce relies on a range of common parameters universal for all countries[13] (usual remuneration, general cultural and educational level), as well as a set of its national-specific features that are difficult to measure.[14] It is rather simple to determine the general features of the workforce—you just have to study several statistical handbooks of the potential host country for the investment. Thus, it is easy to determine that wages acceptable for a Russian worker and engineer are several times lower than those that Western specialists with a similar profile and skills require. The general cultural and educa-

---

12 Bereznoy A.V., Pankin S.M., Slavinsky V.A. et al. *Production Crosses National Borders*. M., 1991. p. 73.
13 See: Supyan V.B. *The Evolution of Labor Force: Qualitative Characteristics* // USA - Economy, Politics, Ideology. 1990. No. 5.
14 Perhaps, the most successful and recognized attempt to measure the workforce's national cultural dimensions is Geert Hofstede's study: Hofstede G. *Culture's Consequences: International Differences in Work-Related Values*. Beverly Hills, L., 1980; Hofstede G. *Culture's Consequences: Comparing Values, Behaviors, Institutions, and Organizations Across Nations*. Second Edition, Thousand Oaks CA: Sage Publications, 2001. See also: Merritt A. *Culture in the Cockpit: Do Hofstede's Dimensions Replicate?* // Journal of Cross - Cultural Psychology, Thousand Oaks; May 2000; Vol. 31; Murphy W.H. *Hofstede's National Culture as a Guide for Sales Practices Across Countries: The Case of a MNC's Sales Practices in Australia and New Zealand* // Australian Journal of Management, Sydney; Jun 1999; Vol. 24; Ulijn J. *Innovation, Corporate Strategy, and Cultural Context: What is the Mission for International Business Communication?* // The Journal of Business Communication, Urbana; Jul 2000; Vol. 37; Veiga J. *Measuring Organizational Culture Clashes: A Two-Nation Post-Hoc Analysis of a Cultural Compatibility Index* // Human Relations, New York; Apr 2000, Vol. 53, and other publications.

tional level of a Russian employee is comparable to that of a Western one. This, in particular, is due to the influence of the multigenerational "school" of industrial production, which, according to some scientists, has been a critical factor in shaping the modern man. It is much more difficult to identify the national-specific characteristics of the workforce. This requires special research.

Modern technologies have one important feature—they substantially increase the role of humans in the manufacturing process. Japanese researcher Masanori Moritani writes, "In our days, the mechanical civilization is undergoing profound change: by acquiring a "brain" [computer], it starts experiencing a strong impact of the cultural environment."[15] A tremendous growth in the importance of creative, knowledge-intensive and information-intensive labor significantly increases the human role in the modern production process. Human mistakes become increasingly more "costly"—the "cost of errors" rises by an order of magnitude.

This latest situation also has a distinctive practical consequence. In developed economies production relies on educated people aged from 25 to 40 years. Even in these countries, over one-third of human resources remains redundant. This accelerating trend will most likely result not in mass unemployment, but in maximum labor flexibility and mobility, individualization of work, and, ultimately, a highly fragmented social structure of the labor market.[16]

The new economy raises the question about the employees' key personal qualities—qualities that were not in mass demand in industrial production. Management adequate to such production regarded labor as any other type of productive resource, since individual, including ethnocultural traits of the workers had a very limited impact on the production process. This type of management begins to falter, not only in the information sector, but—according to the law of connecting vessels—in the whole economy (due to the unity of society as a sociocultural system).[17]

15　Moritani M. *Advanced Technology and the Japanese Contribution*. M., 1986. p. 47.
16　Castells M. (1996, reprinted 1997) *The Information Age: Economy, Society and Culture. Volume 1. The Rise of the Network Society*. Malden, MA; Oxford, UK: Blackwell Publishers Ltd. Pp. 272–280.
17　Lapin N.I. *Sociocultural Approach and Societal Functional Structures*. // Sotsiologicheskie issledovaniia. 2000. No. 7.

It turns out that by many parameters a trained, skilled, and mature worker at some workplaces with a certain type of production process demonstrates the worst possible results, and in another production environment with a different organization of labor—the highest. A key factor underlying these differences is the type of work culture, which generally has ethnic and civilizational features. We should take into account that instead of suppressing, the development of the global economy intensifies the cultural and institutional diversity of nations—societies, promoting at the same time their interdependence.

An analysis of significant differences among the most economically and technologically advanced countries demonstrates this. Here, two dominating models of the new economy are distinguishable. The first—"the service economy model" is represented by the United States, the United Kingdom, and Canada; the second—"the industrial production model"—by Japan and Germany. France in this classification occupies an in-between position leaning toward the service economy. Italy appears to be introducing a third model based on "networks of small and medium businesses adapted to the changing conditions of the global economy, thus laying the ground for an interesting transition from proto-industrialism to proto-informationalism."[18]

Western authors also propose other classifications,[19] which all come to the same conclusion about the diversity of current economic models in the most advanced countries of the world. In this regard, the persistent efforts of radical liberals to squeeze Russia into the American development model always appeared ridiculous.

An important conclusion results from the above. All previous (from the industrial age) assessments of the employees' competencies, the ranking of national workforce / human resources by their efficiency—performance, and the evaluation of successful management methods are now largely a matter of historical rather than practical interest. In this context, it becomes increasingly important to determine how relevant for the new economy are qualities specific for Russian employees and Russian management traditions.

---

18   Castells M. Ibid. pp. 222–225.
19   Lane D. *The Transformation of State Socialism in Russia. From a "Chaotic" Economy to Cooperative Capitalism Coordinated by the State?* // Mir Rossii. 2000. No. 1.

Successful transfer and perception of new knowledge and values directly depend on the workers' cultural characteristics, as well as on the national work and management culture. We should bear in mind that work culture and education are closely interrelated, but these concepts are not identical. With adequate investment, the educational level can be raised rather quickly, whereas the culture of work is a result of national historical development and traditions; therefore, changing it is a rather long-term issue.[20]

National culture, which forms the worker's sustainable behavioral stereotypes, plays a special role in forming the labor potential, especially its innovative component. Currently, applied socio-anthropological studies of ethnic features of the workforce are widespread throughout the world. Over the past decades, multinational corporations have always been relying on information about the ethnocultural distinctions of its future employees whenever establishing business abroad. From individual features and traits, experts synthesize generalized portraits of "typical employees": Japanese, Chinese, Muslim, etc. Based on this data, multinationals plan foreign investment, establish labor incentives, and design the most effective industry structure. Russians also have their cultural distinctions, although in the past, business management never considered this. However, already the first studies have demonstrated that using these distinctions, relying on them can have significant economic value.[21]

Consequently, comparative international studies of the extent to which various national workforce contingents were available and suitable for one or another operation gained importance. Two major lines of research are clearly distinguishable. The first relies on post-evolutionary ideas and addresses the development of the modern man, contrasting him to the traditional type. American sociologist and anthropologist Alex Inkeles is one of the leaders in this line of research. For decades, this scientist led a research program dealing with modernization processes (meaning industrialization accompanied by respective changes in the social environment, culture, and mentality of the popula-

---

20 Santo B. *Innovation as a Tool for Economic Development*. M., 1990. p. 190.
21 See: *The Scientific-Technical Revolution and National Processes* / Edited by O.I. Shkaratan. M., 1987; Perepyolkin L.S., Shkaratan O.I. *Economic Growth and National Development //* Economy and industrial production. 1988. N10. Unfortunately, these studies were later interrupted.

tion) in different European, Asian, African, and American countries. The research identified and empirically verified the specific traits of a modern man, and expressed hypotheses as to the factors of modernization.[22]

The other line of research regards ethnocultural differences between peoples as something given and inalterable in the near future, and based on this, studies the effect of this specificity on the operation of modern enterprises and organizations. This group of scientists seeks to facilitate the international (intercultural) transfer of technology, managerial skills, and personnel, to reduce the "losses" caused by differences in the culture of the donor and recipient countries. Dutch scientist Geert Hofstede is perhaps the best-known representative in this field. He conducted large-scale research of organizational ethnocultural specifics in several dozen countries.[23]

The facts collected by foreign authors, principles underlying their selection, and methods of study are important by themselves. A review of the literature reveals that western science collects information predominantly about the ethnocultural distinctness of the work behavior specific for industrial workers in emerging economies, with a focus on countries hosting major investments of multinational corporations. Research also focuses on the working practices of ethnic minorities, primarily migrants, in developed capitalist countries.

Current studies are designed to identify those components of ethnic culture (associated primarily with traditional culture), which, in one way or another, affect work in the modern economy, the measure and structure of its effectiveness (i.e., quality of the goods, openness to innovation, stability and staff turnover, work satisfaction, etc.). Such components include the following:

---

22 Inkeles A. & Smith D.M. *Becoming Modern: Individual Change in Six Developing Countries*. 3rd edition. Cambridge, MA.: Harvard University Press, 1982; Inkeles A. *National Differences in Individual Modernity* // Comparative Studies in Sociology – Vol. 1. JAI Press, Inc., 1978; Inkeles A. & Diamond L. *Personal Development and National Development: A Cross-National Perspective* // Quality of Life: Comparative Studies. Ed. By Szalai A. & Andrews F. M. L.: Sage Publications, 1980.

23 E.g., Hofstede G. Op.cit.; Gas'kov V.M. *Social Aspects of International Exchange of Industrial Experience*. M.: MNIIPU, 1988; Salk J.E. *National Culture, Networks, and Individual Influence in a Multinational Management Team* // Academy of Management Journal, Mississippi State; Apr 2000; Vol. 43; Spence L.J., Petrick J.A. *Multinational Interview Decisions: Integrity Capacity and Competing Values* // Human Resource Management Journal, L., 2000. Vol. 10 and other.

- The culture's common values
- Traditional values and work standards, and the related work motivation framework
- The hierarchical model of professions and occupations in terms of prestige
- The nature of occupational status symbols and educational aspirations
- The customary distribution of roles attributed to gender, age, and other groups of the population.

Of all the components of national culture, human activity in the modern economy is most affected by the values of the society, social standards and work traditions accumulated throughout the history of this people.

The value system is a universal motivational framework with only a certain national-cultural flavor. It is commonly known that Max Weber was the first to study the impact of the value system on work behavior. He distinguished the ethic component in world religions, i.e. "practical impulses for action which are founded in the psychological and pragmatic contexts of religion."[24] Weber demonstrated that "features of religions that are important for economic ethics shall interest us primarily from a definite point of view: we shall be interested in the way in which they are related to economic rationalism. More precisely, we mean the economic rationalism of the type, which since the sixteenth and seventeenth centuries has come to dominate the Occident as part of the particular rationalization of civic life, and which has become familiar in this part of the world."[25] Weber called this phenomenon "Protestant ethic" and considered it an important factor in the emergence of an effective capitalist economy.

Weber believes that "calling" as the central concept of Protestant philosophy treats rational capitalist enterprise as blessed by God. The Protestant ideal is a "creditworthy respectable person whose duty is to consider augmenting his capital as an end in itself." As for the workers,

---

24 Weber M. *Economic Ethics of World Religions. A Comparative Study of the Sociology of Religion* / Max Weber. Selected works. The image of society. M.: Jurist, 1994. p. 43.
25 Ibid. pp. 65–66; see also subsection of Max Weber's best-known work on this issue, *The Protestant Ethic and the Spirit of Capitalism* / M. Weber. Selected works. M.: Progress, 1990.

"calling" commits them to the "duty to work", to perceive labor as an end in itself, to treat "their earnings with sober self-control and moceration"—and all this in the hope of heavenly reward.[26] Influenced by the values of Protestant ethic, both the employers and the employees develop the motive to achieve (to achieve the best results in their work), a sense of independence and personal responsibility.

Manuel Castells rightly noted that Max Weber's classic essay *The Protestant Ethic and the Spirit of Capitalism* remains the methodological cornerstone for understanding the essence of cultural and institutional transformations, which in history herald a new paradigm of any economic organization. However, historians, who rightly pointed out alternative historical forms that supported capitalism as effectively as the Anglo-Saxon culture, albeit in different institutional forms, subsequently questioned Weber's analysis of the origins of capitalist development.[27]

A similar set of values is true for Buddhist-Shintoist Japan and Confucian China. The most comprehensive studies have been devoted to the phenomenon of the "Japanese miracle". Leading analysts have come to the definite conclusion that skilled leadership, which among other things considered the national features of the Japanese worker, played a significant, if not decisive role, in Japan's accelerated post-war development. Thus, when implementing economic reforms (after World War II), the Japanese elites did not destroy the highly unified community—an archaic collectivist structure, but rather used it as a channe for achieving the government's goals. After all, the community could respond to the objective of economic liberalization better than an underdeveloped individual or a still non-existent civil society.[28] It is common to point out that the miniature products of the modern Japanese electronics industry are successors of the traditional national art of miniaturization (the famous "Bonsai" and "netsuke"—miniature trees and sculp-

---

26 Weber M. *The Protestant Ethic and the Spirit of Capitalism* / M. Weber. Selected works. M.: Progress, 1990. pp. 73, 83.
27 Castells M. (1996, reprinted 1997) *The Information Age: Economy, Society and Culture. Volume 1. The Rise of the Network Society.* Malden, MA; Oxford, UK: Blackwell Publishers Ltd. p. 194.
28 Kitahara A. *The Reality and the Community's Ideal Image (Japan and Thailand)* // Philosofskiye nauki. 1996. No. 1–6; Taichi Sakaiya. *What is Japan?* M.: Partner Co. Ltd., 1992; Pronnikov V.A., Ladanov I.D. *The Japanese.* M.: Nauka, 1983.

tures). This painstaking work, which for centuries has been creating exquisite masterpieces, now lives in high-precision industrial products.

Of course, modernization of the Japanese economy and society was the result of a long and diligent study of western (and in certain areas also Russian) experience. However, what makes Japanese reforms internationally significant is that they relied on old values to create modern institutions. Linking cultural traditions with the achievements of the industrial world made Japan the first ancient civilization to leap into modernity.[29]

Value systems based on Protestant, Buddhist-Shintoist, and Confucian ethics, i.e., on a specific attitude to labor as a person's responsibility, duty, and calling, proved to be the most effective for modern societies. Although these ethical standards were developed by certain Western European and East Asian societies, the works of sociologists, social psychologists, and experts on management demonstrate that it is possible to purposefully promote relevant value and motivational frameworks in societies with different cultural traditions.[30]

This process involves adapting a worker to production, and there are many examples of successful adaptation of this kind. Thus, literature describes the experience of an American company, which located its enterprises in the United States, Canada, and Mexico.[31] In the 18 months of work, the Mexican enterprise's labor productivity reached 75% of that in the U.S.A. with the quality of manufactured engines between the Canadian (lower) and U.S. ones. The authors attributed these achievements to three factors:

---

29 Yemelyanov Yu.V. *The Birth and Death of Civilizations.* M., 1999. pp. 394–395.
30 See: McClelland D.C., Winter D.G. *Motivating Economic Achievement. Accelerating Economic Development through Psychological Training.* N.Y., 1960; Arthur Rich. *Economic Ethics.* Translation from German. M.: Posev, 1996; T.B. Koval. *Backbreaking Benefit. Christian Work Ethics. Orthodoxy. Catholicism. Protestantism.* M.: Institut Etnologii i Antropologii RAN, 1994; idem. *"The Spiritual Christians": Religious Distinctness and Work Ethics //* Mir Rossii. 1993. No. 1; idem. *Orthodox Work Ethics //* Mir Rossii. 1994. No. 2; Lewis R. *When Cultures Collide. Managing Successfully across Cultures.* Translation from English. M.: Izd-vo Delo, 1999; L. Kolesnikova, V. Perekryostov. *Organizational Structures and Business Culture //* Voprosy Ekonomiki. 2000. No. 8.
31 Shaiken H., Herzenberg S. *Automation and Global Production. Automobile Engine Production in Mexico, the United States and Canada.* San Diego, 1987.

- The workers in Mexico, although inexperienced, were well-educated and highly motivated
- Team work arrangement and quality control groups contributed to successful operation
- Managers and engineers from all over the world monitored the production process.

The social standards of each people are much more stable and specific. Even in modern enterprises, they largely mediate "impersonal relations" of the "employee-employee" and "manager-employee" type. Work traditions are quite a stable element of the national culture. This includes the customary nature, intensity, and mode of work; techniques, skills and practices learned through family and social upbringing. The entire system of traditional education focuses on principal local activities. Modern production has to adapt to them, and this forced "concession" sometimes produces unexpected and high results.

The modern economic thought has not remained indifferent to the new role of man in the manufacturing process. Economists increasingly regard the national-specific features of the workforce as one of the most important inputs in the classical model of the demand and supply of factors of production (such as excess or shortage of skilled labor, raw material and energy prices, etc.).[32] When considering new strategies for restructuring business entities in the process of capitalist transition from industrialism to informationalism (the 1980s-2000s), many authors emphasize the priority of new management methods initially generated by Japanese companies in the context of the Japanese national culture. The same applies to the high performance of the Chinese

---

32   *The Political Economy of Japan: The Domestic Transformation* / Ed. by Yamamura Kozo, Jasuba Yasukichi. Stanford, 1987. Vol.1. P.40; Michael E. Porter. *The Competitive Advantage of Nations*. N.Y., 1990; *Post-Fordism. A Reader* / Ed. by Ash Amin. Oxford, 1994; Lewis R. *When Cultures Collide. Managing Successfully across Cultures*. Translation from English. M.: Izd-vo Delo, 1999; Myasnikova L. *Russian Mentality and Management* // Voprosy Ekonomiki. 2000. No. 8; Faltsman V. *Russian Business from the Perspective of Christian Morality* // Voprosy Ekonomiki. 2000. No. 8.

business model based on family firms and cross-sectoral business networks often controlled by one family.[33]

In other words, established experts believe that in the modern global economy the newest international division of labor is closely interacting with the national diversity of organizational forms and work behavior of different institutional and cultural origins. Development of the national economic and industry structure incorporated into the global economy requires relying on the ethnocultural characteristics of human resources, in particular their innovative capacity. In the new environment, all previous (from the industrial age) criteria for selecting promising types of employees and managers largely become impracticable. A rare exception is Russia, which for decades, if not centuries, has been persistently trying to adopt foreign management practices without attempting to distinguish universal characteristics of the economy from its specific institutional and cultural features. In this context, developing the advantages of Russian employees and Russian management traditions and making them globally appealing becomes a critical issue. What are Russia's chances to win this competition and what is required for this?

Many authors currently note that the center and periphery repeatedly changed places in the course of the development of mankind. History was never a unilinear process; it was always a combination of different civilizational models. Current globalization "was (and remains) the resultant of many attempts to organize a common space where peoples and nations live together based on different civilizational models".[34] Suffice it to recall the well-known fact that from the twelfth century until at least the middle of the sixteenth century, Asia and not Europe was the center of trade, economic, and to a large extent industrial progress.

Apparently, influenced by China's spectacular achievements in the period from 1980 to 2014, Yury Granin has collected a "bunch" of data about the faster development of leading Asian countries in pre-colonial times. He recalls that by their military power, as well as cultural and

---

33 Castells M. *The Information Age: Economy, Society and Culture. Vol. III. End of Millennium.* Oxford, 1998. Part 4. Toward the Pacific Era? The Multicultural Foundation of Economic Interdependence. pp. 206–309.
34 Granin Yu. *Globalization or Westernization? On the Nonlinearity of Historical Forms of Unification of Mankind //* Svobodnaya Mysl'. No. 1. 2013. p. 59.

political influence, the Asian empires were significantly superior to any European state. He also provides data on the use of gunpowder for military purposes, and on the construction of ocean-going fleets, "...even production of pig iron in China was based on advanced technology (using coke and continuous blast furnace purging), which in England became known only 500 years later, with such enterprises employing hundreds of workers. The country had an extensive transport network and a developed financial system. By the fourteenth century, China had many prerequisites for the industrial revolution, which, according to historians, England had developed only by the end of the eighteenth century. Researchers believe this was "a relatively well-developed market economy", which encouraged the desire to generate profit and promoted rapid dissemination of advanced technology".[35]

The history of mankind taken over a considerable stretch of time demonstrates that throughout history the European civilization did not and does not have a monopoly on dominance. It is just a coincidence that our current debates are taking place at the time of Eurocentrism both in theory and in the development practice of most nations representing spiritually and technologically advanced Western civilizations.

The idea of the periphery's catch-up development resulted from the logic of unitary approach as a conceptual basis of the development of countries and civilizations, alignment of their development levels by following the same historical path as countries of the European civilization, which formed the first echelon in the progress of mankind. However, the perception that the development of backward countries consisted in catching up with the European civilization could be considered reality only until the end of the twentieth century. An analysis of the fantastic achievements first of Japan and Russia—the USSR, and later the so-called Asian Tigers and finally the giant—China revealed that these countries used the experience of the European civilization, but relied on their own civilizational features, which gave them advantages in the competitive environment shaped by global modernization.

Richard R. Nelson, Professor of economics at Columbia University, speaking at the Leontief Prize award ceremony emphasized that "in the twenty-first century, in order to catch up a country needs to develop

---

35   Ibid. p. 60.

considerable indigenous strength in the relevant fields of science and technology". This process includes training in the West, advice of Western experts domestically, and rapid development of the local education system. As conditions for obtaining support from the developed countries tighten, the catch-up states are beginning to change their strategy and focus on advanced training and development of the research framework. Simple copying, imitating the experience of developed countries usually does not produce the desired result, i.e., it does not constitute real catch-up development.[36]

The authors of the *China and Global Modernization Report Outlook (2001–2010)* noted, "In all strata and in all aspects of global modernization we can easily find many universals—in the lives of the people and their mindset. Similarly, in each area or phase of global modernization it is easy to see many differences in national standards, rates of development, forms, etc. The similarities and differences of global modernization do not repel each other; they manifest two forms of an objective law".[37]

Since the late 1990s, theories of non-European modernity, of multiple forms of modernization have been receiving quite extensive coverage in Western literature. Researchers increasingly refuse to interpret modernization as Westernization and conduct large-scale comparative studies of different civilizations. The British sociologist Nicos Mouzelis rightly criticizes the trend dominant in Euro-American literature to regard the development trajectories of the non-European world (in the past, present, and future) as an imitation of the specific western development model. He indicates that western modernization was historically the first to appear, but it is no longer the only one in the world. Moreover, although it is still dominating, this does not mean that such a situation will continue into the next century. (These words were written in 1999, and proved true in the next few years). Mouzelis did not exclude (and he proved to be right again) that in the near future "quasi-

---

36 Yevstigneeva L., Yevstigneev R. *The Mystery of Catch-Up Development* // Voprosi Ekonomiki. No. 1. 2013. pp. 88–89.
37 *China and Global Modernization Report Outlook (2001–2010)*. Ed. He Chuanqi. Translation from Chinese. M.: Izdatel'stvo Ves' Mir, 2011. p. 232.

authoritarian Asian capitalism may prevail over its more liberal Anglo-Saxon competitor".[38]

These ideas are especially popular in developing countries, where the authors emphasize the limitations of existing social theories, which are inapplicable for analyzing non-European forms of the modern society. It is worth noting that even in the Western academic community the supporters of the long-dominating unilinear approach to the development of mankind increasingly encounter reasonable opposition. The prominent Swedish scholar B. Wittrok wrote, "True enough, a set of technological, economic, and political institutions, with their origins in the context of Western Europe, have become diffused across the globe at least as ideals, sometimes also as working realities. These processes of diffusion and adaptation, however, do not at all mean that deep-seated cultural and cosmological differences between, say, Western Europe, China, and Japan are about to disappear. It only means that these different cultural entities have to adapt to and refer to a set of globally diffused ideas and practices.

In their core identities, these societies remain characterized by the form they acquired during much earlier periods of cultural crystallization, whether these periods are located in the axial age or in the tenth to thirteenth centuries. These core identities have, of course, always in themselves been undergoing processes of change and reinterpretation, but they have continued to structure the most profound cosmological and societal assumptions of their civilizations, and it would be exceedingly naive to believe that they are now suddenly about to disappear. The existence of this common global condition does not mean that members of any single cultural community are about to relinquish their ontological and cosmological assumptions, much less their traditional institutions."[39]

The foregoing clearly indicates that the place of a particular civilization in the overall global development ranking is not established once and for all. When discussing the development of local civilizations, in our case primarily the Russian one, we reject the Eurocentric approach

---

[38] Mouzelis N. *Modernity: A Non-European Conceptualization* // British Journal of Sociology. Vol. 50, No. 1. 1999. p. 153; Maslovsky M.V. *Contemporary Theories of Modernity and Modernization* // Sotsiologicheskiy zhurnal. No. 2. 2008. pp. 31–44.

[39] Wittrok B. *Modernity: One, None or Many? European Origins and Modernity as a Global Condition* // Daedalus. Vol. 129, No. 1. 2000. pp. 54–56.

as the key principle. For centuries, European countries were not in the first ranks of world economic and cultural development. Right now, in the first half of the twenty-first century, the order of civilizations appears to be changing once again, and not in favor of Europe.

Chapter II.
Foreign professionals (expatriates) in national economies

The term "expat" (shortened from "expatriate", i.e., literally "out of the native country"), although sounding unusual for the Russian ear, is a well-established notion in the countries of the European civilization. Presumably, it appeared with the emergence of nation states, when the notion of a native country and citizenship acquired independent meaning. In the broadest sense, expatriates are people living extensively outside their own countries or people who have renounced their citizenship in favor of another country. This definition can be found in the Merriam-Webster's dictionary, one of the best-known American dictionaries, starting from the edition of 1812.[40] By the way, it is quite natural that it was the Western European culture that enriched the world's vocabulary with this term. Two aspects promoted the spread of this phenomenon. On the one hand, state borders were quite relative in densely populated Europe and therefore highly permeable. On the other hand, Europe's rich colonialist experience pulled Europeans out of their familiar environment for lengthy periods, sometimes for the rest of their lives, to conquer new territories and cultures.

The classic definition is still applicable, however, in the current globalization era, the notion of "expat" acquires a new, specific meaning. In an effort to secure access to new production opportunities and markets, large multinational companies increasingly use expats as certain "cuttings" to cultivate locally the required organizational culture, business practices, and technology (or, in other words, the specific human capital critically needed to make the local branches competitive and meet the company's strategic objectives). New practices generate new opportunities, but they also raise new challenges. Thus, the first systematic attempts to study various aspects of expat activities in different countries emerged already in the 1960s-1970s. However, it soon became clear that cross-cultural interaction at the micro-level was an

---

40   *See, e.g.,* Merriam-Webster's Collegiate Dictionary. 11th Ed. Encyclopedia Britannica Company, 2004. p. 439.

extremely complex, internally contradictory phenomenon, since for both parties (i.e., the expatriates and the host culture) such interaction involved not only mutually beneficial exchange and enrichment of experience, but also potential conflicts, stress situations, and other dramatic events. In this chapter we would like to elaborate on the findings already presented in academic literature and outline in more detail the context of our own research underlying a significant part of this book.

It is worth noting that any expat-related research pertains predominantly to sociology of work, cross-cultural management, and human resource management in general. However, its applied, narrowly-disciplinary focus is quite understandable. The demand for such research originated primarily from major international companies that were seeking theoretically substantiated recommendations on enhancing management practices for their international branches and multinational workforce. In this respect, we can clearly emphasize that academic interest in the topic of expatriates is far from exhausted, as research, for example, from the broader sociological and sociopsychological perspective (e.g., interaction of the expatriates with the host culture, institutional context, etc.) is still scarce. Six principle lines of research are distinguishable in the existing range of expat-related studies represented in current academic literature:[41]

1) Selection and recruitment
2) Training for expatriation
3) Adjustment at the new location
4) Performance
5) Level and nature of compensation
6) Repatriation

The first four areas of focus are of the greatest interest for the topics raised in our book; therefore, we will briefly dwell on the state of research in each of them.

---

41   We encountered at least two independent reviews of research in this field, which agree on this classification: 1) Dabic M., Gonzalez-Loureiro M., Harvey M. *Evolving Research on Expatriates: What is 'Known' after Four Decades (1970–2012)* // The International Journal of Human Resource Management. 2013; 2) McEvoy G.M., Buller P.F. *Research for Practice: The Management of Expatriates* // Thunderbird International Business Review. Vol. 55. No. 2. 2013.

The first area of focus deals with the motives, socio-psychological, and professional qualities, as well as different circumstances affecting the people's decision to expatriate. Typical and preferred profiles of candidates for expatriation is a related issue, since appropriate knowledge allows substantially mitigating the risks related to the expatriates' integration in a new location. Thus, research suggests that other things being equal, such universal traits and competencies as knowledge of respective foreign languages, cross-cultural awareness and sensitivity, open-mindedness, a cosmopolitan orientation, high tolerance for stress, a collaborative negotiation style and willingness to compromise, etc. facilitate the expatriates' effective integration.[42] In turn, we can assume that a typical profile over time will become more universal, and the expatriates will increasingly resemble each other regardless of their cultural origin, simply due to natural and artificial (i.e., corporate) selection procedures. However, it is well known that reality substantially adjusts any theory. In particular, actual practice shows that even in major companies, the process of recruiting expatriates for international assignments is rarely structured, formal and rational, focused on selecting candidates compatible with the above profile.[43]

The second area of focus is perhaps the most debated one in modern literature. It concerns training candidates for expatriation and addresses the fundamental possibility of "cultivating" such qualities in future expatriates that would facilitate their seamless integration into the new culture and at the new workplace. In general, a number of researchers[44] point out the critical importance of providing customized training for expatriates when assigning them for positions abroad; however, a classical bibliographical reference in this respect is the compar-

---

42 Black J.S., Gregersen H.B. *The Right Way to Manage Expats* // Harvard Business Review. Vol. 77. No. 2. 1999; Hailey J. *The Expatriate Myth: Cross-Cultural Perceptions of Expatriate Managers* // International Executive. Vol. 38. No. 2. 1996; Mendenhall G., Oddou G. *The Dimensions of Expatriate Acculturation: A Review* // Academy of Management Review. Vol. 10. 1985.

43 McEvoy G.M., Buller P.F. *Research for Practice: The Management of Expatriates* // Thunderbird International Business Review. Vol. 55. No. 2. 2013. p. 217.

44 Black J.S., Mendenhall M. *Cross-Cultural Training Effectiveness: A Review and a Theoretical Framework for Future Research* // Academy of Management Review. No. 15. 1990; Kealey D.J., Protheroe D.R. *The Effectiveness of Cross-Cultural Training for Expatriates: An Assessment of the Literature on the Issue* // International Journal of Intercultural Relations. No. 2. 1996.

ative study performed by professor R. Tung (U.S.A.) simultaneously in U.S., European, and Japanese multinationals.[45] The general idea of training is based on the *theory of met expectations,*[46] the essence of which is reduced to a simple formula: "forewarned is forearmed"—if a person knows what lies ahead, he is better prepared to face the forthcoming challenges and insures himself against possible disappointments. Standard training for expatriation usually includes acquiring the necessary language competencies, a general introduction to the host culture, an analysis of common conflict situations, etc. Special trainings may be conducted both prior to departure from the home country and after arrival in the host country. Some studies suggest this has no fundamental effect on the success of the adjustment[47]—it is the fact that matters, because this reduces the risk of incompatibility with the host culture. Another significant factor promoting or impeding seamless adjustment is the family, which foreign employees often bring with them on long-term assignments. Such situations are fraught with the so-called *spillover effect,* when family conflicts related to unsettled family members and cultural contradictions spill over to the work environment and multiply the expatriates' negative perceptions, which they may experience in the process of adjusting at the new workplace.[48] Thus, in situations when the expatriates move to their new job location together with the family, researchers insist that family members may also need tailored training, because their adjustment is no less important for the adjustment of the expatriates themselves.[49]

The third area of focus—adjustment of the expatriates in the host country—is perhaps central to the entire field of research. Moreover,

---

[45] Tung R.L. *Selection and Training Procedures of U.S., European, and Japanese Multinationals* // California Management Review. Vol. 25. 1982.

[46] Caligiuri P., Phillips J., Lazarova M., Tarique I., Burgi P. *The Theory of Met Expectations Applied to Expatriate Adjustment: The Role of Cross-Cultural Training* // International Journal of Human Resource Management. Vol. 12. No. 3. 2001.

[47] See, e.g., Selmer J. *To Train or Not to Train? European Expatriate Managers in China* // International Journal of Cross-Cultural Management. No. 2. 2002.

[48] Bhagat R.S. *Effects of Stressful Life Events on Individual Performance Effectiveness and Work Adjustment Processes within Organizational Settings: A Research Model* // Academy of Management Review. No. 8. 1983.

[49] Tung R.L. *Selecting and Training of Personnel for Overseas Assignments* // Columbia Journal of World Business. No. 16. 1981; see also: McEvoy G.M., Buller P.F. *Research for Practice: The Management of Expatriates* // Thunderbird International Business Review. Vol. 55. No. 2. 2013. p. 218.

this is one of the key topics of our own study; therefore, we will depict it in more detail than the other ones.

One of the first influential theories that emerged in this line of research was the *culture shock theory*, widely known in cross-cultural studies. Its original provisions were formulated in the writings of American anthropologist Kalervo Oberg.[50] "Culture shock" generally refers to psychological distress caused by an inner cultural conflict, which latently develops as the individual adjusts to a strange cultural environment. The cause of this conflict is asynchronous adjustment, on the one hand, and reduction of uncertainty, on the other. Acclimation typically occurs slowly, while more and more situations that cause misunderstanding and even hostility accumulate extremely quickly. Eventually, this concept became widespread. Numerous studies devoted to the adjustment of foreigners in other countries surged with the development of the international education market and the penetration of large corporations into the economies of other countries. Earlier versions of this theory were based on a U-curve model of cultural adjustment (accumulation of contradictions—crisis—adjustment). Current literature, however, is skeptical about this thesis, because in actual practice a tremendous number of factors (duration of stay, distance between the cultures,[51] individual features,[52] etc.) affect the "culture shock". In general, no one denies the existence of "culture shock", since anyone who has to spend an extended period of time in an unfamiliar cultural environment one way or another encounters this problem. Moreover, the standard expatriation training package includes the concept of "culture shock" and an introduction to this theory.

The *uncertainty reduction theory* developed by Charles Berger and Richard Calabrese contributes to describing and explaining the dynamics of the expatriates' adjustment at the new workplace. This theory assumes that expatriates are inherently motivated to develop interpersonal communication due to the high level of uncertainty of the envi-

---

50 Oberg K. *Cultural Shock: Adjustment to New Cultural Environments //* Practical Anthropology. No. 7. 1960.
51 Parker B., McEvoy G. *Initial Examination of a Model of Intercultural Adjustment //* International Journal of Intercultural Relations. No. 17. 1993.
52 Black J.S., Mendenhall M. *The U-Curve Adjustment Hypothesis Revisited: A Review and Theoretical Framework //* Journal of International Business Studies. No. 22. 1991; Ward C., Bochner S., Furnham A. *The Psychology of Culture Shock.* 2nd Edition. Philadelphia, PA: Routledge, 2001.

ronment, which they face on their foreign assignments.[53] In this case, language is the main barrier to developing intensive interpersonal communication,[54] as well as a mismatch of social norms facilitating communication (e.g., specific types of local leisure unacceptable for representatives of one of the cultures). Therefore, raising their awareness about what is organized in the company and how it functions, what leisure arrangements exist for the employees, what measures are taken for the employees' mutual socialization, etc. is one of the principal and most effective strategies for the expatriates to adjust to the local sociocultural environment. It is a kind of informal insider information, which allows reducing the overall degree of uncertainty and psychological distress inevitably resulting from a collision with a new and unfamiliar environment. In fact, for this reason expatriates sometimes find it more difficult to adjust to the non-work environment than to the work one, because a priori they are usually better informed about the situation in the company than about the local culture in general.[55]

Researchers consider expat adjustment as a complex phenomenon, which includes adjustment in three relatively autonomous fields rather than just in one: 1) *intercultural interactions adjustment*; 2) *work adjustment*); and 3) *adjustment to living conditions*.[56] Besides, the adjustment process consists of three key components—factors, mechanisms, and outcomes. Factors usually comprise individual (personal traits, competencies, past experience, etc.), situational (objectives, work roles and responsibilities at the place of destination), organizational (corporate support, special training), and sociocultural (distance between the host and the home cultures, family circumstances, etc.) ones. Mechanisms involve various adjustment tools, techniques, and

---

53 Berger C.R., Calabrese R.J. *Some Explorations in Initial Interaction and Beyond: Toward a Developmental Theory of Interpersonal Communication* // Human Communication Research. No. 1. 1975.
54 Triandis H.C. *Culture and Social Behavior.* New York: McGraw-Hill. 1994.
55 Saks A.M., Ashforth B.E. *Organizational Socialization: Making Sense of the Past and Present as a Prologue for the Future* // Journal of Vocational Behavior. No. 51. 1997.
56 *See, e.g.,* Holtbruegge D. (Ed.) *Cultural Adjustment of Expatriates. Theoretical Concepts and Empirical Studies.* Rainer Hampp Verlag, 2008; Zimmerman A., Holman D., Sparrow P. *Unravelling Adjustment Mechanisms: Adjustment of German Expatriates to Intercultural Interactions, Work, and Living Conditions in the People's Republic of China* // International Journal of Cross-Cultural Management. Vol. 3. No. 1. 2003.

strategies. Outcomes generally include a certain degree of harmony with the local cultural environment, psychological well-being, and achievement of goals associated with the new assignment.

Thus, according to *theories of acculturation*,[57] the modes of an individual's adjustment to *intercultural interactions* are identical to different outcomes of the conflict between the old and the new cultural identity. Researchers distinguish four modes of adjustment:[58] 1) *assimilation* (individuals adopt new cultural norms instead of their own); 2) *separation* (individuals reject the new cultural norms and maintain their own cultural identity); 3) *marginalization* (the old and the new cultural norms are mutually incompatible, which leads to confusion); and 4) *integration* (seamless synthesis of the old and new cultural norms).

On the other hand, the mode of *work adjustment* can be described using the so-called *theory of work-role transitions*, proposed by Nigel Nicholson in 1984.[59] This theory in its original version answers the question of how employees adjust to a change in role requirements (be it due to changes in the organization or a new workplace). Nicholson argued that this happened mainly through two alternative ideal-typical strategies. Under the first—*role innovation*—strategy, employees tend to be more proactive and try to influence the situation so that the role assigned to them is more in line with their own requirements. The second—*accommodation*—strategy is by definition passive and implies personal development of the employee to fit the new role requirements. The extent of the employees' integration into the local context, i.e., the success of their role transition directly depends on how successfully they implement any of these two strategies. In actual practice, however, both strategies are implemented in different combinations, for example: 1) passive adoption of the new role (*replication*); 2) adjustment to the new role through active behavioral and personal change (*absorption*); 3) active role development without personal change (*determination*); or

---

[57] Berry J.W., Kim U., Minde T., Mok D. *Comparative Studies of Acculturative Stress* // International Migration Review. Vol. 21. No. 3. 1987; Bochner S. *Cultures in Contact. Studies in Cross-Cultural Interaction.* Oxford: Pergamon Press, 1982; Furnham A., Bochner S. *Culture Shock: Psychological Reactions to Unfamiliar Environments.* London: Methuen, 1986.

[58] Janssens M. *Intercultural Interaction: A Burden on International Managers?* // Journal of Organizational Behavior. Vol. 16. 1995.

[59] Nicholson N. *A Theory of Work Role Transitions* // Administrative Science Quarterly. No. 29 1984.

4) search for a new balance through role and personal development (*exploration*).

However, adjustment to new circumstances and the new culture are not always aligned. Thus, J. Black distinguishes three key aspects of successful adjustment.[60] The first, more general one, is associated with the overall perception of the new culture (for example, the ability to adequately perceive local traditions, customs, cuisine, etc.). The second one concerns the more direct interaction with people both in the work and non-work environment (for example, the ability to find common language with colleagues, the nature of socializing outside work, etc.). And, finally, the third aspect is the degree to which employees feel comfortable in the new workplace, how seamlessly they perceive their new roles and responsibilities.

Finally, *adjustment to living conditions* can be either more *conservative* or more *adaptive*. In the first case, expatriates seek to retain their cultural identity in the domestic sphere through commitment to their own habits and desires; in the second one, they change their habits and practices in line with the environment.

We believe, one of the most relevant studies in this regard is a relatively recent study of adjustment dynamics of German expatriates working in branches of major German corporations in the Chinese province of Guangdong.[61] The authors pursued the objective of determining how foreign employees adjust to working and living in an unfamiliar cultural environment; what adjustment mechanisms are used and how they relate to the specific environmental context; and finally, how these mechanisms are influenced by individual and organizational factors. The empirical part of the research was performed on the basis of in-depth interviews with 18 expatriates.

The authors established that in intercultural interactions the Germans generally use the strategy of integration and frequently its extreme form—assimilation. Specifically, this is manifested in the attempt to learn Chinese, even to a little extent. According to the respondents,

---

60 Black J.S. *Work Role Transitions: A Study of American Expatriate Managers in Japan //* Journal of International Business Studies. No. 19. 1988.
61 Zimmerman A., Holman D., Sparrow P. *Unravelling Adjustment Mechanisms: Adjustment of German Expatriates to Intercultural Interactions, Work, and Living Conditions in the People's Republic of China //* International Journal of Cross-Cultural Management. Vol. 3. No. 1. 2003.

this is crucial for successful adjustment. However, there are subtler cultural norms, which practically all German specialists consider worth mastering in order to establish better contact with the local population. Such norms include indirect communication allowing discreet dual interpretations of various agreements; unacceptability of open criticism and a more subtle, than in the western culture, attitude to reputation and the concept of "face"; establishment of personalized relationships with partners and colleagues rather than purely business contacts, etc. Consequently, the expatriates themselves consider integration and assimilation strategies as the most desirable and effective in such situations.

The situation with work adjustment is somewhat different. It is no secret that expatriates are generally sent on foreign assignments to address specific management issues and organize production processes. This involves certain standard perceptions of the respective functions and roles, as well as formal obligations, this setting a rather rigid framework for implementing alternative adjustment strategies. Among the most common work-related problems that Germans face in China, the respondents indicated lack of initiative and reluctance to take responsibility demonstrated by Chinese employees, as well as their inability to use systematic procedures (certain authors, however, note that due to the positive effects of the reforms in education, some of these features are no longer common for the new generation of the Chinese). Since expatriates regard this as a source of inefficiency, passive strategies for them are not an option. Compromise tactics include explanation, active teaching, and closer control over the work of subordinates and colleagues. In the proposed classification, this corresponds to role innovation or determination. The only aspect in which the Germans are more flexible (i.e., they adjust by absorption and sometimes by exploration) is the art of establishing beneficial relations and networks (the phenomenon of "guanxi" widespread in China), which significantly facilitates achieving the company's objectives.

As for adjustment to living conditions manifested in leisure activities, sports, eating habits, etc., the authors identify a broad range of potential strategies. For some expatriates, the lack of familiar dishes in restaurant menus is not a problem and they easily switch to local food. Others are sufficiently motivated to visit regularly metropolitan cities

(Hong Kong, for example) to satisfy their requirements and wishes in the "Western style". In this case, the key factors are the availability of respective goods and services, on the one hand, and the commitment to certain habits, on the other hand.

Factors facilitating the expatriates' adjustment to the local cultural environment include friendly relations and support by Chinese colleagues who help to get used to the local environment and learn the local language. Such acquaintances also help to enhance significantly the adjustment capacity through the availability of strategies involving assimilation of local cultural norms and personal change. Previous experience of socialization in other countries with a similar cultural profile is no less important for the expatriates. By the way, the interviewed Germans emphasized that these factors gave far more advantages than cross-cultural training often practiced in the event of such assignments.

Finally, after adjustment, performance on the global assignment is the next focus of research in the literature on expatriates. Performance is frequently regarded as a function of adjusting to the cultural environment of the host country; therefore, these aspects often correlate with each other.[62]

Actually, defining "performance" in such works is a separate issue. Generally, the situation when expatriates for whatever reasons terminate their contract prematurely and return home early is regarded as a measure of utmost "ineffectiveness".[63] Research of this type usually distinguishes a technical performance dimension related to an employee's job performance and a more general ("contextual") one, which determines the expatriates' ability to find a common language with the

---

[62] See, e.g., Caligiuri P.M. *Assessing Expatriate Success: Beyond Just "Being There"* / Saunders D.M., Aycan Z. (Eds.) New Approaches to Employment Management. Volume 4. Greenwich, CT: JAI Press, 1997; Kraimer M.L., Wayne S.J., Jaworski R.A. *Sources of Support and Expatriate Performance: The Mediating Role of Expatriate Adjustment* // Personnel Psychology. No. 54. 2001; Shay J.P., Baack S. *An Empirical Investigation of the Relationships between Modes and Degree of Expatriate Adjustment and Multiple Measures of Performance* // International Journal of Cross-Cultural Management. No. 6. 2006.

[63] See, e.g., one of the pioneering and most influential writings on this subject: Tung R.L. *Selecting and Training of Personnel for Overseas Assignments* // Columbia Journal of World Business. No. 16. 1981.

host national employees. In this case, the attitude of the latter to foreign specialists becomes a performance criterion.[64]

Surprisingly, specialists recognize that expatriate performance (i.e., the ability to perform their work assignments successfully, and otherwise facilitate the work of the host branches and host national employees) is one of the least developed topics in respective literature.[65] It is likely that lack of serious progress in this field is due, on the one hand, to excessively pretentious definitions of "performance", and on the other hand, to the fact that this notion is hardly operationalizable (as other options are unavailable, most studies still rely on verbal, therefore, rather subjective, statements when assessing performance). Nevertheless, the most comprehensive studies in this field[66] indicate that the expatriates' performance/success largely depends on their sociopsychological and cultural profile, as well as their success in adjusting to a new cultural environment (which actually not in the least depends on the traits of the expatriates themselves).

Besides, academic literature has relatively long ago provided evidence that multinational companies, which practice recruitment of personnel with different national and cultural backgrounds, are often more competitive than traditional monocultural companies employing exclusively local workforce.[67] This is due to the higher flexibility and open-

---

64 Kraimer M.L., Wayne S.J., Jaworski R.A. *Sources of Support and Expatriate Performance: The Mediating Role of Expatriate Adjustment* // Personnel Psychology. No. 54. 2001; Shay J.P., Baack S. *An Empirical Investigation of the Relationships between Modes and Degree of Expatriate Adjustment and Multiple Measures of Performance* // International Journal of Cross-Cultural Management. No. 6. 2006.

65 See Dabic M., Gonzalez-Loureiro M., Harvey M. *Evolving Research on Expatriates: What is 'Known' after Four Decades (1970–2012)* // The International Journal of Human Resource Management. 2013. p. 17; and also McEvoy G.M., Buller P.F. *Research for Practice: The Management of Expatriates* // Thunderbird International Business Review. Vol. 55. No. 2. 2013. p. 219.

66 *See, e.g.,* Mol S., Born M., Willemsen M., Van der Molen H. *Predicting Expatriate Job Performance for Selection Purposes: A Quantitative Review* // Journal of Cross-Cultural Psychology. Vol. 36. No. 5. 2005.

67 Cox T.H. *Cultural Diversity in Organizations: Theory, Research and Practice.* San Francisco: Berrett-Koehler, 1993; Kirchmeyer C., McLellan J. *Capitalizing on Ethnic Diversity: An Approach to Managing the Diverse Work Groups of the 1990s* // Canadian Journal of Administrative Sciences. No. 8. 1991; Tung R.L. *Managing Cross-National and Intra-National Diversity* // Human Resource Management. No. 32. 1993.

ness to change in a fast-moving environment,[68] internal cultural diversity, stimulating creativity and a more intensive exchange of expertise, ideas and knowledge within the work teams,[69]—and these are not allegations. Studies show that there is indeed a stable relationship between the companies' cultural diversity and formal indicators of competitiveness (such as productivity and profitability).[70]

Nevertheless, we believe that the above list of subject areas comprising the current body of literature on expatriates lacks a rather important component, namely, the *interactive* communication between the host culture and the culture of expatriates. In a sense, the existing literature can be described as "expato-centric", since it regards the host culture primarily as an external static context, which serves to analyze the expatriates' role and personal changes, their performance and progress in the organization. Actually, some contemporary scholars[71] also point out that mutual cultural adjustment as such has hardly been investigated (when expatriates help representatives of the host culture to adjust, and representatives of the host culture help expatriates to adjust). Moreover, the lack of interactivity in the cases considered manifests itself not only in disregard of potential mutual adjustments, but also in the resistance of the personal attitudes of the two interacting parties.

---

[68] Mowshowitz A. *Virtual Organization //* Communication ACM. No. 40. 1997; Snow C.C., Snell S.A., Davison S.C., Hambrick D.C. *Use Transnational Teams to Globalize your Company //* Organizational Dynamics. No. 32. 1996.

[69] Maznevski M.L. *Understanding our Differences: Performance in Decision-making Groups with Diverse Members //* Human Relations No. 47. 1994; Watson W.E., Kumar K., Michaelson L.K. *Cultural Diversity's Impact on Interaction Process and Performance: Comparing Homogeneous and Diverse Task Groups //* Academy of Management Journal. No. 36. 1993; Marquardt M.J., Horvath L. *Global Teams: How Top Multinationals Span Boundaries and Cultures with High-speed Teamwork.* Palo Alto, CA: Davies-Black, 2001.

[70] Ng E.S.W., Tung R.L. *Ethnocultural Diversity and Organizational Effectiveness: A Field Study //* The International Journal of Human Resource Management. No. 9. 1998.

[71] Zimmerman A., Holman D., Sparrow P. *Unravelling Adjustment Mechanisms: Adjustment of German Expatriates to Intercultural Interactions, Work, and Living Conditions in The People's Republic of China //* International Journal of Cross-Cultural Management. Vol. 3. No. 1. 2003. p. 63.

In this respect, we would like to refer to an interesting study conducted in the Silicon Valley.[72] Observing the work of American and Israeli specialists and relying on a series of in-depth interviews with representatives of both parties, the authors attempted to compare their behavior and work attitude based on the extent of boundary rigidity/permeability related to the ethnocultural background (*permeability of culture*). A theoretical synthesis of earlier research by such renowned scholars as G. Hofstede, E. Hall, and F. Trompenaars[73] served as the conceptual basis on which the authors built their understanding of this meta-dimension of culture. The situations when this meta-dimension could be potentially realized included, for example, the styles of communication and interaction between employees (*expressive boundaries*), their attitude to job responsibilities, formal procedures, and principles of business ethics (*bureaucratic boundaries*), perception of time (*temporal boundaries*), perception of boundaries between personal life and work *(boundaries between work and non-work roles and relationships)*, and certain others.

The study revealed that in all of the above situations, the Israeli specialists as compared to the American ones acted as representatives of a more "unbound" culture. Thus, for example, Americans are in most cases perplexed (and even irritated) when their Israeli colleagues habitually interrupt the interlocutors during conversation or presentation at a business meeting. The Israeli's "unboundedness" also manifests itself in their frequent disregard of formal constraints, inability to plan and strictly adhere to the adopted plans, highly expressive communication, mixing personal and professional life, etc. Both parties equally capture these differences, but, curiously, virtually no respondent can give a definite assessment of these specific features in terms of their effect on accomplishing one or another organizational task—the Israelis and the Americans equally perceive that "unboundedness" as a general cultural dimension has both negative and positive aspects. Thus, the ease with

---

72　Shamir B., Melnik Y. *Boundary Permeability as a Cultural Dimension. A Study of Cross Cultural Working Relations between Americans and Israelis in High-Tech Organizations* // International Journal of Cross-Cultural Management. No. 2. 2002.

73　Hofstede G. *Culture's Consequences: International Differences in Work-Related Values.* Beverly Hills, CA: Sage Publications, 1980; Hall E.T. *The Hidden Dimension.* New York: Doubleday, 1966; Trompenaars F. *Riding the Waves of Culture: Understanding Diversity in Global Business.* New York: Irwin, 1994.

which the Israelis switch into top gear in case of emergency work and which is less typical of the American colleagues (in their own opinion!), besides causing bewilderment also invariably earns the approval and even admiration of the latter. In this respect, the authors emphasize that different cultural dimensions realize their comparative advantages in different situations, and this, in turn, has high practical value for effective human resource management.

It is, however, noteworthy that the findings of the research are nevertheless a rather gross generalization obtained through reconstructing the most notable features of both cultures using stereotyped reactions of the employees to various instances of their professional experience. Such an approach does not allow revealing subtler differences between representatives of the same culture and demonstrating what these differences can be attributed to. Besides, we found it strange that the authors did not discuss the "background" characteristics of the employees, primarily, the Israelis, because the "unboundedness" that they had revealed could be attributed not only to cultural distinctions, but also to a certain "tourist effect". In a foreign country, people may initially feel less constrained and ignore established local cultural standards, since "as foreigners" they expect the host party to treat them with indulgence. This alternative explanation emerged as we were familiarizing ourselves with the above study, so we thought it would be reasonable to use it as a hypothesis in our own research.

Finally, the recently published monograph of American sociologist Jeffrey Hass, *Power, Culture and Economic Change in Russia: to the Undiscovered Country of Post-Socialism, 1988–2008*[74] deserves special attention in the context of discussing model methodologies for studying cross-cultural interaction and transformation. Drawing on extensive sociological and ethnographic material, the author attempted to understand the reasons for success and failure of various economic agents in the course of transition from socialism to a market economy. For this purpose, the author develops a rather complex but reality-focused theoretic and methodological toolkit, which synthesizes the ideas of several disciplines: *economic sociology, neo-institutionalism*, and *the sociology of Pierre Bourdieu*.

---

74   Hass J. *Power, Culture and Economic Change in Russia: to the Undiscovered Country of Post-Socialism, 1988–2008*. Routledge, 2012.

According to Hass, the "*power-culture*" concept that he developed based on the above theories is fundamental for the understanding of social change. This concept assumes a link between its components—*power*—in Weber's understanding as the capacity of different agents to influence actively the surrounding social reality; and *culture*—as a system of knowledge, meanings, as well as rules and practices, determining familiar ways of interpreting various events and reacting in different circumstances. Oversimplifying this central idea, we can summarize the following. Hass believes that the firm intention of an actor wielding power and available relevant resource by themselves are insufficient to implement fundamental change involving breaking down the existing practices—this is largely impeded by the legitimacy of the existing structures underpinned by the respective culture. Change is possible only when it is accompanied by a corresponding transformation of the elements shaping culture.

To demonstrate the validity of his concept, Hass resorts to an extremely detailed and meticulous analysis of different cases from Russian reality. One such case studies the example of two small companies established in the 1990s—a travel agency providing services to foreigners visiting Russia and a publishing house engaged in translating and publishing professional literature for entrepreneurs and economists. The companies were selected on the basis of similar initial conditions (such as the scope of the activities, staff, etc., and, not least, the strategic view of their leaders as to how the companies should be organized in order to achieve success in a market environment.

Hass notes that at the outset both companies equally experienced problems typical for Russian enterprises of that time—poorly developed corporate procedures, weak discipline and motivation of the staff, informal atmosphere in the team, extremely high value of moral authority, disregard for formal status and responsibilities, etc. At the same time, he pays tribute to their teams, since, in his own admission, both companies offered competitive and in a sense unique products, occupying and maintaining a specific niche in their field of activity. Incentives for development were also the same—the leaders and founders of the companies were focused on profit and were emotionally attached to their business, treating it as their brainchild.

Nevertheless, Hass shows that in the long run only one of the companies managed to overcome the syndrome of the post-socialist enterprise related to the above mentioned problems and become a truly market company (according to Western standards) with a clear segregation of roles and responsibilities, focus on high professionalism, rigid discipline, etc. The American sociologist demonstrates that the reason for this success appears to lie in the complex mechanisms of translating organizational innovations involving, as mentioned earlier, 1) the capacity to actively influence the situation (through successful and effective exercise of power) and 2) synchronizing innovations with successful changes in culture (work culture in this case). For Hass, the key actor of these changes is an expat—a manager of American origin hired by the travel agency and facing the need to implement new practices in a rather inert team. The main problem was that neither the executive position, nor the respective sanctions of the company founder were sufficient to implement the required changes, since all attempts to influence the situation met strong resistance from the employees (including open sabotage!) who were not ready to give up their familiar ways and practices. Another factor impeding change was the informal, almost family atmosphere in the team supported by the paternalism of the founders. This placed significant constraint on the leverage that the new manager could resort to (e.g., dismiss certain employees or provide financial incentives). However, in spite of these difficulties, the manager succeeded in changing the staff's "socialist mentality", i.e. not just implemented new practices, but also made them routine. Hass names the following factors that among others contributed to the success. First, the ability of the manager to respond to the situation in order to become an "insider" and compensate for the lack of power and authority required to implement the planned changes. Second, an adequate understanding of the employees' "mentality" as a given factor, shaped in other circumstances and, what is important, unable to change automatically in a new context. Hass uses this example to demonstrate that *practices* (i.e., people's familiar actions or sets of actions in typical situations), which are part of this "mentality" do not exist by themselves. To understand their sustainability and reproduction, it is necessary to distinguish the underlying *logic*, i.e., the meanings prescribing the use of relevant practices in particular circumstances.

Obviously, the presented brief overview does not cover the entire field of research on which we focus in this book. Our aim was to update the reader on current research and to give an idea about the range of theories and methods at the disposal of scholars and experts engaged in studying cross-cultural interactions on the example of such a specific social group as the expatriates. One can see that some key aspects of high practical and utilitarian interest for major multinational corporations, which actively engage expatriates in their international operations, have received extensive in-depth coverage. Nevertheless, the field of our research still has "exposed" areas, which can be of interest to scholars. In any case, the provided overview should demonstrate that the phenomenon of expatriation and the growing rate of cross-cultural exchanges, which are objective consequences of increasing globalization, consist of extremely complex aspects and processes, which require further study.

Chapter III.
External and internal origins of the Russian work culture

We proceed to analyze the factors that shaped the specific features of the Russian national work culture in the long historical process To date, studies addressing various components of its genesis have produced numerous results. Summarizing the conceptual approaches prevailing in literature, we have identified the following factors, which created the "core" of the Russian work culture: *civilizational-economic, geo-climatic, ethno-environmental, and ethno-religious.*[75]

The key premise of our analysis is that originally, Russian work culture is a global phenomenon, as it was shaped not only by domestic circumstances, but was largely a response to the external geo-cultural and geopolitical challenges and threats typical for Russian history. In an ironic twist of fate, these challenges and treats are still relevant today, and this means that the Russian work culture has not lost its unique potential in the current political, economic, and cultural configuration of the world.

Civilizational-economic factor. We shall first take a look at the more general issue, which has been a topic of discussion for many generations. Do specific national (ethnocultural) features influence economic development and work performance at all?

Since the 1980s, this question implicitly pervaded all discussions regarding Russia's ways of development. Most supporters of the liberal choice were convinced that neither specific national features, nor any civilizational characteristics should have any impact on determining the economic strategy. Their main heroes included two personalities—the British Prime Minister Margaret Thatcher and Chilean dictator general Augusto Pinochet. Perhaps, many of our fellow liberals were more Thatcherite than the most ardent admirers of the distinguished British lady in her home country. Meanwhile, advocates of the civilizational

---

75 This analysis further develops the ideas set forth in the work: Shkaratan O.I., Karacharovskiy V.V. *The Russian Work and Management Culture. A Study in the Context of Economic Development Prospects* // Mir Rossii. 2002. No. 1.

identity were mainly to be found among the opponents of market reforms who were in favor of preserving the failed planned economy. The spirit of the purest universalism triumphed in the actual policy of economic reforms. Non-market institutional factors of economic growth were ignored. Research findings on the comparative sociology of civilizations, comparative management, and the modern institutional economic theory were discarded. It would seem that the sad experience of the 1990s is a clear indication that the supporters of a rational combination of universalism and particularism were right; however, this painful issue is still debated. Views are extremely polarized.

In this respect, one of the first discussions in the context of reconsidering the role of the national factor in economic and civilizational development is very indicative (the process started in the 2000s). The discussion *Economy – Language – Culture (2000–2001)* was launched on the pages of the *Social Science and Modernity (Obshchestvennye Nauki i Sovremennost')* journal. Following is an excerpt from it.

A.V. Kiva wrote, "What does world experience demonstrate? The archetypes of the people, the national culture, the nature of the religion, etc. in fact do not play a crucial role in the economic progress of the country. This is evidenced by the stunning progress of countries significantly varying in these characteristics, such as, for example, the United States, Germany, Japan, China, the "new industrialized countries", and others. Even Islam, the dogmas of which contain many premises that would seem to impede business development, has not prevented the rapid economic progress of a number of Islamic countries."[76]

It would seem that the distinguished professor is a pure universalist. However, further on in the same article he notes, "However, Japan addressed the problems of economic development quite differently from the United States. It made a stake on collectivism, solidarity, patriotism, the achievement of consensus on issues vital for the nation, whereas the USA relied on individualism, on settling all issues within the "majority – minority" paradigm. In other words, countries with both individualist and collectivist traditions achieve enviable success in their development." Whether intentionally or unintentionally, the author once again noted the main thing—the seamless use of specific cultural traditions in

---

[76] Kiva A.V. *"Economy - Language - Culture" through the Prism of Virtual Reality //* Obshchestvennye Nauki i Sovremennost'. 2001. No. 4. p. 46.

work and management is an important tool for achieving success on the common way to the modern developed economy.[77]

By contrast, V.A. Naishul drew attention to the need and possibility to seek support for market and democratic reforms in the depths of the national culture, "I believe the existence of a distinct relationship between the country's economic achievements and its culture is one of the most important lessons of the past decade. In fact, economists specializing in culture studies have long been addressing this issue, but currently a lot of new data have emerged, which illustrate the interaction between culture and the economy and provide a fresh perspective of these processes." In this respect, Naishul provides the following example: "In the late 1980s–early 1990s, a number of states launched post-socialist reforms. Today, we are witnessing significant differences in this process in the Western and Eastern Christian countries. Where the Western Christian societies (both Protestant and Catholic) are transforming their economy more or less successfully, the Eastern Christian societies have landed in the position of losers, and this observation is not confined to the CIS borders. Recall Bulgaria and Romania, and the fact that the economy of Greece—the only Orthodox EEC country—is not in the best shape. This fact alone raises the question of the link between economy and culture."[78] To avoid any misunderstanding, we will remind that the author of these judgments—one of the initiators of market reforms in Russia—was and remains an advocate of this way of national development. He is convinced, "In my opinion, Russian culture is meant for a market-based order."[79]

This dispute is not casual. By origin and content, social sciences are Eurocentric. The theories and conceptual frameworks dominant in the world economic and sociological sciences can be clearly understood and interpreted only when applied to societies based on private property, civil relations, and individualism. However, they do not adequately reflect the realities of societies with other institutional structures, other cultures, and other socio-economic relations. This applies first of all to Marxism with its theory of successive socio-economic for-

---

77   Ibid.
78   Proceedings of the round table *Economy-Language-Culture* // Obshchestvennye Nauki i Sovremennost'. 2000. No. 6. p. 35.
79   Ibid. p. 46.

mations—from slavery to "Paradise on Earth", the theoretical utopia of communism. Karl Marx's "deviations" and his contemplations about the Asiatic mode of production are a separate topic; however, typical for the Marxist worldview was the idea of a unitary linear development of humanity with nations and countries differing only by their level of development.

Liberalism is no different in this respect. It also recognizes that there is no alternative way of development—from the traditional society to the bourgeois one based on private property, or (according to Francis Fukuyama)—from tribalism to slavery, from slavery to theocracy, and finally, to a democratic-egalitarian society crowning the historic path. Countries and peoples are assessed as being at different "levels" (at different stages) of moving to a common ideal—universal Western democracy and liberal capitalism.

It appears that both the Marxist and the liberal unitarianism with their non-alternative evolution of mankind are by no means indisputable. Less than ten years after Fukuyama's famous essay *The End of History?*—the manifesto of triumphant liberalism—was published, the realities of life questioned the validity of the idea of the complete victory of Western democracy.[80] The problem is reduced to disclosing the relation between the essential features of socio-economic systems and the core elements of different civilizations. Here we cannot but recall Professor Samuel Huntington's prediction (which increasingly proves to be true) about the inevitable clash of the ever more rallying civilizations.[81]

Despite their diversity, all the existing paths of social development are ultimately based on the differences between two dominant types of civilizations, which can be termed symbolically as "European" and "Asiatic". The former originates from the antique polis and constitutes a

---

[80] Fukuyama F. *The End of History?* // Voprosy Philosophii. 1990, No. 3, pp. 134–148; see also Fukuyama F. *The End of History and the Last Man.* L.- N.Y., 1992; Fukuyama F. *Trust. The Social Virtues and the Creation of Prosperity.* N.Y.: Free Press, 1996.

[81] Huntington S. *The Clash of Civilizations?* // Foreign Affairs / Summer 1993; translation see: Huntington S. *The Clash of Civilizations?* // POLIS. 1994, No. 1. pp. 33–57; an in-depth analysis of this situation and the emerging struggle of mass movements against the "new global order" see in the work of M. Castells which unfortunately has not been translated into Russian: Castells M. *The Information Age: Economy, Society and Culture. Vol. II. The Power of Identity.* Oxford: Blackwell Publishers. 1997. p. 1–462.

chain of societies characterized by private ownership, balanced "civil society—public institutions" relations, a developed personality, and a priority of individualistic values. The latter is historically associated with oriental despotism, the dominance of state ownership, omnipotence of government institutional structures in the absence of a civil society, with citizenship, the priority of communal values, and suppression of individuality. This type of civilization prevailed in world history, both in space and time.

Over millenniums (although changing its phenomenological features, this type of civilization is incapable of restructuring its social organisms by itself, without external influence) such societies were based on the following core elements:

- The state as an omnipotent divine power standing over the entire population
- Power and legal hierarchy
- Social status determined by power and prestige rather than difference in wealth
- Dependence of individual wealth on the proximity to the authorities
- Dominance of collective ownership of the rural agricultural commune and the state personified by the supreme ruler
- Land appears to be no man's property
- Centralized withdrawal of the surplus product in the form of rent-tax executing simultaneously the function of state authority (tax) and the function of title to land (rent).

Yegor Gaidar, the theorist of Russian liberalism, could not ignore this essential dichotomy of world history. The more so that in recent years only the lazy failed to write about the similarity of the Asiatic mode of production and the socio-economic realities of the Soviet society. But like the other liberals, he attributes this to the past of most world nations, associating the paths of development and the bright "Tomorrow" with a uniform type of economy, a uniform type of civilization—liberal capitalism. Hence the conclusion about the need to adhere to "a single global tradition" based on "the separation of state and private ownership, on the legitimacy of the latter, on respect for human rights, et cetera. Our first task is to enter into that space, and establish ourselves there."[82]

In general, the radical-liberal point of view always perceived the second type of civilization as a catch-up civilization. Although, perhaps, the assumption that another viable alternative path of development was possible should not have been excluded. After all, if we acknowledge that so far humanity has been developing in a non-linear way, why should we refuse to recognize this nonlinearity with respect to the future; why should we not accept nonlinearity, the diversity of paths of development as a law of history? What is Russia's place in the interaction between these two dominant civilizations?

We can reflect on the contemporary events and attempt to reveal the essence of the present "...without inventing anything, but just by trying to understand the logic of Russia's development," its twelve centuries of history.[83] Russian authors Yu. Pivovarov, A. Fursov, I. Chubais, A. Susokolov[84] and many others note the crucial role of the following specific factors of Russia's history, its economic and social life, national culture and mentality: dispersal of the population over vast territories and initially weak links between local communities; exceptional importance of the struggle for survival in a harsh northern climate; and finally and most importantly—the centuries-old process of gathering lands, i.e., extensive growth for about six hundred years. Constant territorial expansion demanded statehood in the form of autocracy and militarization of the country, and as a consequence—tremendous challenges for the population.

We believe it is important to consider the concept of Yu. Pivovarov and A. Fursov, which states that the core element of Russian history is "Power—not political, state or economic, but Power as a metaphysical phenomenon. Power as such. It collapsed every time when it acquired too many state, political or class features. It collapsed itself and destroyed everything around as soon as it started transforming the Russian reality into a Western-style reality—bourgeois or anti-bourgeois—

---

82 Gaidar Ye.T. *State and Evolution*. M.: Eurasia, 1995. p. 41 and others.
83 Chubais I. *Russia in Search of Itself*. M.: Izd-vo NOK Muzei Bumagi, 1998.
84 Susokolov A.A. *The Russian Ethnos in the Twentieth Century: Extensive Culture Crisis Stages* // Mir Rossii. 1994. No. 2.

inconsistent with it..."[85] The authors believe that such power relations stem from the rule of the Golden Horde in Rus'. It was the Horde that brought the principle "Power is everything; the people are nothing" to Rus'. Power is the only significant social subject.[86] It appears that the Mongol invasion changed the national genetic code from a European one to some other:

> "...The Mongol yoke not only radically changed the power relations in Rus'—it molded, shaped an essentially new mutant actor, hitherto unprecedented in the Christian world.
> Actually, in pre-Mongol Rus', power was dispersed among the angles of a quadrilateral: the Prince—Veche [popular assembly]—Boyars [the nobility]—the Church. ... In no case was the prince the only authority—Authority with a capital letter. On the whole, the situation was similar to the European feudal society.
> ... The Horde resolved the issue. It gave the Russian princes who served it—Alexander Nevsky and later the Moscow Danilovich princes—the needed "critical mass" of coercion, which neutralized the power of the boyars and Veche...
> ... By definition, the Christian world is a multi-actor one. This implies the existence of two or more parties. In the Christian world, of which Russia was a part, such actors included individuals, corporations (guilds, universities), cities, rulers. The Horde created a situation where Power and the Church acting as its agent became the only authority."[87]

V.M. Mezhuev arrives at similar conclusions,

> "For all the differences, power in present-day Russia exhibits astonishing similarity with monarchism and Bolshevism...
> There is a Russian word that can perhaps provide a name for this tradition. The word is autocracy, which is semantically close to the notion of 'authoritarianism', but has a Russian flavor more understandable for us. It is just another name for Russian government that many generations of Russian history researchers have tried to puzzle out...
> ...There is no society beyond power in Russia; there is only the people—a faceless, homogeneous, and voiceless ethnic or religious (Orthodox people) community. Power in Russia identified itself not with regard to society but with regard to the people (Power is the subject, people are the object); hence its patrimonial rather than

---

85 Pivovarov Yu., Fursov A. *Russian Power, the Russian System, Russian History /* Krasnye Kholmy. Anthology. 1999. M.: Publishing house Gorodskaya Sobstvennost', 1999, pp.188–189.
86 Ibid.
87 Pivovarov Yu., Fursov A. *The Russian System and Reforms //* Pro et Contra. V. 4, 1999, No. 4. pp. 182–183.

political nature. The people and society in Russia are mutually exclusive concepts."[88]

The Horde replaced the emerging but not yet developed feudal class society with oriental despotism, Asiatic (state) mode of production, and a loose classless social structure without private property and without social groups of proprietors.

Private ownership of land and other assets along with civil rights for the privileged minority emerged only in the second half of the eighteenth century. In 1762, Emperor Peter III issued a Decree, according to which the nobles were released from mandatory service to the state without losing title to their land. However, this document did not introduce much certainty with respect to the status of the land and the peasants who worked on it (previously they were owned by the sovereign). Nevertheless, since then, a class of free subjects not dependent on the state appeared in Russia. In 1765, Catherine II issued a Decree declaring estate owners de jure owners of land even if no documentary evidence was available. Finally, in 1785, the Empress signed the famous Charter of the Nobility granting the "noble Russian gentry" full and inalienable title to their property, i.e., to the lands populated by the peasants. By comparison, England had achieved practically the same six hundred years earlier, while in Germany the notion of "property" came into general use as early as the first half of the thirteenth century. The Charter declared "the liberty and freedom of the nobility" and the voluntary nature of their service to the state.

In the same year 1785 Catherine II signed the Charter of the Cities, by which city dwellers were divided into two estates—merchants ("kupechestvo") and townspeople ("meshchyane"). Both estates were entitled to possess and use movable and immovable property.[89] As for the peasants, who made up the majority of the population, their transformation into owners of the land they farmed by 1917 was still not completed. In general, it can be concluded that on the eve of the Octo-

---

88 Mezhuev V. *The Tradition of Autocracy in Contemporary Russia //* Svobodnaya Mysl'. 2000. No. 4, pp. 94, 95.
89 Pipes Richard. *Property and Freedom.* M.: Moscow School of Political Studies, 2000. pp. 248–249, 251; Mironov B.N. *The Social History of Russia at the Times of the Empire (18th-early 20th centuries): Genesis of the Individual, Democratic Family, Civil Society and the Rule of Law.* Volumes 1–2. Second edition. SPb.: Dmitry Bulavin, 2000.

ber Revolution, the European line of development was starting to prevail. However, for the majority of Russians private ownership had not yet become a tradition. The reforms of Pyotr Stolypin had too little time to transform members of a rural commune into independent farmers. The dual development trend, which existed at that time in Russia, explains why the Bolsheviks had to eliminate tens of millions of people in order to "build socialism", but in fact to establish the Asiatic mode of development.

These dual development trends give a clue to understanding why a regime could come to power on Russia's own national basis (not imposed from outside), which crushed the bourgeois, proprietary society emerging in the country and resulted in the triumph of the Asiatic line of development. However, this could not be fully implemented because psychologically and historically Russia was much closer to the West than, say, China or India.

It seems that the idea of a Eurasian culture can become an important system element for analyzing transitive processes in contemporary Russia. It can help understand the nature of the changes taking place in Russian society—whether they indicate a movement towards Westernization, an attempt to overcome etacratism (statism) and corporate Eurasianism or whether they mean the emergence of a specific social reality. Many years ago, Yury Lotman suggested an interesting idea: Eurasianism formed "to the West of the boundary, which separated the settled European civilization from "The Great Steppe" and to the East of the religious boundary dividing orthodox from heterodox Christianity. Rus', being the core of this Eurasian world, identified itself both with the center of the world and its periphery. It managed to focus simultaneously on isolation and integration."[90] Throughout its history and geography, Russia has been for centuries a Eurasian society; alternately, it sought closer ties with its European neighbors or by its way of life gravitated towards the Asiatic world.[91]

Many authors highlighted the similarity between the essential features of the so-called Soviet socialism and the system, which Karl Marx

---

90 Lotman Yu. *Writings on Landmark Systems*. Tartu, 1972. Issue 15, pp. 5–6.
91 *World of Russia - Eurasia. Anthology.* M., 1995. *The Russian knot of Eurasianism: The Orient in Russian thought. Collected studies of Eurasianists.* M.: Belovod'ye, 1997.

termed "the Asiatic mode of production" and our contemporary researchers prefer (absolutely reasonably) to call "the state mode of production" (in this context, we refer to the writings of our Russian authors—L.S. Vasiliev, R.M. Nureev, and Yu.V. Pavlenko).[92] The similarity is really striking. In terms of the issue we are studying, this identified relationship can help understand and explain the specific features of the Russian mentality and work behavior.

In a series of articles under the indicative heading *The Decrepit Orient and the Bright Future,* A.V. Pimenov gave a detailed account of the discussions regarding the obvious relationship between Soviet etacratism and oriental despotism (with the sad fate of their participants in the Soviet era) and presented the results of his own comparative analysis of the two phenomena—oriental despotism and totalitarian societies of the twentieth century. The articles were published in 1999 in the *Mir Rossii* journal. He rightly points out, "The fact that 'real socialist' societies closely resemble the despotism of the Ancient Orient is no longer news; it is common knowledge... However, the nature of this similarity is still unclear."[93]

We consider the Soviet and early post-Soviet Russian societies to be a distinctive socio-economic and political system, which is neither capitalist nor socialist. Etacratism is an independent stage and a parallel branch of historical development of the contemporary society with its own functioning and development laws. With the establishment of etacratism, historical development seems to follow a coil of the gigantic spiral where authoritarian societies emerge again. Following are the characteristics of an etacratic classless society:

- Segregation of property ownership as a function of power; dominance of "power-property" relations
- Prevalence of state property; increasing state dominance
- State-monopoly mode of production
- Administrative-planned system

---

92 Vasiliev L.S. *The History of the Orient.* M.: Vysshaya shkola, 1994. V. 1. Introductory Section. Essence of the Issue. pp. 13–48; Nureev R.M. *The Economic System of Pre-Capitalist Formations.* Dushanbe: Donish, 1989; Pavlenko Yu.V. *Early Class Societies: Genesis and Ways of Development.* Kiev, 1989.
93 Pimenov A.V. *The Decrepit Orient and the Bright Future //* Mir Rossii. 1999. No. 1–2, p. 59.

- Domination of centralized distribution
- Shortage economy
- Development of the informal economy
- Dependence of technology development on external stimuli (technological stagnation)
- Militarization of the economy
- Hierarchical estate-strata stratification
- Corporate system as the dominant form of implementing power relations
- Social mobility organized from above and focused on promoting people loyal to the system
- The absence of a civil society, the rule of law and, accordingly, the existence of citizenship and particracy
- Multi-ethnic imperial type of national-state order.[94]

At first glance, the seven post-revolutionary decades were a period when development based on "Asiatic" historical traditions triumphed. That was the time when socially significant horizontal ties collapsed, the infrastructure of personal development degraded in many respects, the right to freely choose life models disappeared, and a de-privatization of virtually all aspects of life was under way. All this resulted in a reproduction of aggregate typical "averaged" individuals. In this sense, we can say that there was no truly civilized mode of existence in the Soviet (etacratic) society.

However, in the same years, the increasing globalization of world economic and social processes and the current level of mass communications could not but result in the etacratic society adopting the latest forms and achievements of civilization (this concerns the urban space, transport, architectural solutions, elements of social services, etc.). In counterbalance to the development logic of the Soviet system, this contributed to expanding and consolidating the basis of European culture, the basis which was focused on embracing the market and the civil society. In other words, just as in the previous period of national development, the Russian society was characterized by dual forms of life.

---

94 For a more detailed characteristic of etacratism see: Shkaratan O.I. *Type of Society, Type of Social Relations* // Mir Rossii. 2000, No. 2. pp. 63–108.

Classifying Russia as a society of the statist (etacratic) type is only the first step in explaining the concept of national culture and its impact on work ethics, production behavior, and the specific features of Russian management. Drawing on the writings of social philosophers, historians, and sociologists allows distinguishing Russia and Russians from the totality of countries and nations with a statist historical destiny and makes it possible to pass from an overly generalized typology (West – East) to a more specific typology of local civilizations. At any time, there is a certain set of local civilizations that usually assemble around world religions. In this context, Russia can be confidently attributed to the Orthodox civilization, in which it has held leading positions for centuries.[95]

Western cultural figures perceived Russia as a country of a different order than Europe. Thus, Hegel did not even include Russians in his list of "Christian nations of Europe". And already in the twentieth century Herbert Wells wrote about Russia as a semi-Oriental, semi-Western country. Many observers came to the conclusion that Russia was a certain Eurasian hybrid with no clear features of either part of the world. Oswald Spengler argued that Russia was a centaur with a European head and Asiatic body. With the victory of Bolshevism "Asia is winning Russia back after Europe had annexed it in the person of Peter the Great".[96] It is interesting that the same author perceived Russia as an "undeveloped" culture. In Spengler's typology of world civilizations Russia was classified as an "emerging" developing culture, which will still assert itself to the extent of its enormous development potential.

However, in the fair judgment of Pitirim Sorokin, Spengler in his philosophy of history and in the assessment of Russia reiterated all the fundamental postulates of the outstanding Russian scientist, historian,

---

95 Huntington S. *The Clash of Civilizations and Russia* // Moscow News. 1995, No. 5, 22–29 January 1995. p. 5; idem. *The Clash of Civilizations?* // POLIS. 1994, No. 1. p. 37–38; Yakovenko I. *What was Huntington's Mistake? Monologue of a Cultural Studies Scholar* // Znanie-Sila. 2002, No. 1. pp. 11–19; Orlova I.B. *Modern Civilizations and Russia.* M., 2000; Pastukhov V.B. *Post-Communism as a Logical Eurasian Civilization Development Phase* // Polis. 1992. No. 5–6. pp. 59–75; Mezhuev V.M. *The Russian Civilization - Utopia or Reality* / The Post-Industrial World and Russia. Publishing editors: Khoros V.G., Krasilshchikov V.A. M.: Editorial, URSS, 2001. pp. 287–601.

96 Spengler O. *The Decline of the West. Essays on the Morphology of World History. V. 1. Gestalt and Reality.* M.: Mysl', 1993. p. 110.

and sociologist Nikolay Danilevsky.[97] In his famous work *Russia and Europe* (1869), Danilevsky outlined his theory of cultural-historical types and dwelt on the idea that Russia had not yet completed its civilizational development; on the contrary, it was only at the beginning of the journey. In his opinion, Russia had yet to form its civilization, based on its own moral principles. Danilevsky deeply felt the distinctiveness of the Russian cultural type. He did not recognize the universalism of the Romano-Germanic culture. He did not criticize the Western European culture, but he rejected the view that it was the one and only type of culture; he perceived himself as a representative of another culture, equal and equivalent to the European one.[98]

In the opinion of Arnold J. Toynbee, a distinguished British historian of the twentieth century, Russia "is part of the world's great non-western majority". Russians have never been western Christians. "Eastern and western Christendom have always been foreign to one another, and have often been mutually antipathetic and hostile, as Russia and the west unhappily still are today, when each of them is in what one might call a 'post-Christian' phase of its history."[99] Russia has endured the challenge of nature, the Asiatic challenge, and the Western challenge. A harsh environment forced Russia to develop extensively by expanding its geographical borders. Settled agriculture and consolidation of Orthodoxy became a response to the Asiatic challenge, namely, the Mongol invasion.[100]

Thus, the Eurasian space between the West and the East has created the largest "frontier" civilization—Russia.[101] It is this specific disposition in the external environment that has shaped the ambivalence of the Russian culture—not only its conceptual duality, but also the coexistence of equally pronounced polar properties of mentality. However, "frontier-ness" is a factor that is likely to have limited potential impact on

---

97   Sorokin P. *Social Philosophies of an Age of Crisis*. Boston, 1951. p. 359. Taken from Pivovarov Yu.S. *Nikolay Danilevsky in Russian Culture and in World Science* // Mir Rossii, 1992, No. 1, pp. 167–168.
98   Danilevsky N.Ya. *Russia and Europe. An Inquiry into the Cultural and Political Relations of the Slavic World to the Romano-Germanic World*. Sixth edition. SPb.: Izd-vo SPbGU: Glagol, 1995.
99   Toynbee A. *Civilization on Trial*. Collected works. SPb.: JUVENTA, 1995. p. 156.
100 Toynbee A. *A Study of History*. M.: Progress, 1991.
101 See, *e.g.*, Akhiezer A.S. *Russia: A Critique of Historical Experience*. Volumes I-III. M.: Philosophical Society of the USSR, 1991.

the development of culture. Following the logic of Lev Gumilev's passionarity theory of ethnogenesis, such a feature as "frontier-ness" is hardly an inherent feature of a civilization; more likely, it characterizes a certain stage in its development.[102] Besides, the "erosion" and inner polarization of Russian culture is only one side of the duality arising from "frontier-ness". The other side is fantastic flexibility and capacity to quickly adopt and internalize foreign values without losing its own national identity.

Geo-climatic factor. Speaking about the specific features of Russia's development, it is impossible to ignore the geo-climatic factor and the respective set of ideas that the uniqueness of the Russian economic culture is largely related to the "unavoidable" system properties of the Russian territory.

In pre-industrial societies, the natural environment played a huge role in shaping the type of economy, the whole system of human activity, work skills, abilities, etc. The best experiences and practices were consolidated, and they served to form ethnic work and land development traditions. These traditions could not fail to leave an imprint on the national mentality (when this type of labor activity and certain work traditions were widely adopted by the people). Educational systems developed over generations were primarily focused on shaping a worker with labor skills and psychological traits required by the existing economic practices. Studies of individual nations show that even when the type of economy changes, traditional education systems continue largely shaping the work skills and mentality of a significant part of the population. *We are dealing with a frequent case of inertia of ethnic tradition.* One can either use it or strive to overcome, but in any case one cannot ignore it.

The geo-climatic concept substantiates the uniqueness of the Russian work culture by the fact that it was formed in an area with specific natural and geographic conditions, such as variable natural processes, harsh climate, vast territories, etc.[103]

---

102   Gumilev L.N. *Ethnogenesis and the Biosphere of Earth*. M.: Tanais DI-DIC, 1994.
103   See, *e.g.*, Golts G.A. *Culture and Economy of Russia over Three Centuries, XVIII - XX Centuries*. Novosibirsk: Sibirskiy Chronograph. 2002; Ilyin V.V., Akhiezer A.S. *The Russian Civilization: Essence, Boundaries, Potential*. M.: Izd-vo MGU, 2000; Parshev A.P. *Why Russia is not America. A Book for Those Who Remain Here*. M.: Forum, 2001.

Russian historian Vasily Klyuchevsky already noticed the relationship between climatic conditions, labor activity, and national traditions He wrote, "A Great Russian is certain of one thing—that he should value a clear summer workday, that nature grants him little good time for farming, and that the short Great Russian summer can be shortened even more by untimely and unexpected bad weather. This causes a Great Russian peasant to hurry and work hard to achieve a lot in a short period and be off the field in due time... Thus, a Great Russian has grown accustomed to overexert himself over a short term, to work quickly, feverishly, and efficiently, and then to relax during the forced autumn and winter idleness. No other people in Europe is capable of such short-term overexertion; but it seems that nowhere in Europe can we find such a lack of habit for regular, moderate, and continuous labor as in the same Great Russia."[104]

A century later James Billington, another distinguished historian, continued Klyuchevsky's line of thought, "Famine was also never far away in the north where the growing season was short and the soil was thin; and where grain could not even be planted until trees were arduously uprooted and soil upturned with fragile wooden plows. But the forest also gave rise to special fears: of insects and rodents gnawing from below and of fire sweeping in from without. ...Even when he had cleared and planted a field and built a hut, the muzhik of the north was plagued by an invisible army of insects and rodents burrowing up through the floorboards and gnawing at his crops."[105]

These practices of "ragged", inconsistent, and irregular work have become deep-rooted behavioral stereotypes. They affect all types and kinds of labor activity. In his time, the Russian scientist Ivan Pavlov noted that such qualities as diligence, concentration, and consistency in performing their tasks were not typical of Russian people, "...For us, recommending features are not focus, but pressure, speed, and charge. This is what we obviously regard as an indication of talent; diligence and patience for us fit poorly with the notion of giftedness. ...As soon as a person focuses on one issue, our people immediately pass

---

104 Klyuchevsky V.O. *Writings in eight volumes*. M.: Gospolitizdat, 1956–1959. V. 1. pp. 313–314.
105 J. Billington. *The Icon and the Axe. An Interpretive History of Russian Culture*. M.: Rudomino, 2001. p. 52.

the verdict, 'Ah! This is a boring specialist.' But look what weight such specialists have in the West; they are valued and respected as experts in their field. No wonder! These specialists drive our entire life, but for us it is boring... We believe in pushing everything to the limit, regardless of any circumstances. This is our main feature."[106]

Studies conducted by Boris Mironov demonstrate that the so-called "ethics of idleness" is an element of Russian work culture shaped by the above mentioned factors. This is a value system based on the tradition not to consider time as one of the most valuable resources of economic activity. Data of the late nineteenth—early twentieth centuries show that in the 1850s, Russian peasants had 230 non-working days per year, of them 95 holidays; in 1902—258 non-working days, of them 123 holidays![107] As we see, the "ethics of idleness" as a characteristic of culture had quite objective reasons.

Collectivism as a Russian person's feature is often attributed to the geo-climatic factor. However, this feature in Russian culture clearly stands apart. The issue of whether a Russian person is more inclined to collectivism or individualism remains open. There are many examples when Russians showed tremendous capacity for mobilization and joint actions. On the other hand, we cannot ignore other, directly opposite, facts demonstrating the Russians' extremely individualistic behavioral patterns. Suffice it to recall the example of Russian diasporas abroad, which are traditionally the least united.

Indeed, collectivism in Russia has always been a forced measure, which made survival in a harsh climate and under conditions of territorial fragmentation possible. However, precisely this forced and essentially artificial rapprochement of the people generated a directly opposite feature of culture—inner denial of collectivist values on the backdrop of the externally imposed need to abide by them. Collectivism has become a functional and intrinsically syncretic feature of culture having produced its antithesis—extreme individualism, which manifests itself whenever the external threat requiring cohesion disappears.

The role of the geo-climatic factor can be questioned, since technical progress has completely changed the quality of life in the modern

---

106 Pavlov I. *On the Russian Mind* // Literaturnaya Gazeta. 1991, No. 30.
107 Mironov B.N. *Attitude to Work in Pre-Revolutionary Russia* // Sotsiologicheskie issledovaniia. 2001. No. 10. pp. 100–103

world. As a result, the essays of James Billington and Vasily Klyuchevsky seem to be now only of historical interest. However, these features are retained on the level of archetypes, and the factors underlying them are still valid, albeit in a modified form. Thus, in his book *Why Russia is not America*, Andrey Parshev advances the idea that the cost of maintaining a certain level and quality of life in Russia is disproportionately high as compared to other countries, and the cost to produce any goods is always greater than in other parts of the world. Following are some more debatable but shrewd judgments. Regarding transport: "The density of the population directly affects transport expenses. Should ...the population of each country be evenly distributed across its territory, the distance between the British, Germans, and Japanese would be 60 meters, between the Thais and the French—100 meters. As for the Russians, this distance would be 570 meters."[108] The same applies to the notorious oil factor: " ... Our wealth in energy resources is quite relative. < ... > Yes, we have oil, but in India it is enough to open the window to heat the room." [109]

Geo-climatic conditions, which made the results of labor unpredictable and therefore lowered the value of efforts and commitments, which forced the people to a high degree of unity, gave rise to a "ragged" work schedule and the need to mobilize efforts over the short term while devaluing time as an entrepreneurial resource, were a significant factor, which shaped the fundamental features of the Russian work culture.

Their role in Russia's development has always been ambivalent. Because of them, Russia lagged behind the world's leading countries, and due to them Russia was always capable of demonstrating fantastic civilizational breakthroughs. So far, this potential has not been exhausted.

Ethno-environmental factor. Along with the civilizational-economic and geo-climatic factors, the social "environmental niche" where the ethnos formed and developed was no less important.

The first notable issue in this respect is the degree of monoethnicity of Russia's population. If the Soviet Union united people with a different

---

108 Parshev A.P. *Why Russia is not America. A Book for Those Who Remain Here* M.: Forum, 2001. p. 73.
109 Ibid. p. 65.

historical destiny, with relatively integral economies, an established statehood, and prevalence of the "titular" ethnos on its territory, the new Russian state that emerged, among other things, differs from the former USSR by its predominant monoethnicity. Here, people of one culture and one historical destiny—the Russians—prevail clearly and definitely. By the national culture and language, Russia is currently one of the most homogeneous states in the world. Respecting the rights of all peoples of Russia to their cultural identity, in state-building and economic policy we cannot ignore the factor of prevailing monoethnicity. According to the 2010 census of the population, Russians constitute 77.7 per cent of Russia's total population. A comparison of these figures with the 1989 population census shows an obvious decline in the share of the Russian population (then the proportion of Russians was almost 82%). But even in light of these changes, we see an unconditional domination of Russian population in the country.

In our view, a state's ethnocultural homogeneity enhances its dynamism, its potential in economic development. Small and numerous peoples alike have an ethnic territory as a basis for reproduction, a specific ethno-environmental niche, which is the main resource of preserving and developing the national language and culture. In fact, all rapidly developing contemporary states are either monoethnic (like Japan) or are based on an ethnic core of a numerous people (WASP [White Anglo-Saxon Protestants] can be considered such an ethnic nucleus in the United States). "Deviation" from the model of a monoethnic state usually involves the risk of conflicts and additional difficulties in development. A nation state significantly enhances the viability of the ethnos. We obviously mean a common language and culture rather than the racist unity "based on blood". We take into account that the density of communications within societies united by a common language and culture is higher than between different ethnic groups. The outstanding Russian humanist Nikolai Berdyaev wrote in 1923, "A nation reveals all its potency through the state. On the other hand, the state must have a national basis, although the tribal structure of the state can be very complex and diversified... A state without a national core and national idea cannot have a creative life."[110]

---

110 Berdyaev N. *The Philosophy of Inequality*. M.: IMA-PRESS, 1990. p. 103.

Monoethnicity, however, is just one characteristic of the environmental niche of the Russian ethnos, whereas their totality is reflected in the writings of the contemporary Russian author Alexander Susokolov who has formulated the ethno-environmental concept of Russia's development.[111]

He considers the specific political, social, and cultural changes in the Russian ethnos over the twentieth century as a consequence of the Russian civilization transitioning from the extensive to the intensive type. The Russian ethnos is apparently the only one on the Eurasian continent that had almost continuously expanded its territory over at least six hundred years—until the middle of the nineteenth century. This allowed it to engage new land and other natural resources (forests, minerals, etc.) into the life sphere. Human resources also grew continuously as the Russian ethnos had high natural population increase rates almost throughout its entire history, especially in the late nineteenth—early twentieth centuries at the time of demographic transition. The extensive development of the ethnos on the basis of unlimited resources of all kinds allowed reconciling differences as they were arising within its units without fundamentally changing its structure. Thus, the stability of the core ethnic unit—the rural Russian commune—was achieved by an outflow of "superfluous" people beyond the main settlement area of the ethnos.

The extensive nature of development distinguished Russia from both the cultures of Western Europe where such opportunities had been exhausted by the twelfth-fourteenth centuries, and the civilizations of South-East Asia, in particular, China, Japan, and Korea. Cultures that have become reference ones for us, developed over many centuries as predominantly intensive ones.

Challenges arising in the process of extensive urbanization were met by engaging virtually unlimited human and natural resources. This produced a vicious circle, which was broken by the first crisis of the extensive development model. The Great October Revolution became the political embodiment of this crisis. The main cause of the crisis was the still existing opportunity for extensive development based on agricultural technologies traditional for the Russian ethnos. At the same

---

111 Susokolov A.A. *The Russian Ethnos in the Twentieth Century: Extensive Culture Crisis Stages* // Mir Rossii, No. 2, 1994.

time, this first crisis was overcome only due to the accelerated development of those traditions that formed the foundation of the ethnic culture at the time of crisis. This development stage of the Russian ethnos lasted for three generations and corresponded to the period of constructing "real socialism"; it was historically necessary because it demonstrated that the traditional principles of extensive culture were inconsistent with the new situation.

In the 1920s-1930s, the Russian ethnos was not prepared to develop democratic government institutions meeting the requirements of the European model, nor was it ready to "introduce" market relations. Masses of people had been displaced from the rural areas to the cities, where they were marginalized; their mentality could not serve as a basis for developing such institutions. It was in the process of building socialism that significant changes in the system of values prevailing among the majority of the population took place. These changes allowed taking a new step from the extensive to the intensive model of development.

The exhaustion of three sources, which for centuries allowed engaging unlimited resources to settle internal conflicts, is a prerequisite for the transition to an intensive development model. These sources are: high natural population increase, newly developed lands, and extremely cheap raw materials (ore, energy resources, etc.). Faced with the need for radical restructuring, at the first stage of transition the ethnos is capable of following only those traditions, which are inherent in it at the beginning of the crisis. Therefore, its first reaction is boosting the previous principles of extensive development, bringing them to the utmost limit. This stage of development corresponds to the period of "building socialism", which ends in a second extensive development crisis.

At the end of the twentieth century, the Russian ethnos entered into a new stage of its development—the final transition from an extensive development model to an intensive one. This process involves qualitative changes, which affect both the structure of the ethnos and the substance of the Russian culture in the broad sense of the word. The structural changes that are under way include primarily differentiation of the Russian ethnos, emergence of sustainable groups (territorial, social, and ethnocultural), development of real urban culture and qualitatively new urban local subcultures.

At the new stage, the role of competition as a factor affecting all aspects of the social life of the Russian ethnos becomes more important, since in the process of extensive development competition was suppressed by engaging additional resources. Accordingly, the role of social and cultural mechanisms regulating the impact of competition (in particular, law as a governance principle of society as compared to personal decrees) also grows. The inconsistency between the principles of extensive and intensive culture are manifested at the inter-group level (for example, between groups that had adopted principles of intensive cultures and groups committed to extensive norms), as well as at the intra-group one, this resulting in increased psychological tension within the ethnos.

In general, the Russian ethnos will inevitably adopt the core principles of the intensive development model. However, its culture originally developed as an extensive one, and it remains to be seen whether the restructuring will not result in the loss of its best qualities or even integrity. Besides, the Russian culture is the last extensive culture on Earth; therefore, it is extremely important to determine whether it can survive in the new environment, since its loss could be fatal to the world civilization.

Ethno-religious factor. The ethno-religious factor underlying Russian work culture is the result of three traditions interacting (intertwining) in Russian history—paganism, Byzantine Orthodoxy, and sectarianism. They have emerged in this chronological order and formed three layers of the Russian national mentality.

Here, we cannot ignore the obvious "foreign trace". Indeed, we know that Orthodoxy was initially a phenomenon imported from Byzantium, whereas, for example, Russian founders of the "Spiritual Christian" sects (Doukhobors and Molokans), famous for their economic patterns exceeding the Orthodox village in efficiency, were admirers of European theology. This means direct or indirect foreign influence in both cases. It was exercised either through visiting preachers or directly through European religious texts reaching Russia. Perhaps paganism is the only source of Russian work ethics with truly national roots.

Each of the three traditions plays a specific role in shaping the spiritual nature of the Russian people. Paganism historically laid down certain "initial conditions", which later accommodated Byzantine Orthodoxy and "fused" with it. Sects showed that types of economy close to the Western ones can be established in Russia; however, they succeeded only in creating marginalized groups. Orthodoxy served as a powerful integrating factor, as a unifying basis on which the type of personality "modal" for Russia emerged.

Linking the "spirit of capitalism" with Protestant ethic, Max Weber emphasized the fact that Protestantism had been preceded by a long tradition of monastic asceticism. The Church in the West had fostered this tradition since the end of the 400s "prescribing in addition to prayer also manual labor (up to seven hours per day) and daily academic studies. <... > This contributed to the development of a cultural layer in the monastic environment of medieval Europe, which became a repository of economic culture and 'Roman' education". [112]

In ancient Rus', Orthodoxy was accepted as ethics adequate to traditions of a totally different nature. Lev Gumilev showed that one of the main reasons why Prince Vladimir chose Orthodoxy was because its ethical standards were acceptable for the existing traditions. Thus, "Prince Vladimir turned down the Muslim mullahs by the well-known words: 'Drinking is the joy of Rus'...'"[113]

Of course, the role of Orthodoxy as an independent ethic was much more significant, and Lev Gumilev noted that. Highlighting its importance in controlling pagan elements, he writes, "The goodness and wisdom of Christianity in 988 fought with Perun and the pursuit of profit... Baptism gave our ancestors the highest freedom—freedom of choice between Good and Evil, and the victory of Orthodoxy gave Russia a thousand years of history."[114]

Ksenia Kasyanova developed this viewpoint in a singular manner. According to her, Orthodoxy was a tool to overcome the negative national "genotype", which is characterized by features of aggression. She writes, "...the unusually strong emphasis on submissiveness in Ortho-

---

112 Karsavin L.P. *Monasticism in the Middle Ages*. M., 1992. Chapter 3.
113 Gumilev L.N. *From Rus' to Russia: Essays on Ethnic History*. M.: Ecopros, 1994. p. 59.
114 Ibid. p. 61.

doxy is apparently the cultural response to the genotype."[115] However, she believes it is meaningless to speak about any complete victory of Orthodox ethics over "pagan elements". "When the mechanism of submissiveness and the sense of guilt fail, then... paranoid and maniacal ideas emerge, such as: 'Moscow is the Third Rome'—in the era of Ivan the Terrible; turning Russia into 'real' Holland-type Europe—during the reign of Peter the Great; or building socialism in one single country—in Stalin's time."[116]

Thus, from the very beginning there was a certain specific coexistence of the two ethics—pagan and Orthodox, with the elements of each of them manifesting themselves in different periods and in different spheres of life. James Billington rightly notes, "Brooding pagan naturalism seemed to stand in periodic opposition to a Christianity that had been brought in relatively late from more sunlit southerly regions. ...In Great Russia there was not so much a duality of belief as a continuing influx of primitive animism into an ever-expanding Christian culture."[117] Paganism continually made itself felt.

In Russia this was largely manifested in rituals (processions of the cross, pleading prayers) and specific "folk wisdom", the ideological foundation of which was absent in Christianity per se.[118] A study of Russian folklore gives many illustrative examples. In particular, V. Ivanitsky provides a curious example—a widespread belief that the best properties of the holy water are in its top layer. "...Everyone rushes to scoop water before the others, disrupting the church decorum by cries and bickering, incredible hustle and bustle as at an ordinary bazaar."[119] There are many other examples. V. Verkhovin, another Russian researcher, demonstrates the results of numerous observations on the reflection of market exchange ethics in the popular mind: *"If others pay, we drink all we can"*; *"Others' possessions are fenced off by fear"*; *"That who stole has one sin, that from whom was stolen has ten sins"*;

---

115 Kasyanova K. *On the Russian National Character.* M., 1994. p. 244.
116 Ibid.
117 J. Billington. *The Icon and the Axe. An Interpretive History of Russian Culture.* M.: Rudomino, 2001. p. 48.
118 See., *e.g., Russians. Ethnographic Essays* / Publishing editors: Alexandrov V.A., Vlasova I.V., Polishchuk N.S. M.: Nauka, 1999. p. 191.
119 Cit. ex: Ivanitsky V. *Archetypes of Success and the Russian Fairy Tale* // Znarie – Sila. 1997. No. 8–10. p. 127.

"If goods catch your fancy, your mind will not object" and the like.[120] Such management "recommendations" can hardly originate from anything but paganism.

In this respect, Andrei Konchalovsky voiced an indicative opinion, "Presently, the national culture has successfully abandoned the European tradition once forcedly imposed by Peter the Great, as well as the European traits acquired over three hundred years. This manifests itself in the current re-establishment of the Muscovy rule, the Horde syndrome <...> The people largely remain pagan, as they always used to be."[121]

So where is the contribution of Orthodoxy? Indeed, it is often criticized for a "weak" and "inefficient" Orthodox work ethic. Let us start with what is considered the main virtue of Protestantism—the "competitor" of Orthodoxy. L. Myasnikova has an interesting comment in this respect, "Protestantism implies equality at the start, civil equality (before law), but it does not exclude subsequent material, economic differentiation, that is, it is seamlessly consistent with market relations <...> On the contrary, Orthodoxy implies equality at the finish, that is, it is completely inconsistent with the spirit of market relations and capitalism."[122] In the opinion of E.V. Zhizhko, "Russian Orthodox hagiography makes virtually no reference to any work patterns. <...> the folk religious consciousness has basically failed to capture any work patterns, because they were neither 'prestigious', nor 'promising' in terms of the Orthodox concept of salvation". Indeed, the Orthodox doctrine outlines a very special way to become favored by God—if "a person diligently prays and suddenly achieves a result, this means that he is favored by God... The idea of labor as a process is lacking in the images of the saints, however, the idea of the result is present. More accurately—the idea of instant result due to a miracle."[123] The origins of Orthodox indifference to economic life are to be found in the Byzantine Orthodox tra-

---

120 Verkhovin V.I. *Patterns of Economic Behavior and their Verbalization in Russian Folklore* // Mir Rossii. 2001. No. 1. pp. 109, 111, 116.
121 Interview with A. Konchalovsky. 30.04.2013 / http://top.rbc.ru/viewpoint/30/04/2013/856341.shtml
122 Myasnikova L. *Russian Mentality and Management* // Voprosy Ekonomiki. 2000. No. 8. pp. 40–41.
123 Zhizhko E.V. *The Russian Work Ethics in the Socio-Psychological Context of Economic Reform* // Russian Society at the Turn of the Century: Touches to the Portrait // Publishing editor Butenko I.A. M.: MONF, 2000. p. 204.

dition, which "represents labor as punishment, retribution, a consequence of sin ... wealth is considered to be a sin, and poverty—a virtue ..."[124]

T.B. Koval makes an important comment when analyzing the Byzantine Orthodox tradition, "...although the monastic "community", which focused on prayer, asceticism and contemplation, had a great impact on society, it was indifferent to the spiritual destiny of the outside secular environment. ... The social and economic life of the secular community remained entirely under the influence of pagan elements. Daily work, occupational activity, and the relations between people in the process of production and consumption did not conform to their faith and were not dedicated by the supreme sense of serving God and others."[125]

We see that one of the main features of Orthodox ethics consists in the fact that its influence does not encompass the everyday aspects of labor. It is therefore quite understandable that in Orthodox Russia work culture was never well developed. Recalling the original pagan nature of Russia, it becomes quite understandable that the removal of certain state restrictions (as happened, for example, in the 1990s under contemporary Russian "capitalism") makes the economy an area "beyond morality".

However, even if limitations of any nature prevented the manifestation of "pagan elements" in economic practice, Orthodoxy per se could not offer a clear and attractive alternative to them.

We can judge about this by referring once again to the example of Byzantium—"...the Byzantines did not seek to enhance their tools either in agriculture or in urban crafts. The skill of the craftsman rather than the tools served as a guarantee of success. The craftsman relies only on his hands.

Orthodox theology in its own way supported this idea considering that tools were useless without a skilled craftsman who was able to

---

124 Ibid. p. 203.
125 Koval T.B. *Back-Breaking Benefit. Christian Work Ethics. Orthodoxy. Catholicism. Protestantism.* M.: Institut Etnologii i Antropologii RAN, 1994. p. 82. See also: Zarubina N.N. *The Orthodox Entrepreneur in the Mirror of the Russian Culture* // Obshchestvennye Nauki i Sovremennost'. 2001. No. 5. pp. 100–101; Faltsman V. *Russian Business from the Perspective of Christian Morality* // Voprosy Ekonomiki. 2000. No. 8. p. 47.

transform raw materials into a masterpiece. Thus, the craftsman and his skills was all that mattered. As a result, archaic production tools were typical both for the agriculture and for craft workshops."[126]

Orthodoxy taught people to perceive work not as a profit-generating craft, but as a skill with a totally different purpose, purely of a moral or ethical nature. Orthodox ethics largely blocked the classic component of work motivation (work as a source profit)—"...In the Orthodox Byzantine society, the attitude to profit derived from crafts and trade was negative."[127]

It is also necessary to mention another aspect of the influence that Orthodox ethics had on the perception of wealth by Russians. Orthodoxy articulated the importance of the method by which wealth was acquired, the fairness and moral integrity of this method. It thus formed in workers, craftsmen, and entrepreneurs moral qualities that often prevailed over the principle of economic benefit.[128]

Although the Orthodox doctrine was not capable of creating its own work ethic similar to the Protestant one, the Russian Orthodox Church, according to N.N. Zarubina, "has nothing against business enterprise" and "the institutions of the Orthodox Church were themselves active entrepreneurs in Russia."[129] Orthodoxy did not suppress the pragmatism and drive to act typical of paganism. However, it simultaneously introduced a competitive set of values into the consciousness of the Russian people, thus shaping a worldview, which allowed for a flexible approach to ethical issues in economic practice. It is quite reasonable to consider the mix of Orthodoxy and paganism as a separate, Russian type of economic (business, work) ethics.

The Old Belief and sectarianism (the so-called "spiritual Christianity") can rightfully be considered the third most important source of Russian work culture. M.M. Zhunin notes, "The forced separation from the state in the seventeenth century subsequently often gave Old Believers serious spiritual advantages as compared to the masses of people

---

126 Koval T.B. *Back-Breaking Benefit. Christian Work Ethics. Orthodoxy. Catholicism. Protestantism.* M.: Institut Etnologii i Antropologii RAN, 1994. p. 77.
127 Ibid.
128 See: Afanasiev E. *On Some Orthodox Principles for the Development of a Market Economy //* Voprosy Ekonomiki. 1993. No. 8; Platonov O.A. *The Russian Civilization.* M.: Rada, 1992 and other.
129 *The Current Modernization Challenge and Russian Alternatives. Round table proceedings //* Mir Rossii. 2001. No. 4. p. 34.

blindly following the dominant Orthodoxy strictly regulated by the Empire." The sense of being different from the rest of the society along with high-level literacy skills shaped not only another worldview and another attitude to knowledge in the Old Believers, but also a particular type of motivation consisting in the desire "to show in practice their ability to build a prosperous, beautiful Christian life."[130] Indeed, according to P.I. Melnikov-Pechersky, a brilliant expert on the Raskol [Schism in the Orthodox Church], in Old Believer monasteries "...daily chores preceded spiritual feats... Within the walls of the commune, work was in full swing from morning till night every day except holidays."[131]

The example of "Spiritual Christian" sects—Doukhobors and Molokans—is also interesting in terms of the relation between economic success and work ethic. According to T.B. Koval, their work ethic, like that of the Old Believers, was different from the Orthodox one, and the "economic ethos" they created "allowed them to organize their work and life in such a way that their living standards were always much higher than those of their Orthodox neighbors."[132]

The following example can serve as evidence of this fact. The St. Petersburg newspaper *Morning Star* wrote in 1910, "The Molokans of the Amur Region headed all sectors of the economy and social life in the area. They organize and manage shipping companies, timber trade, flour milling, cheese production, and credit institutions."[133]

Expulsion, exclusion of both the Old Believers and the "Spiritual Christians" from the Russian society could have been one of the possible reasons why these groups were economically successful. In this respect, N.N. Zarubina writes, "the Old Believers... were motivated by their focus on themselves, their isolation, self-confidence, and, definitely, outside pressure. They could rely neither on the state, nor on anyone or anything else, except themselves. All channels of social mobility were blocked for them, except the economic one."[134]

---

130 Here and above: Zhunin M.M. *An Enlightened Merchant is the Pride of the Old Belief* // Mir Rossii. 1998. No. 3. p. 91.
131 Melnikov-Pechersky P.I. *In the Forests*. Book 1. Gorky, 1956. p. 312.
132 See: Koval T.B. *The Spiritual Christians: Religious Distinctness and Work Ethics* // Mir Rossii. 1993. No. 1. p. 22.
133 Cit. ex: Koval T.B. *Back-Breaking Benefit. Christian Work Ethics. Orthodoxy. Catholicism. Protestantism*. M.: Institut Etnologii i Antropologii RAN, 1994. p. 273.
134 *The Current Modernization Challenge and Russian Alternatives. Round table proceedings* // Mir Rossii. 2001. No. 4. p. 33.

Thus, the Russian work culture is a product of the unique fusion of Slavonic paganism with the powerful spiritual system of Orthodoxy, both in its "orthodox" and "European" interpretation. This substantially rather diverse mix of cultural experiences, worldview types and actions, the simultaneous glance of the double-headed eagle to the "West" and to the "East", the potential to develop in different directions, and the eternal choice of the way constitute both the strength and the vulnerability of the Russian ethos.

***

Naturally, the factors we have listed and to a certain extent disclosed do not cover the entire historical background on which the Russian work culture—a fundamental element of Russia's civilization system—emerged. However, they largely exhaust the "list" of relevant factors that have received at least some empirical support.

Chapter IV.
The role of foreign and foreigners in Russian state-building

Russia's example of successfully adopting foreign experience and utilizing the achievements of other civilizations is very indicative. In the eighteenth century, the Russians rather than the Japanese or Chinese were the first in the world to master the achievements of the European development model, at least in the field of military craft and engineering. The Japanese, the Chinese, and the Asian "Tigers" largely relied on our Russian experience. Moreover, during and after the Great Reforms of Alexander II (second half of the nineteenth—the beginning of the twentieth centuries), Russia in competition with Japan and the United States made a leap in its economic and sociocultural development, which astounded the world by its scope and diversity. So the question is, has the Russian civilization exhausted its potential or is it in the process of transforming itself and seeking new ways for another breakthrough? In this respect Yuri Levada wrote, "...no effective (meeting the relevant concepts or plans) changes 'from the top' have ever been possible in Russia—every tide of change imposed by the will of the authorities or by circumstances experienced numerous transformations on its way. Moving in time and space, from the center to the periphery, it created pockets of silent resistance as well as diverse forms of mimicry and adjustment to the changing circumstances. In Russia, resistance to any change (regardless of its direction) has always been based primarily on the inertia of the social and human 'material', and to a lesser extent—on someone's deliberate or habitual opposition."[135]

However, the experience of many centuries of Russian history is by no means pessimistic. After long periods of resisting change, after periods of hesitation and self-doubt, the Russian civilization always achieved success and came out victorious. The brilliant achievements in science and arts demonstrate the enormous potential of the Russian

---

135 Levada Yu. *Searching for Man. Essays in Sociology.* 2000–2005. M.: Novoye Izdatel'stvo, 2006. pp. 275, 276.

civilization. What properties of the national character, of national mentality underlie these defeats and victories?

Europe developed in close proximity to Rus'/Russia. The outflow of the population from Transnistria to the northeast disrupted regular communication with Europe. The interests of the Russians themselves (the future Great Russians) who were forming as a people in the basin of the Upper Volga (which became the main river of the economic and political life) shifted sharply to the East. The future Belorussians and Ukrainians fell under the alien power of the Grand Duchy of Lithuania, having lost both political and, in many respects, economic, and cultural ties with the eastern Russian principalities.

But time passed, and it was North-Eastern Rus' that undertook to gather the Russian lands. As contacts were re-establishing with the not very much advanced western neighbors (Lithuania, Poland, and Sweden), the multi-generational backwardness of the country became apparent. So, since the times of Ivan III, Russia started adopting progressive technical, economic, and also cultural and everyday innovations from the West preserving, however, its institutional framework as well as values and standards. This became familiar routine, which lasted until the era of the great reformer Peter the Great. However, after dynamic progress, this path every time led to long periods of stagnation and irreversibly increased the gap between Russia and the countries that formed the core of the world economy.

James Billington, a unique expert on Russia and its culture, wrote about this, "Repeatedly, Russians have sought to acquire the end products of other civilizations without the intervening process of slow growth and inner understanding. Russia took the Byzantine heritage en bloc without absorbing its traditions of orderly philosophic discourse. The aristocracy adopted the language and style of the French culture without its critical spirit.... The radical intelligentsia deified nineteenth-century Western science without recreating the atmosphere of free criticism that had made scientific advances possible."[136]

By the mid-sixteenth century, Poland and Lithuania had blocked the way to Russia for Western Europeans. Therefore, it was no coincidence that the English expedition sent in 1553 to explore the northern route to

---

136 J. Billington. *The Icon and the Axe. An Interpretive History of Russian Culture.* M.: Rudomino, 2001. p. 687.

India and China found itself in the Russian North. With the opening of the northern gate to Europe, Russia broke out of the centuries-long isolation imposed by the Mongolian conquest. From that time on, for the first time since the middle of the thirteenth century, various specialists resumed coming to Russia. They represented crafts and trades, which had been forgotten by the descendants of the famous craftsmen of the Kievan and Novgorod Rus'—builders of the world famous temples, the pride of our contemporaries.

One of the first striking examples of such cooperation was export-oriented production of rope (strategic goods), which was organized by the English in Vologda and Kholmogory. By 1560, the Russians had mastered this technology, and most English specialists returned to their homeland. Russian production of high-quality ropes for the English navy was strategically important at the time of fierce confrontation between England and Spain for dominance in the Atlantic. Soon (in 1562), the Tsar granted a new privilege to the English—"to explore Vychegda for ore and to build a factory bringing in workers from England with the commitment to train Russians in the new occupation."

Peter the Great understood the urgent need for new technology and the necessity to adapt it to Russian conditions. Rather than taking only finished technical products from the West, he wanted to adopt the technology, to transplant the production to Russia together with its main lever—technical knowledge. This appeal to foreign experience demonstrated not only Russia's backwardness, but also its development, the growth of its complex needs, its ability and willingness to master more complicated tools and move on to more diversified forms of life.

Reforms did not follow any general concept. It was mostly a spontaneous search of innovative ways to develop the country. Thus, under Peter the Great the number of industrial mining enterprises increased fourfold. There was nothing original in this, however, the scope expanded tremendously. With the assistance of western specialists, traditional, outdated technologies were replaced by new, significantly more advanced ones. Actually, European industrialists and professionals contributed to the emergence and development of new industries in Russia. Along with the first iron and steel works in the Urals—the Nevyansk and Kamensk plants established under the guidance of Swedish and English specialists, large-scale shipbuilding was deployed with the participation of the Venetians and especially the Dutch. All of them received pay exceeding manifold the wages of domestic workers. Industry developed on the old feudal pre-market basis. The state could assign enterprises to nobles or merchants for use. However, private entrepreneurs enjoyed only the right of usage. As in previous times, the industry and the mines worked solely for the state.

In addition, many military professionals found employment in the Russian service. Since Ivan IV, the defense of the country increasingly depended on foreigners of Western origin. Already at the end of the seventeenth century, they formed detachments of the tsar's bodyguards. The battle with the Turks at Azov showed Peter I that only European martial arts could help overcome Turkey. It is known that Peter invited individual officers as well as entire foreign detachments for service. He also arranged for Russian servicemen to be trained by experienced foreign veterans. Russia purchased arms on a mass scale, mainly from Holland and Sweden. The Dutch provided Russia not only with stable supplies of arms, but also with cheap credit resources that were crucial for the innovative changes in the country.

In contrast to the positive perception of Peter the Great prevailing among Russian intellectuals, the Eurasianists believed he had actually gravely hurt the national dignity and destroyed the foundations of Russia's inner strength. Thus, he destroyed the institution of Patriarchate, which was essentially important in terms of the principal state-ideological system. The Eurasianists did not deny Peter's patriotism, but pointed out that "his patriotism was peculiar and in Russian life hitherto unknown. Rather than being an attachment to the real, historical Russia, it was a passionate dream of creating a great European state out of Russian material—a state that would resemble other European countries in everything, but would exceed them by territory and the power of its army and navy."[137]

Actually, Peter I had no intention of modernizing the empire either socially or politically. He and his successors, Elizabeth, Catherine, Alexander I, were against the mechanical adoption of European experience, which could undermine the autocracy or affect the stability of serfdom. Treating the West with sound mistrust, he adopted only one

---

137 Trubetskoy N.S. *The Legacy of Genghis Khan. View of the Russian History from the East rather than from the West.* M.: EXMO, 2012.

European political invention—the state governance framework: ten Swedish-type collegiate bodies and the Senate, as well as the form and organization of industrial production (manufactories), the army, the navy, and the form and organization of scientific activity and education, i.e., the Academy of Sciences and the universities (an innovation of the Petrine era that is still functioning today).

The Academy of Sciences established in 1724 became Russia's major scientific center, which developed rapidly. Just two decades after foundation, it was already occupying a prominent place among other academies of the world. At the time, such world-renowned scientists as Leonhard Euler, brothers Nicolaus and Daniel Bernoulli, Christian Goldbach, Georg Bernhard Bilfinger, Joseph-Nicolas Delisle, and other famous European scientists worked there. Initially, the Russian Academy of Sciences consisted of scholars invited from European universities. The outstanding Russian scientist Mikhail Lomonosov played a decisive role in shaping the independent image of the St. Petersburg Academy of Sciences. His work laid the foundation for scientific research in physics, chemistry, biology, and other sciences in Russia. The Moscow University was founded in 1755 at the initiative of Mikhail Lomonosov. From the outset, it became one of Russia's major centers of national culture and science.

The system of scientific research and education adopted from the West was organized purely on an estate basis. Having invited a considerable number of eminent European scientists to work in the Academy of Sciences and having provided them with everything necessary to realize their creative ideas, the authorities used their expanding community to Europeanize the thin layer of Russian nobility. Not only during Peter's reign, but until the second half of the nineteenth century, Russia remained essentially an illiterate country, which in its development relied on tradition rather than social innovations or imported western culture.

Actually, modernization, which at that time was largely synonymous to Westernization, started in Russia with the reforms of Alexander II who made primary education accessible to everyone regardless of their social origin. This dramatically enhanced the opportunity for representatives of virtually all estates, except the peasantry, to obtain complete secondary and higher university education. Since then, the West became a model of development for Russia. The scope of persons invited to teach at the old and newly established universities and otherwise participate in management and social development expanded. Many eminent doctors, teachers, engineers, and pharmacists made Russia their homeland. Precisely then, in the second half of the nineteenth century, cooperation between foreign specialists and their Russian counterparts that had reached similar proficiency levels started developing. It was already possible to apply modern terminology to those relations and discuss the mutual influence of the expatriates and the native residents of the empire. As a result, by the second half of the nineteenth century, medical professors—Russian graduates of national and foreign universities, on the one hand, and their Western colleagues, on the other hand—had built up extensive practice. Russian physician Peter Lesgaft (1837–1909), German surgeon Carl von Reyher (1846–1890), and many others became the pride and glory of Russian medicine. German professor Friedrich Joseph Haass (1780–1853) gained particular prominence and respect, which has long outlived him. He devoted his whole life to the poorest residents of Moscow, especially to prisoners and exiles. No wonder that generations of Muscovites referred to him as "holy doctor".

The reforms of Alexander II brought about the next modernization cycle in the development of the Russian economy. Former adversaries in the Crimean war—France and England—become Russia's partners in that wave of modernization (1870–1910). In that period Russia achieved unique results in industrial development and ranked first in Europe by the average annual growth rate of industrial production. The structure of production underwent a qualitative change with the light to heavy industry ratio shifting from 70:30 in 1887 to 53:47 by 1913. Expatriates engaged by foreign investors played an important role in this modernization. Their contribution was especially significant in emerging industries related to the development of the manufacturing sector, and particularly machine-building. A huge new metallurgical and metalworking district appeared in southern Russia. Of the seventeen major iron and steel works, only one belonged to Russian business; the rest were mostly controlled by French capital that had engaged a large number of professionals from French enterprises. In addition, owing to foreign investors, Russia surged forward to become the world's leading oil producer; it also accounted for 60% of world kerosene exports. The explosive growth in oil production and refining was based on active adoption of advanced foreign technology. In 1913, foreign companies accounted for 98% of investment in the Russian oil industry.[138]

By the time of the 1917 October Revolution, the first place in Europe by economic growth rates was combined with Russia's heavy dependence on foreign capital and highly skilled specialists and workers from abroad. Foreign enterprises were unevenly distributed across Russia, but the most technically advanced ones were concentrated in St. Petersburg. The metropolitan industry consisted of two parts, with state enterprises engaged predominantly in military production forming the significantly larger part. Among them were such world-famous factories as Obukhov and Izhora plants, the Baltic Shipyard, the Petrograd Ammunition Factory, and some others. Expatriates also worked at these enterprises but mainly as part of the engineer staff. As for the workers, generally, a minor part of them were current residents of St. Petersburg of proletarian or petit bourgeois origin, and the majority were otkhodniks [domestic temporary labor migrants], i.e. people whose household remained in the village and who, whenever possible, left the plant to engage in seasonal agricultural work at home.

The second part consisted of private enterprises concentrated primarily on the Vyborg Side of St. Petersburg. They included famous factories, the very names of which spoke for themselves: Siemens & Halske, Siemens-Schuckertwerke, Rosenkrantz, Lessner No. 1, No. 2, Parviainen, Langensiepen, Plant of the Society of Franco-Russian Factories, and a number of others. By the standards of that time, all those enterprises could be classified as high technology ones; therefore, the structure of their workforce differed from that of the state-owned factories. There were virtually no seasonal workers at these plants; most of the personnel were city-dwellers. The lower positions were staffed by many natives of the Baltic provinces (Livonia, Vilna, Kovno); a certain percentage of the workers were from Finland. For a long time, the Vyborg Side was built up with solid, mostly two-storey houses owned by

---

138 Maltsev A. *On the Incompatibility of Autarchy and Modernization. The Russian Confirmation of Global Patterns* // Svobodnaya Mysl', No. 2. 2010

the Balts, Finns, and Germans employed as foremen, heads of divisions, and highly skilled workers at those private factories.[139]

Certainly, in contrast to the time of Alexander II, by 1917 a significant part of the engineers and technicians were Russians who had received sound technical education in Switzerland, France, Belgium, and Germany. However, expatriates still constituted a tangible, albeit decreasing, part of the creative core of these enterprises, which were generally owned by Western businesspeople who had the opportunity to move the workforce between facilities in their native land and those in Russia.

The next modernization breakthrough happened during the Soviet period. The deep and widespread economic crisis, which hit the West in 1929, helped the Soviet Union secure western capital and western workforce. Because of the isolated nature of the Soviet economy, the world crisis did not affect our country. Western business had extremely limited contacts with the Soviet economy in the first twelve years of the Soviet Union's existence. But in the 1930s the situation changed dramatically, because western countries would not have been able to come out of the Great Depression without new markets, including the Soviet one. For that reason, the Soviet Union received wide access to state-of-the-art foreign technology and industrial innovations virtually in all fields of modern technology. Western companies transferred their industrial expertise, licenses, and patents to the USSR, sent their specialists to provide advisory services for the construction and commissioning of industrial facilities, and actively invited Soviet engineers and workers to their enterprises to exchange experience. In the period from 1929 to 1945, the USSR concluded 218 agreements with western companies.

Engagement of foreign extra-class experts acquired even a greater scale in the mid-1940s, when after World War II six thousand German specialists in missiles, electronics, flight control systems, jet aviation, and optics were sent from Germany to the USSR. The following fact demonstrates an example of more in-depth cooperation. In 1946, the Soviet Nordhausen Institute was established on the basis of the German Rabe center in the Soviet occupation zone. About seven thousand

---

139   Rashin A.G. *The Emergence of the Working Class in Russia*. Moscow: Sotsecgiz, 1958, pp. 360–361.

German scientists and workers were occupied at the institute. That was not all. Seven thousand specialists brought in from Germany participated in implementing a nuclear project in the Soviet Union itself. Evidently, these professionals did not work in isolation, but rather in close cooperation with Soviet specialists.

In the period from 1928 to 1940, the Soviet Union imported about 300,000 units of various machinery and equipment. We should also consider the enormous impact these large-scale imports had on the national economic culture. It is important that in many cases the equipment was imported on an integrated basis, which actually meant that whole plants were brought in. That was the case with three tractor works, three automotive plants, such machine-building giants as the Ural Heavy Machinery Plant, Novokramatorsk Machine Building Plant, and others. This was complemented by enormous post-war reparations, under which the USSR received 1,700 enterprises and 123,000 machine tools from Germany, including manufacturing facilities for a number of high-tech industries. It is important that the large-scale modernization processes were based on a solid foundation created by the state. The Soviet Union allocated 10% of its national income for the development of education as opposed to 1.9% of the GNP in the United States.[140]

All subsequent Soviet history the role of foreigners was inconsistent and depended heavily on the political relations between the USSR and the West. The "Cold War", which broke out shortly after and lasted in fact from the second half of the 1940s until the end of the 1980s, definitely reduced the number of foreign specialists working in Russia. Some growth of foreign presence resumed during the so-called period of "détente" of the 1970s, which was again interrupted in 1979 after the Soviet Union intervened in Afghanistan.

Census data (see Table 4.1) are a good illustration of the "tides" of foreign presence in Russia during the twentieth century. The departure of foreign specialists from Russia after the 1917 revolution was disastrous. According to the first census, Russia's foreign population in 1897 included over 7,000 English-speaking residents (Americans and Englishmen), more than 16,000 French, over 14,000 Italians, and about

---

140 Maltsev A. *On the Incompatibility of Autarchy and Modernization. The Russian Confirmation of Global Patterns* // Svobodnaya Mysl', No. 2. 2010.

5,000 Swedes, not to mention the numerous German diaspora numbering about 1.8 million people. The 1926 All-Union Census of the Population registered slightly over 700 English residents, no permanently residing Americans, and a seven-fold, six-fold and two-fold drop in the number of Frenchmen, Swedes, and Italians, respectively.

In the next few decades the number of Western Europeans living and working in Russia only decreased. Interest in Russia somewhat resumed in the early 1970s to be completely lost by the end of the decade. Thus, if in 1970, about one thousand Americans and about as many Englishmen lived in Russia, in 1979 their numbers were 120 and 239 people, respectively (the corresponding figures for RSFRS are 81 and 115 persons). The same is true of the French, Italians, Swedes, Dutch, and other foreigners. The situation did not change visibly even by 1989, despite the weakening of the USSR. Among Germans who historically formed the largest Russian ethnic group, the number of expatriates remained only a little above the "average European" level.

So can we speak about any influence that foreigners exerted during this period on the Russian work culture, technological culture, consciousness and values of the population? Definitely yes! Only *for a certain period of time this influence ceased to be "personalized" and acquired an indirect, cross-border nature.*

Table 4.1. Representatives of some Western European countries and the USA in the ethnic structure of Russia's population (1897–2010), pers.[*]

Census	1897[**]				1926				1939				1959			
	Entire Empire		European Russia		USSR		RSFSR		USSR		RSFSR		USSR		RSFSR	
Nationality	Total	Cities	Total	Cities	Total	Cities	Total	Cities	Total	Cities	Total	Cities	Total	Cities	Total	Cities
Americans	7,054	5,746	6,242	-	-	-	-	-	515	402	462	362	327	-	273	-
English	1,790,489	418,533	1,312,188	-	732	617	535	452	546	468	416	364	399	-	312	-
Germans	1,790,489	418,533	1,312,188	-	1,238,549	184,769	806,301	126,485	1,427,232	298,930	862,504	171,204	1,619,655	-	820,016	-
French	16,433	12,966	13,681	-	2,461	2,055	1,424	1,281	1,637	1,419	1,046	908	1,013	-	535	-
Italians	4,760	3,824	3,618	-	2,328	2,075	1,438	1,300	1,891	1,561	1,226	1,042	1,158	-	525	-
Spaniards	138	112	126	-	-	-	-	-	3,187	1,621	2,495	937	2,446	-	1,615	-
Swedes	14,199	6,969	13,422	-	2,495	1,458	1,394	1,202	1,519	1,010	971	773	-	-	-	-
Dutch	335	225	280	-	1,430	179	1,255	132	742	250	503	183	-	-	-	-

Census	1970 USSR		1970 RSFSR		1979 USSR		1979 RSFSR		1989 USSR		1989 RSFSR		2002 RF		2010 RF	
Nationality	Total	Cities	Total	Cities	Total	Cities	Total	Cities	Total	Cities	Total	Cities	Total	Cities	Total	Cities
Americans	1,039	-	785	-	120	-	81	-	277	225	185	172	1,275	1,230	1,572	1,457
English	903	-	542	-	239	-	115	-	348	301	223	204	529	505	950	914
Germans	1,846,317	-	761,888	-	1,936,214	-	790,762	-	2,038,603	1,075,412	842,295	450,826	597,212 (1,329)***	339,288	394,138 (1,433)***	223,984
French	2,470	-	1,243	-	796	-	305	-	701	651	352	330	819	780	1,475	1,376
Italians	2,040	-	889	-	963	-	356	-	1,337	1,190	627	591	862	819	1,370	1,316
Spaniards	4,107	-	2,631	-	3,039	-	1,961	-	3,172	3,023	2,054	1,968	1,547	1,476	1,162	1,088
Swedes	-	-	-	-	-	-	-	-	-	-	-	-	-	-	264	250
Dutch	1,298	-	643	-	712	-	384	-	794	622	451	348	-	-	417	378

Notes to the table:
* - Consolidated data of the First Universal Population Census of the Russian Empire of 1897; All-Union Population Censuses of 1926, 1939, 1959, 1970, 1979 and 1989; All-Russian Population Censuses of 2002 and 2010. Dashes mean that data was not available. Source: Demoscope weekly (http://demoscope.ru).
** - In the 1897 census, the ethnic structure was based on the native language.
*** - In case of the Germans who historically formed the largest ethnic group in Russia, the figure in brackets additionally indicates the number of people who according to the 2002 and 2010 censuses had German citizenship.

It is a certain irony of history but the "Iron Curtain" and the "Cold War" divided Russia and the West as much as they served to bring them closer to each other.

Indeed, the conflict paradigm implying the presence or proximity of a particular global socio-political environment was historically the first ideological basis of Russia's modern industrial development. Implicitly, this paradigm included the perception of an inevitable and imminent global war with the ideological enemy, the West. Soviet high-tech facilities were established solely as a basis for such confrontation. The main imperative of their development—ensuring the military-technological parity with the leading capitalist powers—was formed accordingly.

Addressing this challenge, the "supreme" monopolist represented by the Politburo of the Communist Party Central Committee was forced to compete with industrial corporations of the "imperialist states", thus acquiring certain features of an oligopoly that heavily invested in development. The civilian sectors of the USSR economy remained almost entirely anti-innovative, but in military technology the country managed to achieve world-class competitiveness. The Soviet military-industrial complex was an enclave of real innovative economy, albeit embracing a limited group of industries with specific development objectives.

To achieve its ultimate goal, the leadership of the Communist Party had also to develop appropriate human resources that would match the similar segment of Western specialists by their level of education and qualifications, and also by the work culture, technological culture, and motivation. For this purpose, the USSR created a technological subculture absolutely not typical for the Soviet society, as well as entire territorial enclaves for its "accommodation" and cultivation. The so-called ZATO (closed administrative-territorial formations) were an example of such enclaves. There, the scientific and technical intelligentsia engaged in the military-industrial field not only enjoyed higher standards of living, but also special working conditions and opportunities for personal development.

Evgeny Starikov describes this quite eloquently, "Against the background of the impoverished Russian province, islands of the 'military-industrial archipelago' stood out like miraculous 'cities of the future' transferred from fantasy novels. Spotless streets, well-tended parks, palaces of culture with shiny windows, modern hospital buildings...—

these townships were so unlike Russian reality. They were separate worlds with their own energy supply, autonomous infrastructure, and almost European quality of life. 'Regime' protected these fantastic cities from the prying eyes of foreign spies or hungry compatriots. Regime included a triple pass system, triple rows of barbed wire, and a plowed security strip along the fenced perimeter with watchtowers from where guards opened fire without warning on anyone who violated the boundaries of the closed 'wonder city'. <...> Professional pride and sense of responsibility almost extinct elsewhere in the country are flourishing here; there is no aggression or widespread hatred; instead, peace and tranquility prevail. <...> Actually one and a half million inhabitants of these numbered cities form a new Russian sub-ethnos ..."[141]

This was true not only of those engaged in the military-industrial complex, but also applied to all occupational estates that were involved in this competition with the West, effectively mastering and exceeding its achievements—in industry, science, art, and sports. Boris Chertok, a veteran of the military-industrial complex recollected, "...The Soviet Union was indeed transformed from a backward agrarian country into a powerful industrial state. <...> 'Physicists' were now in favor rather than 'lyricists'", and "although the 'lyricists' <...> were quite famous, they were also serving the same cause."[142]

The 1990s virtually destroyed this subculture. Geopolitical rivalry disappeared to be replaced by a completely opposite state of expecting the "miraculous" merger with the West. For about a decade this extinguished the competitive field of the Russian work culture, which had historically contributed to the emergence of its best (*read—matching the world benchmark of competitiveness*) properties.

At the same time, it was an era when expatriates started returning to Russia, when they proceeded to develop the emerging Russian market, its opportunities and resources. From that time on we can speak about the largest inflow of foreign specialists back to Russia. Due to this, the 1990s brought Russia a fundamentally different experience of interacting with the West in its contemporary history. Owing to the increasing presence of multinationals, the interaction of the Russian cul-

---

[141] Starikov E. *Different Russians //* Novyj Mir. 1996. No. 4.
[142] Chertok B.E. *The Prospects for Russian Cosmonautics and Science-Intensive Technology //* Economist. 2000. No. 8. p. 4.

ture with foreign cultures moved to the micro level, the level of companies. Cooperation with representatives of other cultures became part of the production process involving specific business practices rather than abstract romanticized values, forcing people to overcome daily their long-term habits and stereotypes, because the company's performance was at stake, and, respectively, the evaluation of their own input.

By the beginning of the 2000s, a macroeconomic environment favorable for Russia emerged, thus making the Russian economy even more attractive for foreign investment (see Table 4.2).

At that time, Russian GDP growth rates exceeded those in any of the world's leading economies, with the exception of China. Growth rates peaked in the period from 2004 to 2007. In those years, the Russian economy increased annually by 6%-8%, as compared to the traditional 2%-3% in the Western European economies.

Even in spite of the more profound drop in 2009 (peak of the financial crisis), the Russian economy recovered relatively faster in the post-crisis period than the leading world economies. Thus, in 2010–2011, Russian GDP grew at 4.3%-4.5% p.a., in 2012—at 3.4%. At the same time, the economies of Europe, the United States, and Japan demonstrated growth rates of 1%-2%, or even sometimes close to zero (e.g., Japan in 2011, France and the United Kingdom in 2012).

Foreign investment figures also indicated interest in Russia in the first decade of the 2000s. In the period from 2000 to 2013, the inflow of foreign investment in the Russian economy in current prices experienced a more than fifteen-fold increase (including a more than three-fold increase from 2005), although this was accompanied by a change in their structure—in particular, a gradual decline in the share of foreign direct investment. In the last five years of the period, Russia's accumulated foreign investment remained consistently at 18%-20% of the GDP, and accumulated foreign direct investment—at 4%-5% of GDP, which is comparable with other countries.

Table 4.2. Selected indicators demonstrating macroeconomic conditions and the scale of foreign participation in the economy of the Russian Federation in the 2000s *

	2005	2006	2007	2008	2009	2010	2011	2012	2013
Russian GDP growth rates in comparable prices (year-on-year, %)	106.4	108.2	108.5	105.2	92.2	104.5	104.3	103.4	101.3
Comparative data for individual countries:									
USA	103.1	102.7	101.9	99.7	96.9	102.5	101.8	102.8	101.9
UK	102.8	102.6	103.6	99.0	96.0	101.7	101.1	100.3	101.8
Germany	100.8	103.9	103.4	100.8	94.9	104.0	103.1	101.0	100.5
France	101.8	102.6	102.2	99.8	96.9	101.4	101.7	100.2	100.3
Japan	101.3	101.7	102.2	98.9	94.5	104.7	99.5	101.4	101.5
Foreign investment in the Russian economy (in brackets - from non-CIS countries), USD billion	53.6 (n/a)	55.1 (40.2)	120.9 (93.6)	103.8 (66.5)	81.9 (60.6)	114.7 (79.7)	190.6 (154.9)	154.6 (113.4)	170.2 (124.8)
Of them - direct investment (in brackets - from non-CIS countries)	13.1 (n/a)	13.7 (7.4)	27.8 (18.7)	27.0 (11.1)	15.9 (6.9)	13.8 (4.3)	18.4 (6.4)	18.7 (5.3)	26.1 (10.6)
Accumulated foreign direct investment from non-CIS countries, USD billion (in brackets - share of GDP, %)	n/a (n/a)	37.1 (3.0)	51.7 (3.8)	54.5 (4.0)	51.2 (4.6)	41.3 (4.9)	45.5 (4.9)	39.6 (4.8)	41.9 (4.0)
Increase in the number of companies with foreign capital in relation to the year 2000, times	1.8	1.9	2.1	2.2	2.2	2.2	2.6	2.4	2.6
Share of employment in companies with foreign and joint capital in average annual total employment, %	4.2	4.5	4.5	4.7	4.6	4.6	4.8	4.6	4.8
Share of companies with foreign capital in the total turnover in the Russian Federation, %	28.8	28.9	28.3	29.8	29.3	38.7	33.9	31.2	36.0

* Compiled from Rosstat (www.gks.ru) and FIRA-PRO (www.fira.ru) data.

In the same period, the number of companies with foreign capital in the Russian economy increases. In 2000–2013, their number had increased 2.6-fold, and their aggregate turnover averaged about one-third (in 2013 - 36%) of the turnover of all enterprises operating in Russia. By the end of the first decade of the 2000s, the average annual number of employees in companies with foreign and joint capital had reached only about 5% of the average annual employment in the economy. The figures in table 4.2 show that this fact was not situational, but was consistently reproduced from year to year.

The resulting picture is remarkable—less than 5% of employees account for over a third of total Russian production. It is precisely in this segment of the Russian economy that the forces of the most high-ranking expatriates are concentrated, and the changes taking place in this corporate segment can significantly influence the economy and its development trends.

High GDP growth rates and an inflow of foreign capital in the Russian economy leads to an increase of foreign specialists controlling such investments. Data on the distribution of foreign professionals working in Russia, by country of origin, and on the shift in their interest to work in Russia in the 2000s are presented in Fig. 4.1.[143]

Since 2000, the number of foreign professionals working in Russia was increasing gradually. In 2004–2005, the steady trend was replaced by explosive interest, which lasted until the active phase of the 2008–2009 global financial crisis. Thus, in 2000–2008, the number of foreign professionals from the United States grew 2.7-fold, from the United Kingdom, Germany, France, and Italy—3.4–3.8-fold, and from the European Union in general—almost 1.6-fold.

However, the active phase of the 2008–2009 global financial crisis had a significant impact on this process and reversed it. Since 2008, the number of foreign specialists from leading world economies officially employed in Russia has been declining and by now has dropped below the level of the year 2000. According to the Russian state statistics, by the beginning of 2014 only about 600 US nationals (1,800 in 2000), 500 British nationals (1,600 in 2000), and 700 German nationals (1,400

---

143   *The Russian Statistical Yearbook*. M.: Rosstat, 2014. Section "Labor", table 5.14–5.15 / http://www.gks.ru/bgd/regl/b14_13/IssWWW.exe/Stg/d01/05-14.htm , http://www.gks.ru/bgd/regl/b14_13/IssWWW.exe/Stg/d01/05-15.htm

in 2000) were employed in Russia. In 2008–2013, the total number of EU professionals formally employed in Russia dropped more than fivefold—from 35,900 to 6,600, which is 3.4 times lower than in 2000.

Today the era is once again changing. We are watching a new outflow of expatriates from Russia. We are witnessing a new round of cooling relations between Russia and the Western world with its satellites... What have we achieved so far? How can we assess the experience in cross-cultural interaction and professional exchange that Russia has accumulated in the past quarter of a century? Can we state that Russia is changing its orthodox perception of "Western" values and "Western" experience as universal and absolute categories identical to development and success—a trend that had formed in Russian culture back in the 1980s? Is it fair to say that the long dominant abstract and idealized perception of "Western" mentality has been replaced by a purely pragmatic approach in evaluating foreigners and their role in the development of the Russian society and economy? And what role can foreigners still play in Russia's modernization?

Towards a New Russian Work Culture

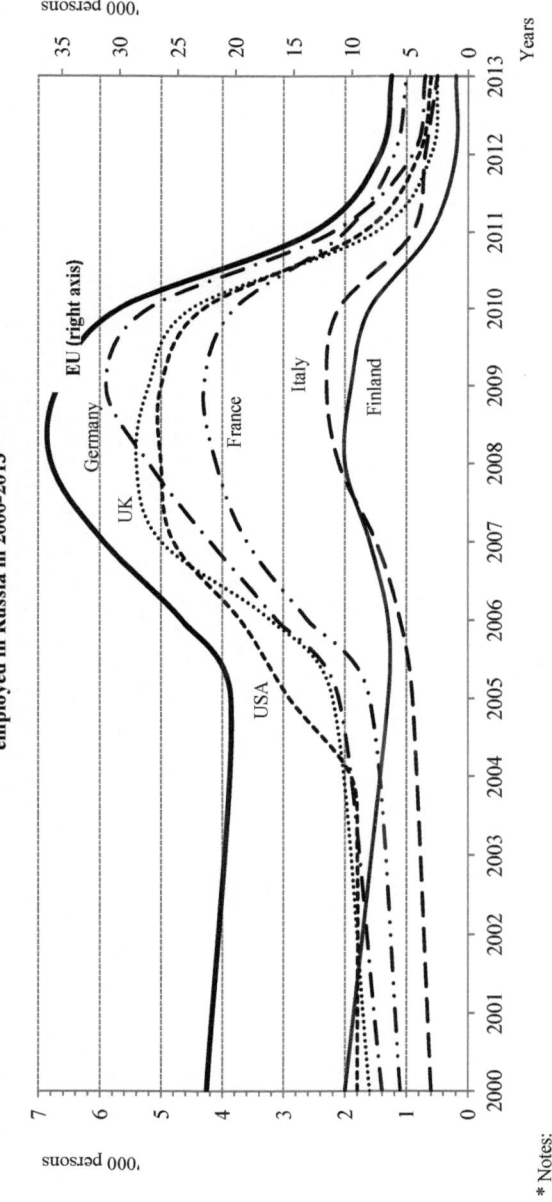

Рис. 4.1. Change in the number of foreign specialists from selected EU countries and the USA employed in Russia in 2000–2013*

* Notes:
1) Compiled from Rosstat data (www.gks.ru). The graphs are based on data for 2000, 2005-2013; for the USA - data for 2000, 2003-2013.
2) The number of foreign specialists includes holders of valid work permits from the following countries:

Chapter V.
Demand of the Russian economy for foreign human capital

All serious experts agree that a surge in innovative development wi l be the objective of the Russian economy for the nearest decade. Technological priorities have been defined in the most general terms. Today, the world is on the threshold of the sixth shift in the techno-economic paradigm, which, by all accounts, will be achieved through breakthroughs in nano-, bio-, information technology and cognitive science. It is absolutely clear that the current fifth techno-economic paracigm based on crucial breakthroughs in microelectronics serves as a foundation for innovative economic growth and promotes the emergence of the sixth paradigm.

However, the disintegration of the Soviet modernization system in the process of building a new Russia brought about unforeseen consequences, which were not associated either with the expectations of the elite, or the anticipations of the main groups of the population. Traditional values and local identities sprang back to life; the society became increasingly archaic and fragmented down to specific ethnic, civilizational, religious, and regional spaces. This is the consequence of the rollback of the Russian economy to peripheral positions in the capitalist world system, which logically reduced the potential social base of the bearers of modern values. A model of peripheral capitalism and its legitimizing values is gradually emerging. The peripheral nature of the economy objectively correlates with identical institutional archaism of the political order.[144] V.S. Magun and M.G. Rudnev note that in the existing model of the post-Soviet society "a strong desire for personal success and wealth is not associated in the minds of Russians with an equally pronounced courage, readiness to act in a new way, take risks, and make independent decisions. Values are based on the 'have fun principle'—high claims without the willingness to make significant per-

---

144 Martianov V.S. *Involution of the Elite in the Modern Society* // Political Expertise, Vol. 6, No. 3. 2010.

sonal efforts and take risks."[145] In contemporary Russia, values of paternalism are firmly blended with extreme individualism. We have outlined these considerations to clarify the challenge in forming sustainable and high performing work teams, which include present-day Russian employees and expatriates and explain why expatriates find it difficult to adjust to the Russian work reality.

The authors of these lines strongly support Russia's re-industrialization, the need to restore its industrial capacity. It is great that our military pilots fly shining, technically advanced, Russian-made aircraft. But it is high time to give every Russian citizen once again the opportunity to fly domestically or internationally aboard domestic planes fully constructed in Russia. For this purpose, it is extremely important to reinstate the key personnel, to rebuild the skills and competencies driving industrial enterprises. In the mid-1990s, one of the authors hereof had the opportunity to interview directors of major enterprises in Moscow and the Moscow Region. The interviewees expressed serious doubts as to their ability to retain the qualification potential of their workforce. Most of them spoke about the lack of orders and the need to secure such orders themselves relying on personal connections. The hopes pinned on potential foreign investment proved groundless. Following are some typical statements: "We are trying to retain personnel by offering them paid work within the enterprise. But, generally, this work does not require high skills"; "It is a pity to lose the people; the young and the most skilled ones are the first to leave." The director of another enterprise, the Yakovlev aircraft manufacturer, states, "The young workers have left. Half of those gone are people aged from 30 to 40. Inadequate wages are the main reason." At the time of the survey (1996), the Yakovlev aircraft corporation had managed to maintain stability only on a small pilot plant. As the director rightly noted, the country was losing its aviation industry. "We find contracts ourselves, including abroad. There, they are buying our 'brains' for next to nothing, but even this little money helps retain the team...there is just enough to cover the wages. We are not investing a single penny in development...we are barely surviving." There is no domestic commercial entity that invests in aviation. This is very "long" money. It pays back on average in eight to

---

145 Magun V.S., Rudnev M.G. *The Russian's Fundamental Values in the European Contact* // Obshchestvennye Nauki i Sovremennost', 2010, No. 4, p. 16.

ten years. It takes from eight to ten years from commencement of production to the creation of an aircraft. All this time the money does not generate any profit; it is "frozen".

Finally, in view of the tough sanctions imposed on Russia by the United States and the European Union, even those who had doubted the need to restore such industries as aircraft construction, joined the camp of re-industrialization supporters. And it is for this that we especially require expatriates who would help us save time and occupy a rightful place in the world market for high-tech products.

We particularly need the expatriates in order to change the industrial development strategy, which for many years has not been focused on innovative development, on using the results of research and development. Unfortunately, for decades, scientific achievements remain without demand. Russia's significant distinction from other industrialized countries is that its research activities are still primarily concentrated in research institutes detached not only from higher education establishments, but also from business enterprises. In the meantime, in other countries corporate research integrated into the real sector of the economy plays a key role in driving innovations. Thus, corporate research accounts for 65% of all scientific research and development in the EU and for 75% in the USA. In this context, it is virtually impossible to make domestic products competitive without restructuring the very strategy of industrial development, without seamlessly incorporating research into the production process.[146]

In order to describe in general the situation in Russia as a country that is experiencing a shortage in expatriates and needs to consolidate its key human capital capable of engaging in creative and highly intensive labor in the context of the emerging sixth techno-economic paradigm, it makes sense to refer to the rather recent past when Russia was already part of the capitalist world. As A. Tarasov rightly points out, Russia is in fact rejoining the world capitalist system after the "Soviet deviation". Moreover, "the country once again finds itself on the periphery of this system and seeks only a 'semi-periphery' position."[147]

---

146   Semenova A. *The Innovative System of Russia* // Voprosy Ekonomiki, 2005, No. 11. pp. 146–148.
147   Tarasov A. *Russia: The Second Edition of Capitalism* // Svobodnaya Mysl'. 2009. No. 1. p. 33.

Evaluating the two "occurrences" of capitalism on Russian soil, the above quoted author clearly opts for its "first edition". He provides the following reasons. "...Pre-revolution capitalist Russia was a *backward* (in terms of developed western countries), but *progressing* country. The capitalist Russia of today, on the contrary, is a *regressing* country. 'Knock-down assembly' is replacing our high-tech and knowledge-intensive industries. Entire sectors of the economy are mothballed...

Tsarist Russia with its thirteen percent of urban population... and masses of submissive, humble peasants heading for the cities is one case... Modern urbanized Russia with a population accustomed to a certain level of comfort and *already* professionally specialized is a completely different case." To complete the picture, the author compares the explosive demographic growth in pre-Soviet Russia with the current population decline due primarily to incredible mortality rates. This means that "the second edition of capitalism" in Russia is taking place in an unfavorable environment in terms of such a crucially important factor as productive forces.[148]

In the past twenty years, Russia has seen serious innovative developments. Most of them have unfolded in provincial regions, rather than in Moscow, namely in Tomsk, Stavropol, Penza, Cheboksary, and towns of the Moscow Region. Dozens of globally competitive companies with sales reaching $100 million are already operating in these and other regions. These companies were established 10–15 years ago. And the biography of every one of them paints a dramatic picture of having to overcome numerous administrative barriers. The Aspect research and development center based in Dubna near Moscow can serve as an example of such a company. Aspect is involved in the development and production of state-of-the-art world-level professional radiation monitoring equipment. Orders from Western countries, primarily the USA, account for 85% of the company's output. The research and development center owes its commercial success to western demand for their unique innovative radiation equipment. The employees of the Center closely cooperate with specialists from the USA and other client countries.[149]

---

148 Ibid. p. 35–37.
149 *Aspect's Evolution //* Znanie-Sila, December 2005.

Another example of the innovative potential and global competitiveness of Russian firms in the global market is Ecwid, a portfolio company of Runa Capital, established in Ulyanovsk and developing software for e-commerce. Today, tens of thousands of stores in the world use this e-commerce platform, of them, 40% are based in the USA, 25%—in the EU, 10%—in Russia, and 5%-8%—in Canada and Australia.[150] The Russian IT sector is growing rapidly. It focuses primarily on western customers, as evidenced by figures of Russian IT exports: average annual growth rate of 30% and $3 billion in export volumes in 2014. Domestic IT companies—mentioned and not mentioned—closely cooperate with foreign businesses, employ foreign personnel and use western projects. For example, the portfolio of the Russian Runa Capital venture fund was evenly split in 2014 between domestic and foreign projects, including those from such advanced countries as Germany, Romania, France, the United Kingdom, and Israel.[151] However, the IT field is not the only one in Russia with a potential for innovation that attracts western specialists. Suffice it to mention such companies as Transas (St. Petersburg), which holds 60% of the world market for marine navigation systems (for example, such equipment is installed on the famous cruise ship *Queen Victoria*); Novomet-Perm (Perm)—a supplier of oil drilling equipment, and ER-Telecom (Perm), which is competing today with Chinese telecommunication companies.[152]

Focus on innovations has clearly emerged as a priority in Russia's state policy in recent years. Important legislative measures have been taken to stimulate innovative processes. However, so far the country has not created a suitable environment for the development of major innovative businesses. Renowned film director Sergei Bodrov comments this, "Why are Russians going to America and creating Google there? Whereas in Russia they fail! This is very-very sad. I consider myself a Russian filmmaker. But all the time I think, why don't we have a Bill Gates or a Steve Jobs? We must ask ourselves such questions

---

150   Shmelyova G. *Designer of Online Stores Ecwid Raises $5 million from iTech Capital and Runa Capital* // http://www.the-village.ru/village/hopesandfears/news/158565-konstruktor-onlayn-magazinov-ecwid-privlyok-5-mln-ot-itech-capital-i-runa-capital
151   *Internet Against Oil* // Delovaya Moskva, 20 January 2014, No. 27 (126)
152   *Innovations are not Flights to Mars. Is Russia Ready for "High-Tech Sanctions"?* // Delovaya Moskva, 15 September 2014, No.42 (141).

even if they are unpleasant."[153] Obviously, the key challenges have not been met yet. We still have to establish hundreds of companies with billions in turnovers.

Such an objective can be achieved only by uniting our national creative forces with the bearers of a higher culture of production, technology and research from Western countries. It is not for nothing that Vladislav Surkov, the former "shadow" supervisor of the Skolkovo project, when asked about the expediency of this "innovation miracle" in view of the already existing numerous research centers with an established infrastructure, replied that "the miracle" will be created by foreigners. "They will themselves say what they need; we will just have to perform. We need a new 'German Community'. We critically need a more advanced culture here...together with its actual representatives."[154] One cannot but agree with those authors who believe that any imported technology we purchase will be obsolete, because no one wants to create their own competitors. Therefore, advanced technology can be developed solely on the basis of domestic research, national technological projects, but only in cooperation with live bearers of this new advanced technical culture.

However, such cooperation encounters many difficulties. Employees raised and educated in different cultural environments and social conditions differ substantially by their work motivation, attitude to the time budget, system of values, and mentality in general. However, Russia's entire historical experience demonstrates that at the time of modernization leaps, which happened during the reigns of Peter the Great and the outstanding emperor Alexander II, in the years of the so-called socialist industrialization and post-war economic development, thousands of foreigners worked side by side with Russian workers and engineers and achieved exceptional results comparable with the best world accomplishments. This issue is once again on the agenda, and it is exacerbated by the losses our industry and other sectors of the economy suffered in the 1990s. Suffice it to recall in this respect the

---

153 *Fear is a Compass Leading to the Brink* // Novaya Gazeta, No. 107, 24 September 2014.
154 Granin Yu. *Exchanging "Necklaces" for Oil. Russian-Style Modernization: Simulation and Formalism* // Svobodnaya Mysl', 2014. No. 1. p. 200.

mass migration of specialists to such countries as the United States, Germany, France, and others.

The effects of policies on groups of highly skilled professionals are well known: it is here that we have suffered the greatest losses due to emigration of competent specialists in the most productive age groups. There are no systematic data to this effect. L. Gokhberg and E. Nekipelova noted that since 1986 statistical records had removed questions about education and specialty field from questionnaires on travel abroad. The *Law on Entry and Exit* enacted in January 1993 abolished exit visas and extended the duration of foreign passports to five years.[155] In such conditions, neither the state nor the public have any reliable data on the actual migration of elite human resources over the years of large-scale "brain drain". We can assume that the outflow from science and associated areas of professional activity was largely due to domestic inter-sectoral mobility. However, in creative fields of activity, the absolute outflow-inflow figures are not comparable by relevance to qualitative parameters.

In 1989, about 70,000 scientists left the country. According to academician Alexander Andreev, already by the beginning of 1993 approximately 40 percent of high-level theoretical physicists and about 12 percent of experimental physicists had left the former USSR either temporarily or for good. From 1990 to the end of 1999, 80 percent of world-level mathematicians and 50 percent of physicists had left the country. This is about eight thousand people, whose departure was critically dangerous for the national science.[156] At that time, surveys of physicists engaged at Russia's leading scientific research centers showed that in fact four out of five young scientists aged under 30 intended to leave the country. As experts had predicted, representatives of unique professions, people with high and very high skill levels prevailed among the emigrants. According to the passport and visa department of the Russian Interior Ministry, an average of about five thousand professionals in science and higher education left Russia in 1992–1996—generally, the most qualified and promising researchers aged

---

155 Gokhberg L.M., Nekipelova E.F. *Emigration of Scientists: Statistical Estimate* // Intellectual Migration in Russia / General editor S.A. Kugel. SPb., 1993. pp. 49–50.
156 Pavlyutkin V. *"Mousetrap" for Academics* // Mir za Nedelyu. 1999. No. 12. 13–20 November

from 30 to 40 years. The resource for emigration of such professionals is largely exhausted. Nevertheless, according to projections, in the coming years Russia will annually lose about 200–300 scientists who have advanced developments in such key areas as computer software, applied mathematics, production of composite materials, and creation of new medicines.

Such large-scale professional emigration can be considered a national disaster. Based on the UN methodology, costs and lost profit from the emigration of one specialist with higher education or an academic degree are estimated at $200,000-$250,000. It is not difficult to imagine that Russia's losses reach tens of billions of US dollars. In general, the "brain drain" in the years of high-level migration cost Russia $25 billion.[157] The Education Department of the Council of Europe assesses the annual losses incurred by Russia from science emigration in 1994–2004 at no less than $50–60 billion.[158] Strategic military losses are also an issue. According to expert assessments, about eight thousand Russian scientists were engaged (as at 1999) in over forty US defense programs; exclusive rights to research findings belong to the American government.[159]

According to data as at 2005, approximately 40,000 immigrants from Russia are engaged in research in the United States and Western Europe. Another 30,000 are constantly traveling to foreign research centers to conduct research. In the United States only, recent Russian immigrants provide about 20–25 percent of the American high-technology market, which is no less than ten percent of the world market.[160]

---

157 *The Russian economy in 2004. Trends and Prospects* / Chief editor Yegor Gaidar M.: Institute for the Economy in Transition. 2005. p. 355.
158 Naumova T. *Science Emigration from Russia* // Svobodnaya Mysl'. 2004. No. 3. p. 127.
159 Vishnevsky A., Zayonchkovskaya Zh. *The Fourth Wave of Emigration* // Moskovskiye Novosti. 1992, 9 February. p. 18; Vishnevsky A., Zayonchkovskaya Zh. *Migration Waves. The New Situation* // Svobodnaya Mysl'. 1992, No. 12. p. 13; Dolgikh E. *Why are Scientists Leaving* // Moskovskiye Novosti, 4 April 1993, p. 11; Pavlyutkin V. *"Mousetrap" for Academics* // Mir za Nedelyu. No. 12. 1999, 13–20 November <reprint from Krasnaya Zvezda >; Akhiezer A.S. *Emigration as a Status Indicator in Russian Society* // Mir Rossii. 1999. No. 4.
160 Kharichev I. *Russian Science: To Be or Not to Be?* // Znanie-Sila. 2005. No. 6. p. 32.

According to the estimate of academician Vladimir Zakharov (September 2003), by the beginning of the 2000s, from ten to fifteen percent of mathematicians and physicists in US universities were of Russian origin. He says, "We made the West an enormous gift. The prospect of irreversible processes is real—in about 20 years from now, when our generation is gone, Russian science will cease to exist."[161]

In the second half of the 2000s, intellectual emigration from Russia, including that of scientists, declined significantly as compared to the 1990s. Emigration of Russian citizens to the United States in 2010–2012 was only 23% of its level during the 1990s and about 63% of that in the early 2000s. And while it is true that the number of Russians receiving US permanent residency did increase slightly from 2011–2012 (going from 8,500 to 10,100), even that level is much lower than it was in the recent past.[162]

At the same time, arguments in favor of denying the substantial harm from the emigration of professionals started appearing increasingly in the press, especially the pro-government one. The publications appeal to official statistics claiming that of all those who had quit scientific activity no more than 2% had actually emigrated. Thus, the "brain drain" risk is proclaimed as over exaggerated, although sometimes the departure of even one person can mean that an entire line of research will be discontinued. Besides, these "not alarming figures" can hardly be trusted. Many scientists, who had left the country for good, did not change their citizenship. Moreover, they are often still registered as employees of one or another domestic institute or university, although their employment is purely formal.

After several years of silence, concerns about the harmful effects of the "brain drain" re-emerged in the mid-2000s and became a widely discussed topic along with the need to develop measures aimed at retaining young people in science. However, the factors driving this interest were different than those in the first half of the 1990s. The economic strengthening of the state became apparent. Accordingly, demands increased for the country's leadership to shift interests and resources towards science and innovation. The new generation of young people

---

161   Izvestia (4) 2003.
162   14 November 2013 http://www.forbes.com/sites/markadomanis/2013/11/14/russian-emigration-to-the-united-states-is-a-lot-lower-than-it-was-in-the-1990s-or-2000s/

studying at the best Russian universities were now more focused on working in Russia.

However, scientists did not benefit much from the enormous influx of petrodollars into the economy. For many young professionals, science remains a transit zone, and "brain drain" abroad is still on the agenda. Based on official statistics, Reuters reported a rise in the emigration figures from Russia—to 186,382 in 2013 from 122,751 in 2012, 36,774 in 2011, and 33,578 in 2010. It is not just political activists and opponents of the political regime that are emigrating. These are the small- and medium-business owners and entrepreneurs, economists and scientists who are afraid of the increasingly constrictive Russian society.[163]

In 2004, science theorists from the Institute of History of Science and Technology of the Russian Academy of Sciences and sociologists from the Institute of Economics and Industrial Engineering of the Siberian Branch of the Russian Academy of Sciences conducted surveys, which showed a growing differentiation within the scientific community. Only five percent of scientists had incomes comparable to those in the business sector (i.e. no less than $500 per month). Research projects (grants from various funds, contracts and agreements with customers) and teaching were principal sources of additional income. However, there is also an evident positive shift—currently, commercial activity unrelated to science is the main source of income for eight percent of scientists only, whereas in the mid-1990s, up to 70 percent of researchers were involved in additional occupations unrelated to science and education.[164] In subsequent years the situation did not change fundamentally.

While in most countries of the world, the number of people employed in research and development is growing, in Russia we are witnessing a downward trend. According to Rosstat, the average annual number of people engaged in science and research was 1,201,000 in

---

163 28 July 2014 http://nationalinterest.org/feature/russias-next-crisis-brain-drain-10961

164 *The Russian Economy in 2004. Trends and Prospects* / Chief editor Yegor Gaidar M.: Institute for the Economy in Transition. 2005. p. 354. Yurevich A. *Clever but Poor: Scientists in Modern Russia.* M.: MONF, 1998. p. 104. Yurevich A., Tsapenko I., Prikhodko A. *How and How Much do our Scientists Earn?* // Naukovedeniye. 2004. No. 1. p. 58.

2000; 988,000 in 2005; 904,000 in 2010; 907,000 in 2011, and 880,000 in 2012.[165]

However, simultaneous work on different projects and often in several organizations does not allow concentrating on serious research, thus negatively affecting performance. According to the Thomson Reuters InCites research analytics tool, the share of Russian publications in total world publications in 2010 was 2.27 percent, whereas in the 1980s this figure exceeded five percent.[166] The integration of Russian scientists into the global scientific community is also rather low. According to the survey conducted by the Institute of Psychology of the Russian Academy of Sciences, only 39 percent of Russian researchers are involved in international programs and projects.

For quite a number of years, surveys showed that most scientists did not anticipate any increase in their income in the coming years. Suffice it to provide the following example. In 2005, even doctors and candidates of science had an average monthly salary of only seven thousand rubles (about $230). The logical question is what groups of interests benefit from such policies? Academician Vladimir Zakharov explained the policy pursued at that time by specific interests of the business elite. "Brain drain" for oligarchic capitalism "...is not a problem. In a resource-based economy, it is easier to purchase the required equipment from oil sales proceeds than develop something in-house."[167] As a result, in those years Russia ranked 43rd in the world by competitiveness of the economy and 28th by index of innovation. As for development of information and communication technologies, Russia was not even included in the list of 44 more or less successful countries.[168]

Such a situation was not very attractive for young scientists. Therefore, many talented university graduates sought work unrelated to science. However, following negative publicity in the summer and autumn of 2005, the authorities decided to raise sharply the salaries of researchers to the level of 30,000 rubles by 2008. The situation changed significantly by 2010 with a reform in the system of compensation for

---

165 *The Russian Statistical Yearbook.* M.: Rosstat. 2013. Section 5, Table 5.
166 Gazeta.ru, 14 January 2013.
167 Izvestia, 13 September 2003.
168 *The Economist. Pocket World in Figures 2003*, p. 56–58.

researchers. The reform allowed achieving a long-targeted result—the salaries of people engaged in research became twice as high as average compensation throughout the country reaching 32,000 rubles and continuing to increase in subsequent years. According to figures for 2012, the average salary in science had reached 42,000 rubles.[169] In this situation it was possible to contemplate inviting expatriates to work in Russian research teams. The issue was not so much the remuneration of the expatriates as the general atmosphere, which had become more favorable.

We would like to remind that by the mid-2000s, every second doctor of science was over sixty, candidate of science—over fifty, and academician—over seventy years old. An age vacuum between representatives of the older generation and the young people emerged.[170] The middle generation of scientists and scholars in the most productive age from 30 to 45 years often left the country upon reaching their creative potential, and those who stayed preferred to work for foreign customers. As a result, the link between generations was broken; schools of thought where Russia held leading positions in the world were destroyed. Reforms in the organization and compensation of scientific work are gradually changing the situation. However, it is obvious that a breakthrough in such complex things as raising a whole generation to replace the one that had dropped out of domestic science will require many years.

By the total number of scientists, we are still holding the third-fourth place in the world, but where we have about 60 scientists per 10,000 inhabitants, Japan, Finland, and Sweden—about 100. Thus, by relative indicators, Russia is far behind. In 1989, the number of researchers in Russia still stood at 1.1 million. In 2010, about 840,000 people were engaged in research and development in Russia against 878,000 in Japan; 549,000 in Germany; 390,000 in France; 320,000 in the United Kingdom; 77,000 in Sweden; and 56,000 in Finland.[171] We will hardly be able to restore the previous number of scientists, and that is not the main issue. The central problem is the deteriorating quality of the edu-

---

169 *The Russian Statistical Yearbook*. M.: Rosstat. 2013. Section 6, Table 9.
170 Naumova T. *Science Emigration from Russia* // Svobodnaya Mysl'. 2004. No. 3. p. 129.
171 *Russia and the Countries of the World. Statistics Digest*. M.: Rosstat, 2012. Section 12, Table 1.

cated part of the society. The quality of the Russian educated population is declining despite the increasing number of educated people. If in 1994–2003, about 500,000 diplomas of higher education were issued annually, in 2012 this figure reached 1,125,000. It is clear that the number of people with higher education not occupied in their field of specialization is also constantly growing.[172]

Returning to the issue of migration. We share the opinion of those who consider the large-scale emigration of the intellectual elite from Russia in the 1990s a national catastrophe. All the more that this process, albeit on a much lesser scale, is still going on. Lower levels of emigration are largely due to the depletion of the most talented human resources in many areas of science and technology. According to Tamara Guzenkova [Deputy Director of the Russian Institute for Strategic Studies], by pessimistic estimates Russia has lost up to two-thirds of its scientific potential, and by optimistic ones—about a third. The hardest hit were those branches of natural and engineering sciences, which are now points of growth for qualitatively new knowledge and technology.[173]

In the meantime, not only countries with administrative exit restrictions but also such relatively poor democracies as India are successfully implementing measures on supporting professionals to reduce their emigration and raise the share of knowledge-intensive products in the GDP. Russia also has such means and opportunities. The problem is the policy pursued by the state.

It is indicative that in the prosperous year 2000, expenditures on science constituted only 2.05 percent of the federal budget and were 30 times lower than in 1990; in 2003 they rose to 2.19 percent and reached 39.9 billion rubles, i.e. about $1.3 billion. Meanwhile, pursuant to the law *On Science and Government Policy in Science and Technology* adopted in 1996, the state has committed to allocate no less than 4 percent of budget expenditures for civil research and development. In March 2002, a new government policy for funding science was developed at a joint meeting of the Security Council, the State Council Presidium, and the Presidential Council on Science and High Technolo-

---

172 *The Russian Statistical Yearbook.* M.: Rosstat. 2013. Section 7, Table 50.
173 *"Brain Drain" and Science Administration. Round table at the Svobodnaya Mysl' editorial office on 24 June 2004* // Svobodnaya Mysl'. 2004. No. 9. pp. 121–123.

gies. It was reflected in the final document titled *Policy Framework of the Russian Federation for the Development of Science and Technology for the Period until 2010 and beyond*. The document stated that the rate of 4 percent was not applicable to civil science in general, but only to fundamental research and promotion of progress in science and technology. The financial part of the document stipulated that the 4 percent minimum was to be reached only by 2010. Thus, the implementation of the 1996 law scheduled to start in 1997 was postponed for 14 years. Under the law on the national budget for 2005, allocations for science amounted to 56 billion rubles ($2 billion), i.e. 2 percent of total budget expenditures. A special emphasis was made on the applied nature of the spending. Obviously, such allocation negatively affected long-term research, which included most breakthrough technologies. In subsequent years, regardless of the overall economic and international situation, the leadership of the country has taken all possible measures to raise public spending on science. Such allocations constituted 3 percent of the executed 2012 federal budget reaching 3.4 percent in 2013. These are very decent figures of budgetary expenditure on science. They already allow involving expatriates in research projects, where necessary. Moreover, in those years the government singled out individual mega-projects envisaging engagement of outstanding foreign scientists, whose role was not only organizing research, but also training talented young people widely involved in such projects.

It is evident that, on the one hand, the needs of the country require a new large inflow of creative workers from abroad, but, on the other hand, the status of these representatives of the middle class, or more precisely, of the core of this class of creatively competent workers is such that it does not promote the activity of foreign professionals in the Russian labor market. For decades, debates have been going on in Russia about the nature, scale and special features of the domestic middle class. Most authors continue to focus on the income level of the middle strata, which brings such representatives of the middle class, as the bureaucracy and some groups of entrepreneurs, to the forefront. However, it is not coincidental that from his first article for the Russian readers, which appeared in 1994, the eminent Finnish sociologist Markku Kivinen has been continuously focusing (like many Russian authors are now doing) on the professional qualities of middle class representatives. This well-known sociologist notes that based on Western experience, the middle class today is the most privileged group of employees. The power resources of the new middle class are related to professional skills and strategies rather than property.

However, in Soviet and post-Soviet Russia, the use of power resources provided by professionalism was limited. Russia never had a domestic market by professional segments. Professions operated within the principal bureaucratic organizations. Moreover, many professions depended on the dominant ideology. The traditional way of thinking and ethos of the Russian intellectuals were far from professionalism, from specialized labor ("craft"). With a rare exception (lawyers, doctors), specialists in Russia were not socially united, had no professional associations representing their interests, and were at the mercy of the state and corporate management. On the other hand, the society was forced to evaluate the performance of individuals and groups of professionals based on the opinion of officials rather than the competent judgment and assessment of their peers. As a matter of fact, this specific status of Russian professionals was unusual for expatriates and impeded their greater integration into the labor market.

Following the 2008 crisis, the problem of attracting highly skilled foreign personnel has been aggravated by the fact that those specialists that Russia requires are generally not jobless, as opposed to the 1930s. Moreover, the labor market in developed countries, especially in the United States, often experiences a shortage of exactly the same people that are so needed by the Russian economy. Therefore, starting from 2010–2011, engaging expatriates has become quite problematic due to financial and economic reasons. This is further complicated by considerable differences in the mentality of employees raised and educated in different cultures.

In this respect, the findings of a recent study of domestic and foreign companies (branches) operating in Russia are extremely valuable. The study included entities with a headcount ranging from 300 to 1,000 people. HR managers, both Russian and foreign, acted as respondents.

The study revealed significant differences in the human resource policies practiced by Russian and foreign companies. Where foreign companies proceed from the premise that employee talent has to be cultivated—"this is the performance and potential" of HR work, Russian companies perceive talent as a given, which cannot be influenced. That is why foreign companies focus on creating a corporate talent pool, while domestic companies mainly engage in HR management and work with individual existing and potential high performers. Western companies primarily focus their HR policies on developing teamwork capacities rather than individual personalities. Foreign companies are distinguished by a comprehensive approach to HR management; they rely on a robust system for working with talented staff. Where Russian companies focus on short-term results of work with talented employees (here and now), foreign firms consider subsequent corporate development and train future talented employees. Russian entities often adopt from foreign companies the most effective practices of managing talented personnel without considering the specifics of the Russian labor market, the existing skills of their employees, and the internal organizational environment.[174]

The issue of intellectual property is especially acute in Russia. The essence of the problem is the existing gap between the source of motivation and ownership of intellectual property. Motivation belongs to the inventors, whereas intellectual property rights *de facto* do not. It is impossible to build a post-industrial economy in such an environment.

We cannot rely only on foreign expertise when addressing the emerging challenges. Our own experience in this respect, as we have tried to show, extends back over centuries. On this long way, Russia knew both stunning success and disappointing failures.

In this respect, how can we evaluate the recent trend discussed in the previous chapter—outflow of expatriates from Russia? Is the Russian economy and the Russian society losing something important with their departure? Both yes and no. Let us ask ourselves—did the Russian economy benefit in the period when the number of expatriates grew from year to year? Can we see any trail left by the foreign cultural experience? The answer to these questions may well be predictable; nevertheless, let us turn to Table 5.1. for some macro- and mesoeconomic indicators.

---

174 Latukha M., Tsukanova T. *Talented Employees in Russian and Foreign Companies* // Voprosy Ekonomiki, 2013, No. 1.

Table 5.1. Some macro- and mesoeconomic indicators demonstrating the nature of foreign participation in Russia's economy in the 2000s *

	2005	2006	2007	2008	2009	2010	2011	2012	2013
The aggregate share of oil, gas, metals, precious stones and their products in Russian exports, % **	84.9	85.8	84.8	86.8	83.3	84.8	85.4	85.5	85.9
The share of engineering products in Russian exports, % **	3.6	3.9	3.4	2.8	4.6	4.2	3.6	3.5	3.7
Ratio of imports to output of engineering products in the Russian economy, %***	57.1	63.8	71.5	100.5	68.9	74.6	87.8	77.2	75.8
Ratio of imports to gross added value created by Russia's mechanical engineering industry, times**	1.9	2.2	2.5	3.5	2.2	2.4	3.2	2.7	2.6
Investment of Russian enterprises in imported machines, equipment, and vehicles as a share of total investment in machines, equipment, and vehicles, %	20.6	19.1	17.8	20.0	20.7	18.0	18.6	16.2	16.1
Including by individual industries:									
Production of air and space craft	36.4	19.2	18.1	31.8	22.0	30.3	23.4	31.3	23.0
Production of cars	22.5	34.0	34.1	56.7	54.1	57.2	56.2	49.1	40.4
Production of electrical, electronic, and optical equipment	31.8	24.5	23.5	23.5	29.2	28.1	26.7	28.2	29.1
Production of radio, TV, and telecommunications equipment	38.2	29.1	15.3	14.5	34.7	38.5	30.4	23.8	22.4
Production of medical equipment	17.3	23.3	27.8	38.6	22.6	22.0	22.1	18.4	35.0
Production of basic pharmaceutical products	16.6	45.2	9.0	15.2	57.7	38.2	38.7	61.3	52.1
Production of drugs	17.5	12.3	23.8	30.3	21.5	35.0	32.6	26.5	43.9
Telephone communications	39.9	40.8	21.8	29.0	21.2	30.3	30.5	29.2	28.9

Ratio of exports to imports for certain types of goods, %**									
Air and space craft, their parts	150.5	75.2	179.0	98.6	85.5	42.4	54.8	20.3	37.3
Aviation engines	56.4	434.7	17.6	n/a	198.5	n/a	68.1	100.8	20.6
Vessels, boats, floating structures	122.2	81.5	108.7	65.3	35.4	139.5	47.6	161.2	104.8
Electrical machines and equipment, their parts; TV and audio equipment	14.5	11.2	7.2	7.2	9.3	6.2	7.5	7.1	6.9
Nuclear reactors, fuel elements, equipment and devices for isotope separation	5,756.3	4,166.9	n/a	1,309.5	9,294.5	n/a	n/a	9,422.9	8,864.8
Metalworking machines	35.0	17.2	18.6	6.5	5.3	9.8	4.9	3.2	1.6
Pharmaceutical products	0.7	0.6	0.9	0.7	0.7	0.7	0.7	1.6	0.9
Organic chemicals	354.0	369.3	293.8	227.4	134.5	140.2	134.1	123.5	125.3

Notes to the table:
* Compiled from Rosstat (www.gks.ru) and FIRA-PRO (www.fira.ru) data.
** Under foreign trade with non-CIS countries

We see a set of quite classic facts:

A. Russia continues to be a resource-based economy with an absolute predominance of natural resources in the structure of exports. This is practically our only link with the global economy. Thus, if in 2000 the share of oil and natural gas in merchandise exports was 54.5 percent, in 2013 this proportion increased to 75.5 percent, with raw materials (including metals and gems) accounting for 85.9 percent of total exports. In contrast, the export share of manufactured goods—machinery and equipment—decreased in the same period from 7.5 percent to 3.7 percent.

B. The bulk of Russia's demand for high-tech goods is currently satisfied through imports, leaving virtually no place for local products even in the domestic market. For example, in 2008, which was a peak year in the pre-crisis period, imports of machinery, equipment, and vehicles reached 100.5 percent (!) of the domestic mechanical engineering output, exceeding 3.5-fold the gross added value created by Russian machine-building enterprises. In 2013, these figures were not as high as in the pre-crisis period, however, they indicated that the problem remained—imports amounted to 75.8 percent of the output of domestic machine-building enterprises, exceeding 2.6-fold the added value created by them. To this day, Russia's technological dependence is enormous, and in fact it is one-sided.

C. Investment in imported machinery and equipment is growing in virtually all domestic high-tech industries—depending on the sector, it constitutes from one quarter to more than a half of total investments in machines and equipment. Some of the highest figures have been registered in the automotive industry (an average of about 50 percent), in the production of basic pharmaceutical products and drugs (from 30 to 60 percent in different years), in the production of electronics, medical equipment, and in the telecommunications sector (from one quarter to one third of total investment). For major products of the domestic industry, imports are a substantial cost element.

D. For an impressive list of key goods, the export/import balance either shifts increasingly in favor of imports or fluctuates around a certain stable level reached in the early 2000s. In 2005, for example, the ratio of exports to imports in the aerospace industry (air and space craft, their parts) was 150 percent; by 2013 it had dropped to 37 percent. For certain types of electronic and electrical equipment, the ratio of exports to imports fell from 14.5 percent in 2005 to 6.9 percent in 2013. Russia is close to losing completely its positions in export manufacturing of metalworking machines—in 2005 their exports amounted to 35 percent of imports, but by 2013 this indicator had plummeted to 1.6 percent. The global pharmaceutical market is virtually inaccessible for Russian producers—exports average 0.7–0.9 percent of imports. Only exports of nuclear reactors, their components, and jet engines are beating records. With some exceptions, the Russian economy is experiencing increasing demand for imports of high-tech products, whereas the global economy is increasingly losing interest in their exports from Russia. The global market balance remains largely unfavorable for Russia—its share in world exports of major high-tech products stays on average at the level of 0.1–0.5 percent (depending on the type of product); equipment for nuclear reactors and radioactive materials are an exception with shares of about 2 percent and 0.8 percent, respectively.[175]

So, where is the **contribution** of expatriates (as representatives of technologically more advanced societies) working in Russia under long-term contracts? At this level there is none. Moreover, there could be none. Academician Natalia Ivanova made a very important remark when asked in an interview about the notorious problem of Russia's dependence on oil exports. She said, "If oil and gas extraction is accompanied by the emergence of world-class science and production, 'lamenting' is irrelevant. If the development of new oil and gas fields in Siberia begins with the purchase of Chinese drilling rigs, then we have a problem."[176]

Can this be the essence of the matter? The expatriate population, which existed until now, served to control foreign capital invested in Russia rather than promote the modernization of the Russian economy. Through no fault of theirs but based on the predetermined system conditions, the expatriates "served" the existing economic system. Definitely, expatriates triggered certain important changes, primarily, on the level of work teams. With their help, Russian employees not only found

---

175 *Russian Innovation Index.* M.: NRU HSE, 2011. pp. 80–81.
176 *Not Until the Last Drop of Oil. Interview with Academician (RAS) Natalia Ivanova //* Oil and Gas. Annex No.156 to the Kommersant newspaper of 30 August 2013. p. 19.

out what "Western-style" working and thinking meant, but acquired hands-on experience. Some lessons the Russians appreciated, some rejected, and in certain cases the expatriates themselves had something to learn. We will dwell on this in the following chapters.

That stage is largely over. Today, the Russian society needs expatriates as much as it requires a change in their composition—along ideological and even class lines. Even the expatriates' occupations and positions demonstrate that *the current expat framework as a specifically designed combination of forces is no longer relevant.* According to Russian government statistics (estimate as at 2012), the majority of expatriates occupy various managerial positions—foreign managers in Russia are double the number of foreign specialists in natural sciences and engineering.[177]

The impression emerges that management is the key problem of present-day Russia. In reality, however, *by being preoccupied exclusively with managerial matters since the 1990s, we have almost lost the intellectual class of researchers and engineers, who with their worldview and motivation can hardly find a place in the existing structure of the Russian labor market. There are also practically no job opportunities for the respective category of expatriates. But it is precisely this category of expatriates that Russia currently needs.*

For foreign specialists to start addressing the task of transforming the Russian economy on the system rather than individual work team level, new foreign top managers and advisors with their universalistic management models are no longer needed. We need to create conditions for changing the very principle on which the work of currently departing expatriates was based. For the most part, *they worked for their companies in Russia rather than for Russia.* The liberal doctrine treats this as almost identical, but in fact, it is not. For example, the situation was fundamentally different during the reign of Peter the Great and Elizabeth. At that time, foreign scientists, engineers, industrialists, and military officers *worked not just in Russia, but on behalf of Russia creating the Russian brand.* That was the case in the later periods of Russian history. That was even so in the early Soviet years. This is the fun-

---

177   *Labor and Employment in Russia.* M.: Rosstat, 2013. Section 5, *Movement of workers and employees, use of working time, and labor migration* / http://www.gks.ru/bgd/regl/b13_36/IssWWW.exe/Stg/05-19.doc

damental class distinction between the role of expatriates then and now. Perhaps, the most important current task in terms of engaging foreign specialists is bringing back expatriates to Russia in this new class and role capacity.

Chapter VI.
Social criteria for evaluating the role of foreign professionals in Russian society

Foreign professionals in Russia: The new "Varangians"? Foreign professionals employed as executives and managers in major companies in Russia are of interest to researchers, since being non-residents, they are in a position to take strategic corporate decisions that can directly influence the social and economic development indicators not only of individual businesses but also of entire local communities. Besides, foreign professionals are bearers of a different culture code, which may be more appealing and effective than that reproduced by the "host" institutional environment.

This is what gives us reason to speak about the potential impact that expatriates can have on the nature and trend of socio-cultural and socio-economic modernization in Russia. The answer to this question is far from straightforward, primarily because the expatriates themselves constitute a rather heterogeneous social stratum.

Our task is to get an understanding of whether it is reasonable to include expatriates into the list of social groups, which, according to modern researchers, are actors of Russian modernization alternative to the state, namely, the "new middle class", professionals occupied in sectors of the new economy ("informationalists"), innovative entrepreneurs, etc.[178] Can this new social stratum of the Russian society, under certain conditions, be able to contribute to the transformation of the Russian economic culture, to its transition to new sustainable forms, more responsive to modern economic and technological challenges?

---

[178] See, in particular, Tikhonova N.E. *Characteristics of Russian Modernists and Prospects of Cultural Dynamics in Russia* // Obshchestvennye Nauki i Sovremennost. 2012. No. 2. pp. 38–52; Tikhonova N.E., Mareyeva S.V. *The Middle Class: Theory and Reality*. M.: Alpha-M, 2009. pp. 261–280; Shkaratan O.I. *Socio-Economic Inequality and its Reproduction in Contemporary Russia*. M.: OLMA Media Group, 2009. pp. 354–370; Karacharovskiy V.V. *Economic Motivation and Innovative Processes* // Problemnyj Analiz i Gosudarstvenno-Upravlencheskoye Proektirovaniye. 2011. Vol. 4. No. 6.

History shows that during periods of modernization breakthroughs Russia usually either extensively engaged foreign professionals in its economic and state-building processes or actively imported values and achievements of other cultures. Like it or not, this fact cannot be ignored. It is also undisputed that this strategy was always accompanied by a phenomenon unique in world history—it took Russia just several years to cover such ground in its development for which pioneer countries had needed decades or even centuries.

At the same time, there are quite a few examples when transplanting the experience, institutions or values from other cultures played a negative role, producing dangerous pathologies in the country's development. In those cases, much depended on the aspects of foreign experience that were being transferred to Russian soil and the "foreign influence" groups that emerged in the country—the goals they pursued, the means they used, how appealing for Russians were the socio-cultural patterns they conveyed, and, finally, their true attitude to Russia and Russians.

Obviously, criteria must exist that would allow predicting the nature, intensity, and focus of foreign influence on the development of the national culture and domestic economy. Herein we explore the conditions under which expatriates can in principle act as agents of modernization. In particular, we will focus on the social image of foreign professionals as an indicator of their role in the development of Russian companies.

Empirical basis of the analysis. The ideas presented herein are based on the findings obtained from 166 in-depth interviews with foreign and Russian professionals jointly working in multinational teams of Russian companies or in Russian branches of international companies.

The interviews with foreign professionals were held in Moscow (74 interviews), Saint Petersburg (37 interviews), Nizhny Novgorod (14 interviews), and Novosibirsk (20 interviews). Respondents representing the following socio-professional groups took part in the survey: 29%—corporate top management, 44%—middle managers, owners or heads of small companies, and 37%—staff employees and freelancers. The sample includes expatriates from the USA (18% of the total surveyed), the Netherlands (15%), the United Kingdom (11%), Germany and Austria (11%), post-socialist EU countries (10%), France (7%), Italy (6%), and Spain (3%). One respondent each represents Sweden, Switzerland, Ireland, Japan, Portugal, Peru, India, Morocco, Pakistan, and some other countries.

Interviews with Russian professionals (21 interviews) were held in Moscow. Among those surveyed 20% were corporate top managers, 40%—middle managers, and 40%—staff employees. Interview guides with Russian and foreign professionals are provided in Appendix 1.

Definitely, interviews with foreign professionals became the main source of information on the topic of our research. We have attempted to identify the ideological basis of the contemporary expatriates' activity in Russia, highlighting among them groups with a fundamentally different potential impact on the development of Russian companies.

We covered companies operating in the following industries and sectors of the economy: information technology and telecommunications, FMCG companies, advertising and marketing, trade, hospitality, tourism, science and education, consulting (business services), financial sector, and industry.

The social image of foreign professionals as an indicator of their role in the development of Russian companies. A key finding of our research is the conclusion that the foreign professional community in Russia is heterogeneous, and this directly determines the different roles, functions, intensity, and focus of their impact on different processes in the Russian society and economy.

Two basic criteria underlie the stratification structure of foreign professionals with different "utility" for Russian companies.

The first criterion is *the nature of integration of foreign professionals into the Russian society.* Here, two polar and one intermediate stratum are clearly distinguishable. One extreme is the stratum of professionals whose attitude is not to be integrated into the Russian society (*staying "out of society"*). In many cases, this is not just an attitude but a contractual provision paid for by the employer. The other extreme are professionals significantly influenced by Russian culture or culturally fully assimilated. Generally, they include staff employees or small business owners, who one way or another were connected with Russia in the past (for example, completed here their higher education). In-between are the professionals whose mission is to find common ground with the Russian business culture and design fundamentally new "culture-centric" efficient business models on that basis. According to the classification proposed by Nigel Nicholson in his theory of work role transitions, these are professionals focused on establishing a fundamentally new balance with the host culture either involving personal change (*exploration*) or without personal change (*determination*).[179]

The second criterion determining the role of Russian-based foreign professionals as agents of influence is their *vision or perception of the Russian society*. Analysis shows that foreign professionals engaged in Russia have shaped quite different perceptions of Russia and Russians, ranging from productive to counter-productive, when an effective cross-cultural exchange of values is either problematic or impossible. Our research has revealed at least three basic ways in which foreign professionals perceive the Russian society. We have tentatively classified these perception types into the following categories: "Cold War-style", "rationally pragmatic", and "allowing for modernization"

***"Russians are not a welcoming society" vs. "Russia as an adventure"*: How expatriates perceive Russia and Russians**. Segmentation of foreign professionals based on the above two criteria allows distinguishing at least *six typological groups,* the representatives of which play fundamentally different roles in the development of Russian entities (see Table 6.1).

---

[179] Nicholson N. *A Theory of Work Role Transitions* // Administrative Science Quarterly. 1984. No. 29

Table 6.1. Segmentation of Russian-based foreign professionals by their role in the development of Russian companies

Type of integration into the host culture / Perception of the host culture	"Cold War-style"	"Rationally pragmatic"	"Allowing for modernization"
Strategy to remain not integrated into the host culture (staying *"out of society"*)	(+) The "reference" culture code remains unchanged; institutional isomorphism of local companies with the "western" type of business culture is provided. (-) High exposure to conflict, the style of imposing ready-made change "templates" ignoring local specifics prevails; gives only temporary effect (as long as pressure is maintained).	(+) The "reference" culture code remains unchanged; institutional isomorphism of local companies with the "western" type of business culture is provided. (-) Narrowly utilitarian perception of the host culture and local companies; effective cross-cultural business exchange at the micro-level is problematic.	—
Focus on establishing a fundamentally new balance with the host culture without personal change (*determination*) or with personal change (*exploration*)	—	(+) High efficiency in dealing with current corporate matters owing to the ability to abide by local rules of the game. (-) Limited desire to give a new impetus to the development of the local system.	(+) Combines the ability to deal efficiently with corporate issues with the desire to give a new impetus to the development of the local system, along with the ability to build the required team spirit. (-) This type is rare among top managers.

Copying (*replication*) or passive acceptance (*absorption*) of the new role in the host culture[*]		(+) Establishes efficient local businesses, sets high performance standards for local competitors. (-) Limited desire to give a new impetus to the local system; contributes no new knowledge to the existing vision of modernization.	(+) Establishes efficient local businesses, sets high performance standards for local competitors. (-) This type is almost isomorphic to the Russian business culture and only replicates the "local" vision of modernization.
	[**]		

Notes to the table:

[*] Elements of the classification proposed by N. Nicholson in his theory of work role transitions have been used (Nicholson N. A Theory of Work Role Transitions // Administrative Science Quarterly. 1984. No. 29).

[**] Rare combination.

The **"Cold War-style" perception** is the rarest of the existing attitudes to Russia and Russians. It is distinguished by its conflict-prone nature.

Following are some judgments specific for this perception type:

> "Russians are not a welcoming society. Moscow is the hardest city I've ever lived. It's difficult, it's aggressive. Russians are aggressive generally." (UK, advisor to the chairman of the board of a bank)
>
> "If they (the Russians—authors' note) fear, they will do it, but if you ask them, they will think that you are weak." (UK, advisor to the chairman of the board of a bank)

In many respects, such a perception demonstrates a kind of "self-fulfilling prophecy"—the initial negative perception creates a conflict, which can eventually really generate higher aggression, confrontation, and sabotage. This type of perception is mainly encountered among foreign employees, who (together with their families) are fully provided for and taken care of by their foreign company. They are the ones who typically adopt the strategy of not integrating into the host culture, this strategy reflecting either their personal attitude or the approach of their foreign employer.

Expert opinion:

> "...their work (the work of the above category of foreign professionals—authors' note) has nothing to do with integrating; on the contrary, their task is to stay not integrated... otherwise they will be unable to implement the corporate policy. ...A person, who is paid over $2,000 per week will in any case respect corporate strategy more than the interests of Russia." (UK, top manager of a specialized publication)

In part, the strategy of non-integration can be justified. Thus, some studies show that consistent reproduction of foreign socio-cultural patterns in Russia often requires that their individual bearer be "shielded" from the influence of local culture and institutions by a high-level status or specific socio-professional environment. "Only those who hold more or less advanced positions in business or are engaged in international cooperation succeed in reproducing this (*"western"—authors' note*) model in practice".[180]

On the one hand, foreign professionals and executives of this type, being shielded (both institutionally and personally) from the influence of

---

[180] Konstantinovskiy D., Voznesenskaya E., Cherednichenko G. *Russians in Western Countries: The Effect of Long-Term Sojourn* / In: Yadov V.A. (ed.). *Impact of Western Socio-Cultural Patterns on Russian Social Practices.* M.: TAUS, 2009. p. 187.

the local culture, are able to stimulate the reproduction of "reference" (by western standards) interaction and activity patterns at the workplace. This increases the institutional isomorphism of local companies with "western-type" entities, thus raising the chances that such companies will be successful in certain segments of the international business community.

The non-integration strategy may be effective if a Russian company wants to match western standards of "proper business". In that case, the expatriate faces the task of adapting local employees to western standards rather than finding common language with them, and if they fail to adapt, to employ others. The less such an expatriate is associated with the local culture, the better he will perform this function. Whether such an approach is reasonable is another question.

On the other hand, the interaction of that type of foreign professionals with local companies is largely based on imposing canonic "western" work culture and management patterns with no consideration for local cultural specifics. First, this often gives only temporary effect (as long as pressure is maintained) with a rather uncertain impact on team performance. Second, the now classic question, which V.G. Fedotova pointed out some time ago, arises—can genuine modernization (of the business or society in general) be achieved by applying the strategy of "...adopting and imitating the existing structures of the western society, which themselves are starting to undergo change"? [181]

However, in combination with the examined perception of the Russian society, the role of such foreign professionals in the development of Russian companies becomes rather ambiguous.

In part, the "Cold War-style" perception may manifest itself after the first few months of staying in Russia. In this case, no integration has happened as yet.

Example:

> "After we had some drinks, a Frenchman virtually interrogated us whether Russia was going to bomb France and whether Russian aircraft were spying on France" or "...The conversation (with an Italian—authors' note) turned to World War II, and he dropped the following phrase, 'Why is Russia so concerned about World War II...

---

181 Fedotova V.G. *Modernization of the Other Europe* M.: IF RAN, 1997. Chapter I, §3.

You had no role to play there, it was the Americans who won the war'." (Russian, engineer in a company producing and distributing medical equipment)

"...Some foreigners come here, because they were not able to secure a good job back home. ... They think we don't have a clue about anything here, that we are all monkeys, and they must urgently teach us, educate us and open our eyes. ...So here they come bursting from their own greatness, although back home they were good for nothing." (Russian lady, head of the innovations department of an FMCG company)

The **"rationally pragmatic" perception** of the Russian society is much more widespread among foreign professionals. This perception is highly skeptical. The Russian society in general is considered to be a static system incapable of modernization—one can "deal with it", but one cannot significantly enhance it. In many ways, such a perception reflects the consumer attitude to the Russian society and economy.

Following are some judgments specific for this perception type:

"...Now foreigners understand that nothing ever changes here. Corruption has always been, is and will be in place. Pulling strings has always been, is and will be a way of getting things done. All public positions have always been filled through networking. Everyone understands it now, but previously we didn't." (UK, top manager of a specialized publication)

"There are many ways in making it (meaning 'do a specific job'—authors' note) more efficient. But it is futile. This is not going to happen. It's been like this over a thousand years." (USA, analyst of a bank's financial department)

Of course, the approach that "nothing will ever change here" is the opinion of the observer, his or her personal attitude or experience. Let us ask whether anything can be changed in Germany, France, or the USA? And do Germans, for example, want anyone to change them? Of course, Russia, like any other country, has its problems, but treating any sustainable difference between Russia and the West as a "problem" is unreasonable. It makes no sense to reproduce imported familiar patterns and expect that here they will function exactly the same way as at home. Foreigners have to be open to values different from theirs and willing to understand the Russian reality—then they will be able to cope with it, because Russians are ready for change and are as unhappy about many Russian problems as the expatriates are.

This type of perception is common for expatriates, who are largely shielded from the local culture by their corporate status or relations with their foreign employer. Observations made by Russians:

"It happens that they (the expatriates—authors' note) travel from home to the office and back by car and encounter no local reality.... They lack understanding, because they live in suburban communities surrounded by similar expatriates or the like. They spend their leisure among their own." (Russian lady, research and development manager of an FMCG company)

"The only obstacle that hampers their (the expatriates'—authors' note) work is lack of understanding as to the size of the country. This generates problems. I have the urge to take them along and show how people live. Very few of them see and understand this." (Russian lady, head of the innovations department of an FMCG company)

Such expat groups share a narrowly utilitarian perception of Russia along with next to no desire to introduce fundamentally new features into the local system that would facilitate its transition to a more advantageous position.

This is apparent from the rationale behind their decision to come to Russia. Expert opinion:

"Currently, there is no deep integration, people are reserved. They used to be more open; they came here and exclaimed, "Oh, what music! Oh, what culture!" In the 1980s-1990s, they used to fall in love with Russia. People are no longer curious; their only concern is money... Russia itself has become more pragmatic and less interesting. ... People come here mainly to earn money—they have no other purposes." (UK, journal editor)

"Some of them (expatriates—authors' note) came to make money doing nothing. They stand out from the crowd. They just came because of the generous compensation package and have no wish to move a finger. There are quite a few of them here. Some people manage to sell themselves well to major companies. They get good pay, do nothing, moreover, the company has to pay them a big parachute just to get rid of them. <...> for many people work in Russia is a step up the career ladder. They do not care what happens to the company in two years." (Russian lady, head of the innovations department of an FMCG company)

Foreign professionals of this type largely share a purely pragmatic and negative perception of Russian capitalism as corruption-prone, bureaucratic, and temporary—existing only as long as oil prices remain high.

Following is a typical opinion:

"The only thing that keeps everything together right now are the high oil prices... I just feel it won't be a safe place to raise a family in." (USA, analyst, financial department of a bank)

"We changed the website, we changed the documentation, and all proposals to bank in Europe, because the reaction to Russian was, 'Ew! Russian? Probably stolen!'... so we called ourselves an international company. And we really changed this attitude. Because people in Europe and USA say that Russia is corrupt. Corruption is everywhere. But it's more popular here." (UK, advisor to the chairman of the board of a bank)

In the meantime, professionals and managers of this type can be very efficient in dealing with current corporate matters owing to the willingness and ability to abide by local rules of the game. However, it is obvious that the situation could have been quite different if their initial perception of Russia and Russians would not have been negative.

Opinion:

> "They (Russians—authors' note) are drivers for results. If you give them a task, they will have it done." (USA, manager, research and development department, an FMCG company)

The last quote brings us to the third typical way in which foreign professionals perceive Russia and Russians—**"perception, allowing for modernization"**. First, this type of perception implicitly does not reject the Russian society and Russian capitalism from the start; second, it does not consider Russia as a static system; and third, it focuses on a positive perception of Russian specifics.

Following is an opinion characteristic of this perception type:

> "If in Germany, for example, you are taken to court or do something wrong, or get a penalty notice, you know what to expect. Here (in Russia—authors' note), anything can happen... It took me long to decide whether I need to switch a stable good job in Germany for an adventure in Russia." (Germany, top manager of a recruiting agency)

Please note that this opinion, in general, is rather critical and definitely reflects the complex nature of life in Russia; however, its perception is completely different—it generates no conflict and contains no skepticism. Let us compare the "Cold War-style" and "modernization" perceptions of the Russian society—*"Russians are not a welcoming society"* vs. *"Russia as an adventure"*. The modernization perception of Russia is far from being an isolated case among foreigners. This approach is rather widespread among professionals and managers of different nationalities. Following are some typical examples:

"There are many things I like about Russia. For example, I meet young people in Moscow, in whose eyes I see the future. There is a feeling of movement, of progress, and of change." (East European country, top manager of an engineering and construction company)

"I think I will never live in America again. I love being American. I'm definitely American, I've been American all my life, but America for me is very boring. Americans don't know about the outside world. I think that Russians know a lot more about America, than Americans know about Russia." (USA, editor and columnist of a specialized publication)

"There is more work here, more money, and more opportunity for experiments." (Eastern Europe, top manager of an engineering and construction company).

"Russia is considered to be a promising market; there are business and career development opportunities here ... I am here for this, because the salary in Russia is the same as in Japan. A global unified wage scale is our corporate policy." (Japan, leading manager of an international automotive concern)

"Russia is a developing country. Everything is growing. Traffic jams, crowded metro. The people are very hospitable." (Germany, engineer at an industrial enterprise)

"I like it here. It was my choice. The country is interesting, and I find that the people are interesting, good, and kind. I am never bored here. The city is lively and the people are lively." (The Netherlands, head of the Russian office of a consulting company)

"I am excited. I am concerned about Russia and want it to become a developed country. I am very optimistic about Russia's future." (Japan, director of a national center)

"The people in Russia are more open than the Westerners; they are more spontaneous and straightforward, and less formalized. They can find different solutions based on logics rather than laws. Their only negative trait is disorderliness." (Poland, programmer in a Russian bank)

Russians also confirm the existence of this type of foreigners:

"There are normal foreigners who realize they have come to a large country that no one understands. They have the knowledge of processes and methods. They are ready to share their knowledge. There are foreigners who are in love with Russia and have no intention of leaving." (Russian lady, head of the innovations department of an FMCG company).

Definitely, this is the most valuable type of foreign professionals in terms of transferring new cultural elements to Russia, consolidating them, and, therefore, achieving a new level of value and business exchange, at least in the sense, in which many professionals of this type see their mission in Russia:

"Western companies want to extend their influence, that's why they are sending them (the expatriates—authors' note). They want to influence local subsidiaries with a western mindset. So the goal of the expatriate is to bring the capability up so that future leaders are Russians." (USA, manager, research and development department, an FMCG company)

Expatriates of this type combine the ability to deal effectively with corporate matters through building the required team spirit with the desire to give the local system a fundamentally new development impetus by merging aspects of the Russian ("host") business culture with those of the "guest" culture, which they (foreign professionals) represent.

This type is also widespread among high-ranking expatriates:

"The Russians' reputation could not be worse. There is no other nation with a poorer reputation. But if there is understanding and trust between you, Russians are the most practical people of all. And that is very important. <...> If we look reasonably at what Russia has achieved in the past twenty years, it is mind-blowing." (USA, partner in a financial company)

However, the attitude to Russia within this group can also be quite pragmatic—far from missionary ("modernist" is just an ideal type; actual people, useful in this respect, are quite practical). Here are two viewpoints expressed by one person:

"The main distinction is that Russians are very particular about the words friend, acquaintance, and pal. In America, it is different—there, the word friend means nothing. Here, if I have a friend, and that friend has a problem, it is also my problem, and let us deal with it together. An American can just fail to react, even if you ask him ... This is something I appreciate very much, that is why I am here. This is very much to my liking... I am now writing a book to tell Americans what Russians are like, to tell them that there are no bears roaming the streets here. The perception of Russia has remained unchanged over the past 50 years or so, and that is very sad."

Compare the above with his own following opinion:

"I have two children, and I would not like to raise them here. I have friends in Russia, but I think one should stay as long as one is young. There is nothing for the elderly here. As long as I am young, I get along well here. But of course I love the sea and the sun, so I would like to retire somewhere to Italy... Here, the business opportunities, especially for the young and ambitious ones, are good. That is why I am here." (USA, board member of an energy company)

Therefore, one should not confuse those, whom we call modernists, with romantics in the sentimental sense of the word. The latter, of course, exist as well, but they are few and generally have little potential for transformation. On the contrary, Russia often "reshapes" such expatriates. Most often, they are to be encountered among individual freelancers. Following is a typical example:

> "One must accept difficulties as a fact and bravely endure them. Russia helped me understand that life is not a bed of roses..., helped me see life as it is, and taught me to accept everything.... In Italy, people live, as if everything depends on them, as if they know life, but here that is not possible. Here... life is more like the real thing." (Italy, teacher of Italian at a university)

The expatriates delegated by companies generally undergo respective training before taking up a position in another country. Therefore, they usually know what to expect. If they have come to Russia, this must have been their rational, deliberate choice. Indeed, the "modernists" have a mission—to change something for the better, and in that sense they are idealists. However, they are far from expecting the other culture to be a plastic substance that will immediately change under their touch. They find extreme assignments challenging. Like surfers, they want to catch and ride the wave.

The "modernist" type of perception, like the "rationally pragmatic" one, is widespread among middle managers, well-paid professionals working in major Russian and joint companies, and Russian branches of international companies, as well as among business owners in Russia.

Based on the type of integration into Russian society, we can distinguish *two groups of* professionals sharing this perception. The first group includes people whose integration is based on finding a completely new balance between the interacting cultures and designing hybrid high performance models. The second group includes those who have adapted to the Russian business environment through replication and passive acceptance of the Russian culture.

The majority of those whom we have provisionally classified into the "first" group of modernists keep their distance, socializing with Russians only at work or for business purposes:

"In general, they are normal pleasant people that are good to work with. There are few "despots" or extreme careerists among them that would squeeze you dry giving nothing in exchange. They socialize among their own and tend to stick together. They don't hang out a lot, since most of them are hard workers, but they know how to maintain friendly relations." (Russian, marketing specialist at an FMCG company)

"Out of office, they (the expatriates—authors' note) are very open and easy to communicate with.... As for his or her private life, there is a red line that no one is allowed to cross. This line is much more distinct than the one my Russian acquaintances have." (Russian, software developer, an IT company)

Respondent: - The Arabs are absolutely loyal towards Russians (from Saudi Arabia and Syria), almost like the Serbs and many other European Slavic nations. The French are loyal, but in a cool sort of way. The Germans, Austrians, and the British are reserved.

Interviewer: - Perhaps, they are just "reserved" by themselves, not only towards Russians?

Respondent: - Maybe... Nevertheless, it was from them that I didn't feel any specific attitude." (Russian, engineer in a company producing and distributing medical equipment)

However, there is a completely different (provisionally "second") group of expatriates-modernists. Generally, they are professionals or small and medium-size business owners, who one way or another were connected with Russia in the past (for example, completed their higher education). Usually, they have been living in Russia for quite some time and successfully play by the local rules of the game. Largely, this is their rational choice, which demonstrates clearly the strategy of adjusting to a new role through active behavioral and personal change (*"absorption"* or *"replication"* according to N. Nicholson's terminology).

Following are some typical examples:

Question: "Are there any specific aspects of Russian behavior that you do not understand and that interfere with your work?" - Answer: "I see many things like a Russian now. You should have asked me this question when I had just arrived, then I would have probably noticed such aspects."

Question: "What is your current religious affiliation?" - Answer: "I don't know (laughs)... it depends on the weather." (North African state, leading engineer in a construction company)

"After 20 years I will no longer be able to work in Switzerland. I will definitely continue working here, but when I retire, I will return home." (Switzerland, partner in a company providing printing services)

"My nature has not changed, but what has completely changed is my perception of Russia; I see it as an insider rather than an outsider." (The Netherlands, advisor in a consulting company)

"I have become more Russian. Another positive effect is that I am no longer as tense as I used to be." (Germany, line director at an IT company)

"Today, I am more Russian than Irish. I have also become slightly less well-mannered in shops and parking lots, when I need to park my car. In contrast to Ireland, people in the streets never smile here. At first, I went around smiling like an idiot. Now, I smile no longer." (Ireland, CEO, an IT company)

The last type of foreign professionals is almost isomorphic to the Russian business culture and its representatives only replicate the Russians' "domestic" vision of modernization. Generally, they can contribute no new knowledge to the development patterns already assimilated by the Russian culture. However, they usually establish rather efficient local businesses, setting high performance standards for Russian colleagues and competitors.

Chapter VII.
The cultural distance between Russian and foreign professionals

This chapter attempts to evaluate the extent and nature of cultural differences between Russian and foreign professionals working in multinational teams in Russia, as well as the degree to which the initial nationally determined cultural distance between representatives of both parties is subject to change due to extended joint work.

Applying quantitative methods to measure cultural differences as a research task

A quantitative approach to the analysis of cultural differences. The below analysis of the cultural differences between Russian and foreign professionals working in multinational teams in Russia is based on the CVSCALE methodology proposed by Boonghee Yoo, Naveen Donthu, and Tomasz Lenartowicz.[182] Conceptually, this technique is a development of the widely known approach suggested by the Dutch scientist Geert Hofstede.[183] It allows comparing cultures by measuring five quantitative dimensions—power distance (PD), uncertainty avoidance (UA), individualism/collectivism (IDV/CO),[184] masculinity (MA), and long-term orientation (LTO). CVSCALE was designed as a tool adapted to measuring the respective dimensions on the individual level (rather than the country level, as per Hofstede).

Power distance reflects the degree to which an individual believes that authoritarian management and decision-making are legitimate (re-

---

[182] The technique is described in detail and tested (validated) in the following work: Boonghee Yoo, Naveen Donthu, Tomasz Lenartowicz. *Measuring Hofstede's Five Dimensions of Cultural Values at the Individual Level: Development and Validation of CVSCALE* // Journal of International Consumer Marketing, 23: 193–210, 2011. p. 210.

[183] See G. Hofstede's classical work: Hofstede G. *Culture's Consequences: International Differences in Work-Related Values.* Beverly Hills, CA: Sage Publications 1980.

[184] Hofstede's original technique measured the level of individualism, whereas CVSCALE measures the reverse dimension - the level of collectivism.

gardless of whether this individual wields power or is a subordinate). *Uncertainty avoidance* is the degree to which an individual needs detailed instructions, rigid norms, clear rules, standardized procedures, and feels the urge to strictly abide by them. *Collectivism* expresses the measure in which group interests prevail over personal ones for an individual. *Masculinity* reflects the degree to which an individual (regardless of gender) recognizes the leading male gender role in society. And finally, *long-term orientation* indicates the degree to which individuals are ready and able to sacrifice current benefits for the sake of future ones.

Each of the above five measures is calculated as the average value of answers (expressed in scores) provided by respondents to a specific group of questions/judgments.[185] The response to each question is evaluated using the 5-point Likert scale (where 1 is the lowest and 5 is the highest manifestation of the dimension considered in the question/judgment).

By now, CVSCALE has been used for a significant number of studies in different countries, thus making the technique an effective comparative analysis tool, which relies on extensive accumulated results.

Preceding results and research hypotheses. The aggregate traditional ethnocultural portrait of a Russian worker, as well as its correlation with the typical portrait of an individual representing the "Western" culture, has received quite extensive coverage in academic literature. According to Hofstede's first evaluations of Russia, the local workers were appointed exceptionally high scores for power distance and uncertainty avoidance (93 and 95 points, respectively) and low scores for individualism (39 points) and masculinity (36 points).[186] Similar evaluations for the EU and the USA showed lower measures for the first three dimensions and a higher score for the fourth one: USA (40, 46, 91, 62),

---

185 We used the 26-item questionnaire proposed by the authors of the methodology. The questions underlying the five scales are provided in Appendix 2 - in the original (2A) and in the Russian translation (2B).

186 Hofstede G. *Culture's Consequences: Comparing Values, Behaviors, Institutions, and Organizations Across Nations*. Second Edition, Thousand Oaks CA: Sage Publications, 2001. p. 500–502. The data are provided from: Latova N., Latov Yu. Ethnometric Approaches to the Analysis of Economic and Cultural Values // Voprosy Ekonomiki. 2008. No. 5. p. 85.

Germany (35, 65, 67, 66), UK (35, 35, 89, 66), France (68, 86, 71, 43), Czech Republic (57, 74, 58, 57), and Poland (68, 93, 60, 64).[187]

In our case, however, we consider a special type of Russian worker—highly skilled specialists (professionals), who are in permanent contact with expatriates. Moreover, this contact takes place at the micro level (in the course of business interactions), when each of the parties is directly and permanently influenced by the neighboring culture. This can shift the standard set of values both in the case of Russians and expatriates, resulting in either their convergence or divergence. Therefore, under the first hypothesis we test the existence and intensity of differences between representatives of the two mentioned groups of professionals: *there is a cultural distance between Russian and foreign professionals working together, which manifests itself in the fact that Russians score higher in power distance, uncertainty avoidance, collectivism, and masculinity.*

Studies initiated by Hofstede triggered a whole layer of further research using his methodology, including in Russia. The research demonstrated a rather considerable dependence of the values on the socio-occupational groups that became the subject matter of analysis. It rendered a number of quite contradictory evaluations of Russians that revealed the high internal cultural diversity of the Russian society.

For example, a mid-1990s survey of Russian business school students showed their close proximity to the Europeans. In particular, the power distance and uncertainty avoidance scored 40 and 68 points, respectively.[188]

Another Russian survey carried out in the early 2000s among the engineering personnel of machine-building enterprises yielded even lower power distance measures (=28).[189]

A number of surveys performed in different Russian cities revealed a considerable territorial discrepancy in Hofstede's dimensions: in particular, the measure of individualism in different cities varied from 48 to

---

187 All the indicated figures are available on the web site of the Hofstede Centre: The Hofstede Centre. Cultural Tools Country Comparison (http://geert-hofstede.com).
188 Naumov A. *Hofstede's Dimension of Russia: Influence of the National Culture on Business Management //* Management. 1996. No. 3.
189 Danilova E., Tararukhina M. *The Russian Industrial Culture in Hofstede's Dimensions //* Public Opinion Monitoring. 2003. No. 3(65). p. 55.

82, power distance—from 19 to 91, and uncertainty avoidance—from 91 to 136.[190]

Finally, one of the international studies compared respondents from eleven countries, including Russia (in each case the sample consisted of business students of national universities).[191] The study showed that Russians in the tested sample were distinguished not only by the highest power distance and masculinity measures, but also one of the highest individualism scores (comparable with the value obtained for Americans).

Thus, the very existence of the traditional Russian "cultural type" is contested by many studies that often come up with polar portraits of Russian employees depending on their affiliation with a certain socio-occupational group or territorial community.[192] The factor of the internal cultural polarity of the societies necessitates testing the hypothesis that the "cultural type" of the employee is affected by the competition between the national and group identity: *it is possible to distinguish such multinational groups of expatriates and Russians that demonstrate greater cross-group differences than the teams grouped by nationality.*

The last hypothesis addresses cultural dynamics. The interaction between local professionals and expatriates creates favorable conditions for mutual cultural transformation. The above mentioned close contacts between representatives of different cultures, typical for multinational teams, serve as the first factor in this case. The second hypothetical factor promoting cultural dynamics is the possibility to obtain immediate evidence of the efficacy/utility of a value or ideological principle originating from another culture—a possibility that exists in multinational work teams. In particular, based on in-depth interviews, we

---

190 For an overview of relevant studies, see: Latov Yu.V., Latova N.V. *Findings and Paradoxes of Ethnometric Analysis of Russia's Economic Culture According to Hofstede* // Mir Rossii. 2007. No. 4. pp. 52–53.
191 Schumann J.H., Wangenheim F.v., Stringfellow A., Yang Zh., Blazevic V., Praxmarer S., Shainesh G., Komor M., Shannon R.M., Jiménez F.R. *Cross-Cultural Differences in the Effect of Received Word-of-Mouth Referral in Relational Service Exchange* // Journal of International Marketing. 2010.Vol. 18. No. 3. p. 70.
192 See also: Susokolov A.A. *Culture and Exchange. Introduction to Economic Anthropology.* M.: SPSL-Russkaya Panorama, 2006. pp. 258–259.

captured the existence of strategies for adopting—when reasonable—the business qualities of partners representing other cultures.[193]

On the other hand, there is resistance to cultural change. First of all, this is the classic dichotomy "we–they"—the irrational basis of cultural distance, which may have a decisive impact. Another similarly likely factor impeding cultural rapprochement applies only to expatriates. Being in an unfamiliar symbolic environment, they may deliberately keep their distance from the surrounding culture for psychological or defensive reasons, or due to "culture shock".[194]

We shall test the assumption about the importance of the time factor—the duration of joint work and the frequency of contacts between the two cultures—for cultural dynamics: *the cultural distance between Russian professionals and expatriates is not a consistently reproduced characteristic; it depends on how long representatives of the two cultures work together.*

The empirical basis of the analysis. To test the proposed assumptions, we conducted a survey of Russian and foreign professionals working in multinational teams of Russian companies and Russian branches of international companies in the following sectors: information technology and telecommunications, FMCG companies, advertising and marketing, trade, hospitality, tourism, science and education, consulting (business services), financial sector, and industry. The survey was held in Moscow at the end of 2013—beginning of 2014. Respondents included 104 Russian professionals and 117 foreign professionals from over 20 countries working in Russia. All respondents were highly skilled specialists with higher education, who were employed in line with their training. Direct contact with representatives of another culture in the course of business interactions was a prerequisite for the selection of respondents.

To make the sample more homogeneous, we narrowed the range of respondents to people representing contacts between Russia and

---

[193] Karacharovskiy V.V., Yastrebov G.A., Shkaratan O.I. *Culture and Modernization in the Mirror of Interaction Between Russian and Foreign Professionals in Multinational Work Teams in Russia* // Sotsiologicheskiye Issledovaniya. 2014. No. 8. pp. 69–73.

[194] The original provisions of the so-called "culture shock" theory were formulated in the writings of the American anthropologist Kalervo Oberg, see: Oberg K. *Cultural Shock: Adjustment to New Cultural Environments* // Practical Anthropology. No. 7. 1960.

the West. Russian professionals had to be Russians by self-identification and had to work in Russia alongside foreign professionals from the EU and/or the USA. Foreign professionals (expatriates) had to be Europeans (of any nationality representing a EU country) or Americans (USA) by self-identification and to work in Russia under a contract alongside Russians.

The final sample included 78 respondents from among expatriates and 71 respondents from among Russian professionals. Russian and expat samples differed by age, gender composition and percentage of respondents with subordinates. The Russian sample had a lower average age (32.9 years against 37.9 years, t=-3.62, p<0.0001), lower percentage of males (33.8% against 74.4%, χ^2=24.74, d.f.=1, p<0.0001), and a lower share of respondents in executive positions (39.4% against 69.7%, χ^2=13.62, d.f.=1, p<0.0001). In the course of the analysis we monitored the impact of these differences.

The duration and frequency of cross-cultural interactions between Russians and expatriates were important characteristics of the sample. The selected samples had a high variation in both indicators, which allowed analyzing their impact on the cultural profile of the respondent. In the Russian sample, the average duration of joint work was 6 years (the standard deviation is 4.2 years), in the expat sample—5.3 years (the standard deviation is 5.2 years). Over 46% of Russians and almost 65% of expatriates communicate with each other on a daily basis.

About 41.4% of Russian respondents and 43.1% of foreign respondents represent large businesses (companies with a headcount exceeding 1,000 employees).

By nationality, the expat subsample included representatives of the USA (18%) and the EU (82%): UK, Germany, Austria, France, Spain, Italy, Denmark, Ireland, the Netherlands, Poland, Slovakia, Bulgaria, Hungary, and the Czech Republic. In the entire sample, the proportion of EU representatives from post-socialist countries reached 20.5%.

We distinguished two principal interacting parties: the Russians, on the one side, and EU and US expatriates, on the other side. The premise of the study was that there are less national differences between expatriates of these countries than between them and the Russians; therefore, one can speak about differences between the Western civilization and Russia.

Nevertheless, we performed all calculations for the entire data array (sample "D") and for three separate subsamples representing the nationality of the expatriates with whom the Russians interacted: "A"—expatriates from the EU, excluding post-socialist countries; "B"—expatriates from the US and the EU, excluding post-socialist countries; and "C"—expatriates from the EU, including post-socialist countries. Accordingly, in each case we changed the Russian subsample: "A"—Russians interacting with expatriates from the EU (excluding post-socialist countries), and only with them: "B"—Russians interacting with expatriates from the EU (excluding post-socialist countries) or the US, and only with them; and "C"—Russians interacting with expatriates from the EU, including post-socialist countries, and only with them.

"We" and "they" face to face: the cultural distance within multinational work teams in Russia

1. Cultural differences. Based on the CVSCALE methodology, we evaluated five dimensions (PD, UA, CO, MA and LTO) for the samples of Russian professionals and expatriates working together in multinational work teams in Russia. The results revealed cultural differences between them manifested by the Russians showing lower levels of uncertainty avoidance and collectivism and higher levels of masculinity (see table 7.1).

Differences in power distance scores turned out to be less pronounced. However, the hypothesis about the existence of differences in this dimension (Russians demonstrate a higher power distance) can be accepted at the level of significance of $p<0.100$ (for subsample "B"—at the level of significance of $p<0.106$). No significant differences were detected in "long-term orientation".

Thus, four out of five dimensions evidenced a deviation of the cultural profile of Russian professionals from the traditional portrait of a Russian worker identified in Hofstede's studies. The only exception is the power distance where Russians score higher in line with traditional perceptions.

Table 7.1. Comparative analysis of the work culture of Russian and foreign professionals working together in Russia using CVSCALE dimensions

Dimension / Sample		PD	UA	CO	MA	LTO
A. Russia[2] - the EU, excluding post-socialist countries						
Expatriates (N=48)	Mean (std. deviation)	2.14(0.90)	3.67(0.66)	3.44(0.59)	2.28(0.99)	3.99(0.61)
	Cronbach's α	0.88	0.79	0.68	0.86	0.78
Russians (N=32)	Mean (std. deviation)	2.49(0.69)	3.27(0.68)	2.76(0.81)	2.91(0.90)	3.92(0.41)
	Cronbach's α	0.68	0.78	0.90	0.81	0.60
t-value [3]		-1.82˜	2.52*	4.30†	-2.87**	0.54
B. Russia[2] - the USA and the EU, excluding post-socialist countries						
Expatriates (N=62)	Mean (std. deviation)	2.06(0.93)	3.64(0.73)	3.32(0.61)	2.13(0.97)	3.98(0.58)
	Cronbach's α	0.89	0.83	0.71	0.87	0.73
Russians (N=42)	Mean (std. deviation)	2.33(0.70)	3.35(0.63)	2.80(0.75)	2.90(0.94)	3.88(0.43)
	Cronbach's α	0.70	0.71	0.87	0.81	0.62
t-value [3]		-1.63	2.06*	3.86†	-3.99†	0.93
C. Russia[2] - EU						
Expatriates (N=64)	Mean (std. deviation)	2.21(0.90)	3.62(0.67)	3.28(0.66)	2.34(0.94)	3.98(0.66)
	Cronbach's α	0.89	0.78	0.76	0.84	0.81
Russians (N=60)	Mean (std. deviation)	2.46(0.71)	3.16(0.67)	2.73(0.90)	2.66(0.91)	3.92(0.40)
	Cronbach's α	0.75	0.78	0.92	0.84	0.50
t-value [3]		-1.75˜	3.79†	3.86†	-1.91˜	0.62
D. Entire sample						
Expatriates (N=78)	Mean (std. deviation)	2.13(0.93)	3.61(0.72)	3.22(0.65)	2.21(0.94)	3.98(0.63)
	Cronbach's α	0.90	0.81	0.76	0.86	0.78
Russians (N=71)	Mean (std. deviation)	2.36(0.72)	3.22(0.65)	2.75(0.85)	2.69(0.92)	3.88(0.43)
	Cronbach's α	0.75	0.74	0.90	0.83	0.56
t-value [3]		-1.73˜	3.43***	3.68†	-3.13**	1.04

Notes to the table:
[1] The calculations were made using the CVSCALE methodology: PD - power distance; UA – uncertainty avoidance; CO – collectivism; MA – masculinity; LTO - long-term orientation.
[2] In each case, the Russian subsample was formed according to the nationality of the foreigners with whom the Russians worked: A - contacts with representatives of Western European countries and only with them; B - contacts with representatives of Western European countries and/or the USA and only with them; C - contacts with representatives of Western European and/or Eastern European countries and only with them.
[3] Statistical significance for the t-test: ~$p<0.1$, *$p<0.05$, **$p<0.01$, ***$p<0.001$, †$p<0.0001$.

The identified differences were consistently reproduced in all the surveyed subsamples. The likelihood that the identified differences in power distance, uncertainty avoidance, collectivism, and masculinity are due to the different socio-demographic composition of the Russian and expat samples is low.

Thus, differences in the age of respondents (respondents in the Russian sample are on average five years younger than those in the expat sample) affect neither of the five cultural dimensions.

The different share of respondents in executive positions, which hypothetically could distort the power distance value, in fact has no such impact either in the Russian sample ($t=0.66$) or in the expat one ($t=-1.46$). This indicator has been noted to affect the masculinity value in the expat sample ($t=-2.08$, staff employees demonstrate lower masculinity), whereas the Russian sample has demonstrated no such impact ($t=0.83$). However, as the percentage of respondents in executive positions is higher in the expat sample than in the Russian one, ideally, the gap in masculinity values between the Russians and expatriates should have been even greater, which only emphasizes the sustainability of the obtained result.

The situation is similar with regard to the differences in the share of male respondents in the samples. Gender affects only the masculinity value and only in the Russian subsample ($t=-3.27$, females demonstrate lower masculinity); the expat subsample displays no such impact ($t=-1.31$). Therefore, the divergence of the Russian and expat samples by gender only narrows the gap in masculinity, thus also confirming the sustainability of the obtained result.

So, we can speak about the existence of notable cultural differences between groups of expatriates working in Russia and the Russians. For certain dimensions (uncertainty avoidance and collectivism), the traditional "Russian" and traditional "Western" type change places. What determines this phenomenon? Can it be that we are dealing with a specific group of extremely "Western"-focused Russian employees? Or, on the contrary, we are dealing with expatriates who due to their work in Russia have to a certain extent internalized the attitudes inherent in the traditional Russian cultural type? To answer this question, we compared the cultural profile of expatriates working in Russia with the "reference" cultural profile. In this case, the "reference" profile implies representatives of the "Western" civilization living in their own ethnic environment and not exposed to a permanent influence of other cultures at the micro level.

With certain reservations, we used the sample of Americans (N=213) tested by the CVSCALE authors as a "reference" group.[195] We selected Americans as a nation with traditionally some of the lowest levels of power distance and uncertainty avoidance along with some of the highest individualism scores. Our premise was that the Americans represent the extreme version of the "Western" cultural type.

We obtained the following estimates. No statistically significant differences between our expat sample (we tested subsample "B"— expatriates from the US and the EU, excluding post-socialist countries, N=62) and the "reference" sample were identified for any dimension, except collectivism—power distance (the value for the reference sample = 2.10 (standard deviation 0.93), t=-0.298, d.f.=99.26, p<0.75), uncertainty avoidance (respectively: 3,71(0,78), t=-0.654, d.f.=104,94, p<0.50), masculinity (2.25(0.96), t=-0.859, d.f.=98.44, p<0.39), and long-term orientation (3.97(0.60), t=0.122, d.f.=105.20, p<0.9). At the same time, we identified differences in collectivism—the value in the "reference" sample was below that for expatriates working in Russia (3.05 (0.75), t=2.59, d.f.=273, r<0.01).

This means that the expatriates employed in Russia are practically unaffected by the Russian sociocultural environment and reproduce their traditional cultural profile virtually unchanged. The only exception is the set of properties included in collectivism. Its excessive (as com-

---

195 Boonghee Yoo, Naveen Donthu, Tomasz Lenartowicz. *Measuring Hofstede's Five Dimensions of Cultural Values at the Individual Level: Development and Validation of CVSCALE* // Journal of International Consumer Marketing, 23: 193–210, 2011. p. 201.

pared to the "reference") value for expatriates working in Russia may be a reaction to living in an unfamiliar sociocultural environment, which promotes solidarity.

The second finding consists in the fact that Russians working with expatriates actually represent an extremely "Western"-focused group of employees. Comparing Russian professionals from subsample "B" with the American "reference" sample, we obtain significant differences in uncertainty avoidance (t=-2.81, d.f.=253, p<0.05), collectivism (t=-1.97, d.f.=253, p<0.05), and masculinity (t=4.02, d.f.=253, p<0.0001), less evident but nevertheless captured by statistics differences in the power distance (t=1.52, d.f.=253, p<0.130), and also identical to each other long-term orientation values (t=-0.92, d.f.=253, p<0.300).

The power distance is the main (and only) dimension demonstrating that the cultural profile of Russian professionals has features linking them with the traditional portrait of a Russian worker—a high level of acceptance of the authoritarian nature of power. The fact that a Russian employee combines high power distance, on the one hand, with low uncertainty avoidance (and, therefore, low value of instructions, rules, and regulations), on the other hand, fits well into the logic of the classic Russian rule that "the stringency of Russian laws is offset by their non-observance" (the conventional Russian wisdom articulated by Mikhail Saltykov-Shchedrin, a famous Russian satirist of the nineteenth century). And such a worldview in itself can be characterized as a specific "Russian type".

Thus, we can say that Russians working together with expatriates demonstrate quite a specific cultural profile. It is characterized by a combination of qualities that are closer to the traditional description of a Russian worker (high power distance) and qualities more relevant for the "Western" type of worker (high long-term orientation value and low levels of uncertainty avoidance and collectivism), with the last two dimensions reduced to extremely low values in the case of Russians.

2. Cultural diversity. However, is the layer of Russian professionals internally homogeneous by its cultural profile? The same question is valid with regard to expatriates. Indeed, many studies reveal that value systems within a society can be polarized. This logically leads to the question of the extent to which cross-national differences are more pronounced than cross-group ones, and whether this is actually the case.

The second hypothesis of the study is that certain multinational groups of professionals demonstrate more pronounced cross-group cultural differences than respondents grouped by nationality. To test this hypothesis, we identified groups with polarized cultural characteristics using K-means clustering in the space of the five surveyed dimensions (PD, UA, CO, MA, and LTO), with mandatory designation of two clusters.

As a result, we received pairs of respondent groups differing by three dimensions—power distance, collectivism, and masculinity. Group 1 represents a cultural profile with a low power distance, low masculinity, and a higher level of collectivism; Group 2 represents the opposite cultural profile with a high power distance and masculinity, but lower level of collectivism (see "Entire sample" column in Table 7.2).

The national structure of the group serves as the differentiating factor (χ^2=10.201, d.f.=1, p<0.001): expatriates prevail in Group 1 (expatriates - 64.2%, Russians - 35.8%), and Russians prevail in Group 2 (expatriates - 37.3%, Russians - 62.7%).

Thus, the aggregate national cultural profile of both Russians and expatriates results from a combination of properties of two polar subgroups—the "core" and the marginal ("dissident") one. The "core" group includes most respondents of the given national cohort and represents the cultural profile of the majority; the "marginal" group includes the minority of respondents of the same national cohort who by their attitudes are closer to the majority of people representing the other culture.

We additionally tested this assumption by directly comparing the Russian core and marginal groups (see "Russian sample" column of Table 7.2), and the expat core and marginal groups (see "Expat sample" column of Table 7.2).

Apparently, the most pronounced differences between the compared groups are observed in the power distance dimension (for Russians it is much higher in the core group, and for expatriates—in the marginal one). This is a classic characteristic of the Russian and most oriental cultures.

Table 7.2. Multinational teams of Russian and foreign professionals with polar work culture characteristics

	Entire sample			Expat sample			Russian sample		
	Group 1 (N=67)	Group 2 (N=75)	t-value[1]	Expats from Group 1 (core, N=43)	Expats from Group 2 (marginal, N=28)	t-value[1]	Russians from Group 1 (marginal, N=24)	Russians from Group 2 (core, N=47)	t-value[1]
CVSCALE dimensions									
PD	1.75 (0.50)	2.72 (0.81)	-8.71†	1.59 (0.40)	3.04 (0.83)	-8.64†	2.03 (0.54)	2.53 (0.74)	-3.21*
UA	3.52 (0.73)	3.32 (0.68)	1.70	3.66 (0.76)	3.51 (0.58)	0.89	3.25 (0.52)	3.20 (0.71)	0.30
CO	3.19 (0.77)	2.77 (0.75)	3.24***	3.29 (0.67)	3.02 (0.60)	1.72˜	3.01 (0.92)	2.62 (0.79)	1.81˜
MA	1.70 (0.55)	3.14 (0.70)	-13.6†	1.64 (0.54)	3.11 (0.70)	-10.0†	1.79 (0.57)	3.15 (0.70)	-8.18†
LTO	4.01 (0.64)	3.87 (0.43)	1.53	3.98 (0.74)	3.97 (0.46)	0.05	4.05 (0.41)	3.80 (0.41)	2.35*
Group characteristics									
Av. age, years	36.7	34.3	1.65	39.2	36.7	1.07	33.0	32.9	0.04
Males	50.7%	56.0%		72.1%	75.0%		12.5%	44.7%	
With subord.	59.1%	49.3%		61.9%	78.6%		54.2%	31.9%	
$T_{joint\,work.}$, years[2]	5.68	5.70	-0.02	5.07(5.46)	5.92(5.11)	-0.64	6.75(5.13)	5.57(3.69)	1.00

	National structure of the groups				
Russia	35.8%	62.7%	-	-	100%
USA	17.9%	2.7%	} 100%		-
EU1[4]	37.3%	21.3%		} 100%	-
EU2[4]	9.0%	13.3%			-

Notes to the table:

[1] Statistical significance for the t-test: ˜p<0.1, *p<0.05, **p<0.01, ***p<0.001, †p<0.0001.

[2] Years of joint work with Russians (in the case of expatriates) or with foreigners (in the case of Russians).

[3] Frequency of contacts between expatriates and Russians (1 – virtually no contacts; 2 – no personal contacts, all communications either by mail or phone; 3 – personal contacts several times per year; 4 – personal contacts several times per month; 5 – personal contacts several times per week; 6 – daily contacts).

[4] EU1 - the EU excluding post-socialist countries; EU2 - post-socialist countries of the EU.

Significant differences between the core and marginal groups are also manifested in the masculinity dimension. However, the high masculinity score in the core Russian group (likewise as the low masculinity score in the core expat group) cannot be considered a similarly clear (as power distance) marker of the differences between the "West" and Russia or the "West" and the "East". Thus, according to Hofstede, Russia is rather a feminine culture (MA=36), whereas both China and Germany score identically high in this dimension (MA=66). In addition, gender differences affect the level of masculinity in the Russian sample—there are more males in the core group than in the marginal one (χ^2=7.35, d.f.=1, p<0.01).

Analysis shows that the core and marginal groups within the Russian sample manifest different long-term orientation values—for the core group they are lower than for the marginal one.

At the same time, the core and marginal groups (both Russian and expat) score similarly when it comes to uncertainty avoidance, and the discrepancies in the level of collectivism are less pronounced than when comparing respondents grouped by nationality (distinctions are significant only at the level of p<0.100). However, the trend in the latter case is the same: the majority of Russian professionals demonstrate a lower level of collectivism, whereas the majority of expatriates—a higher one. And vice versa, the marginal group of Russians demonstrates a higher level of collectivism, whereas the marginal group of expatriates—a lower one.

Finally, it is important to note that the duration of joint work does not manifest itself as a differentiating factor either in the core or marginal groups both for Russians (t=1.00) and expatriates (t=-0.64). It follows that generally the emergence of the "marginal" group is not associated with how long the expatriates and Russians work together. On the contrary, this shows that social cohorts manifesting value sets different from the value core of the majority representing the titular culture originally exist both in the Russian and the "Western" societies.

3. Cultural dynamics. Hypothetically, the duration of joint work and the frequency of contacts with representatives of the opposite culture should be powerful factors of cultural transformation. In our case, these factors should have a particularly noticeable effect on expatriates, as, all else being equal, they experience an additional impact—the influence of the local (Russian) environment, the symbolic environment, and social institutions. The estimated impact of these factors on the cultural profile of expatriates and Russians is summarized in Table 7.3.

Table 7.3. The duration of joint work and the frequency of contacts with representatives of the neighboring culture as factors of cultural transformation (logit model)[1]

	Russian professionals			EU and US expatriates		
	Coefficient B (std. error)	Exp(B)	Wald test[3]	Coefficient B (std. error)	Exp(B)	Wald test[3]
	Specification 1 of the Model (N=71)			**Specification 1 of the Model** (N=61)		
Independent variables						
Duration of joint work (years)	0.147(0.083)	1.159	3.134ˇ	-0.136(0.069)	0.873	3.852*
Frequency of contacts[2]	0.496(0.545)	1.643	0.830	1.018(0.588)	2.768	2.999ˇ
Existence of subordinates	1.216(0.600)	3.374	4.111*	-1.043(0.652)	0.352	2.563
Gender (1 -male, 0 - female).	-1.775(0.738)	0.169	5.781*	0.097(0.668)	1.101	0.021
Age (years)	-0.057(0.024)	0.945	5.429*	0.031(0.021)	1.031	2.148
Model Fit						
Test χ^2 for model coefficients	22.992(df=5, p<0.0001)			12.148 (df=5, p<0.05)		
-2 Log Likelihood	75.435			72.416		
R^2 Cox and Snell	0.277			0.181		
R^2 Nagelkerke	0.369			0.241		
Share of accurate predictions, %	70.4			65.6		
χ^2 Hosmer-Lemeshow	5.933(df=8, p=0.655)			5.492(df=8, p=0.704)		
	Specification 2 of the Model (N=71)			**Specification 2 of the Model** (N=57)		
Independent variables						
Duration of joint work (years)	0.142(0.083)	1.152	2.909ˇ	-0.119(0.078)	0.888	2.328
Frequency of contacts[2]	0.542(0.559)	1.719	0.938	1.544(0.683)	4.684	5.116*
Existence of subordinates	1.232(0.606)	3.427	4.132*	-0.820(0.800)	0.441	1.049
Russian top management	-0.302(0.907)	0.739	0.111	1.896(0.987)	6.659	3.692ˇ
Foreign top management	-0.648(0.658)	0.523	0.970	-0.266(0.715)	0.767	0.138
Gender (1 -male, 0 -female).	-1.826(0.757)	0.161	5.813*	-0.172(0.771)	0.842	0.050
Age (years)	-0.049(0.025)	0.952	3.857*	0.012(0.025)	1.013	0.255

Model Fit		
Test χ^2 for model coefficients	24.002(df=7, p<0.001)	18.896 (df=7, p<0.01)
-2 Log Likelihood	74.424	60.123
R^2 Cox and Snell	0.287	0.282
R^2 Nagelkerke	0.382	0.376
Share of accurate predictions, %	71.8	73.7
χ^2 Hosmer-Lemeshow	9.933(df=8, p=0.270)	5.523(df=8, p=0.701)

Notes:
[1] The probability that an individual will be included in Group 1 ("pro-Western cluster") as compared to the probability of being included in Group 2 ("pro-Russian cluster") is estimated. In the training sample, 1 means being included in the "pro-Western" cluster, and 0 -in the "pro-Russian" one.
[2] Dummy variable representing the frequency of contacts between expatriates and Russians (1 – daily personal contacts, 0 -personal contacts several times per week or less frequently).
[3] Statistical significance for the Wald test: ~p<0.1, *p<0.05, **p<0.01, ***p<0.005, †p<0.0001.

The logistic regression method was applied. We estimated the probability that a respondent will be included in Group 1 ("pro-Western cluster") as compared to the probability of being included in Group 2 ("pro-Russian cluster") depending on the duration of joint work and the frequency of contacts with representatives of the neighboring culture (with Russians—in the model for expatriates, and with expatriates—in the model for Russians). In the proposed model, we could speak about the existence of "cultural dynamics", if a longer duration of joint work and more frequent contacts increased the probability of Russians being included in the "pro-Western" cluster and expatriates in the "pro-Russian" cluster. We used two model specifications with different sets of control variables. Under specification one we were controlling for age, gender, and position within the organizational hierarchy (existence of subordinates). In specification two we additionally introduced dummy variables representing the corporate top management's national affiliation—Russian or foreign (a mixed type of top management also exists).

For expatriates in specification one of the model the regression coefficient B for the duration of joint work with Russians is -0.136 (the longer expatriates work in Russia jointly with Russians, the lower is the probability of them being included in the "pro-Western cluster"). Thus, we can say that the expatriates' stay in Russia has a certain impact on their cultural profile, shifting it toward "Russification". This result, however, is not sustainable—under specification two of the model, the effect of the duration of work in Russia is insignificant.

For Russians, the corresponding hypothesis (the longer Russians work in Russia jointly with expatriates, the higher is the probability of them being included in the "pro-Western cluster") can be accepted only at the level of significance $p<0.100$. In the two considered model specifications, the respective regression coefficients B are equal to +0.147 at $p=0.077$ and +0.142 at $p=0.088$; however, the level of significance does not allow speaking of a pronounced effect.

The surveyed expat sample produced another interesting result. The probability of the expatriates being included in the "pro-Western" cluster is higher in the group of expats with daily contacts with Russians (B=1.018, $p=0.083$ in specification one; B=1.544, $p=0.024$ in specification two). Specification two of the model demonstrates a similar effect—the probability of the expatriates being included in the "pro-Western" cluster is higher in the group of expats working in companies where the top management is Russian (B=1.896, $p=0.055$). At first glance, this fact contradicts the intuitive expectation, since the frequency of contacts with Russians should hypothetically increase the probability of the expatriates being included in the "pro-Russian" cluster. However, this may reflect the phenomenon of a culture's resistance when artificially placed in extremely close contact with another culture, in particular, when representatives of different cultures have to work daily alongside each other.

Summary of findings

Close cross-cultural interaction is a typical phenomenon in contemporary societies. The cultural distance between the interacting parties, internal diversity and sustainability of cultural types are the key elements, which help understanding what is good for each culture, what needs to be done to unlock its potential to the utmost, and what path leads it to success. In addition, these are factors which taken into account allow improving the performance of multinational companies.

Analysis revealed that in spite of productive professional exchange, Russian professionals and expatriates are separated by a certain cultural distance, which manifests itself in different attitudes to authority, risk, and group (collective) interests. The aggregate national portrait of a Russian professional represents a specific combination of radicalized features of the "Western" culture and oriental features that continue to coexist with traits typical of the European image.

Russian professionals differ from expatriates working in Russia by lower levels of uncertainty avoidance and collectivism while having comparable long-term orientation scores. This contrasts with the traditional perception of the Russian nature as per G. Hofstede (high levels of uncertainty avoidance and collectivism with low-level long-term orientation).

The power distance is the main (and only) dimension demonstrating that the cultural profile of Russian professionals has features linking them with the traditional portrait of a Russian worker—a high level of acceptance of the authoritarian nature of power. The fact that a Russian employee combines high power distance, on the one hand, with low uncertainty avoidance (and, therefore, low value of instructions, rules, and regulations), on the other hand, fits well into the logic of the long defined Russian rule that "the stringency of Russian laws is offset by their non-observance". This particular combination of work culture features in itself can be described as a specific "Russian type".

Another notable finding is that Russians demonstrate a low level of collectivism, whereas the expatriates—an excessive one. In Russia, collectivism as an element of culture stands apart. The issue of whether a Russian person is more inclined to collectivism or individualism remains open. Indeed, collectivism in Russia has always been a forced measure, which made survival possible. However, precisely this forced and essentially artificial rapprochement of the people generated a directly opposite feature of culture—inner denial of collectivist values on the backdrop of the externally imposed need to abide by them. Collectivism has become a functional and intrinsically syncretic feature of culture having produced its antithesis—extreme individualism, which manifests itself whenever the external threat requiring cohesion disappears.

It is interesting that the expatriates, contrariwise, demonstrated an excessive level of collectivism in comparison not only with Russians, but also with representatives of historically more similar cultures. In particular, this result was obtained when comparing a combined sample of expatriates from the USA and the EU with a sample of Americans living in the USA, with whom these expatriates demonstrated similarity in all dimensions, except collectivism. An excessive level of collectivism demonstrated by the expatriates may be a reaction to living in an unfamiliar sociocultural environment, which promotes solidarity.

An analysis of cultural diversity within the national cohorts yields some important results. The aggregate national cultural profile of both Russians and expatriates results from a combination of properties of two polar subgroups existing "within" each culture—the "core" and the marginal ("dissident") one. The "core" group includes most respondents of the given national cohort and represents the set of values characteristic of the majority of this national cohort; the "marginal" group includes the minority of respondents of the same nationality who by their attitudes are closer to the majority of people representing the other culture. The most apparent difference between the core and marginal groups is observed in the power distance dimension (for Russians it is much higher in the core group, and for expatriates—in the marginal one). A high power distance is the classic distinctive feature of the Russian and most oriental cultures.

The attempt to explain the nature of the occurrence of marginal groups within each culture as a consequence of cultural dynamics (by such factors as the duration of joint work and the frequency of contacts of the Russians with foreigners and the foreigners with the Russians) provides no clear result. In the case of Russians, the joint work duration factor has an unsustainable effect. In the case of expatriates, however, an extended stay in Russia has a certain (although not pronounced) impact on their cultural profile, shifting it toward "Russification".

We captured the culture resistance effect in the surveyed expat sample. The expatriates who work in close contact with Russians or in companies with Russian top management are more likely to demonstrate qualities specific of the "core" group of their culture than those expatriates whose contacts are less frequent.

Chapter VIII.
Effectiveness of business and cultural exchange in the segment of highly skilled labor

In Chapter VI we mentioned that the characteristics of the social stratum of expatriates in Russia is a factor determining their potential as agents of influence and actors of modernization. It is obvious that the result of the interaction depends not only on expat features, but also on the properties of the Russian host culture. Chapter VII was devoted to quantifying the cultural distance between Russian and foreign professionals and assessing the extent of its sustainability. In this final chapter we will rely on qualitative data to demonstrate the specific results of cross-cultural business and professional exchange in the segment of highly skilled labor.

Competition of values and society development scenarios. Close and constant contact with a particular culture changes the society. This impact can have either a positive, educating effect, or be destructive, pathological. The outcome is always determined by the competition of two cultural systems—their effusiveness, the appeal of their inherent sociocultural patterns, the ability to absorb values of the other culture while maintaining its own identity, etc.

Indeed, the national business culture is a phenomenon, which, on the one hand, is highly resistant to external institutional and cultural influences, but on the other hand, is capable of transforming under their influence in cases where the external cultural code proves to be "stronger" or more appealing as compared with the cultural code reproduced by the local ("host") institutional environment.

Samuel Huntington expressed this idea with the utmost clarity. He distinguished four development scenarios for modernizing societies experiencing the expansion of "Western" values and the "Western" type of consciousness: (1) rejection of the unfamiliar foreign system of values along with rejection of the very idea of modernization ('Rejectonism'); (2) modernization based on the society's indigenous culture without reference to foreign values ('Reformism'); (3) modernization based on foreign values fully replacing the national type of consciousness

('Kemalism'), and also (4) an intermediary option where "Initially, Westernization and modernization are closely linked, with the non-Western society absorbing substantial elements of Western culture and making slow progress toward modernization. As the pace of modernization increases, however, the rate of Westernization declines and the indigenous culture goes through a revival."[196] In Huntington's diagram, the latter scenario is depicted in the form of a parabola in the "Westernization—Modernization" axes (see Fig. 8.1).

This latter scenario is rather interesting because it adequately depicts the nature of modernization leaps typical for Russia virtually throughout its history.

We are concerned with the current manifestation of the Russian work culture. What scenario do processes developing in the current Russian society resemble? One of the best techniques to find this out is to observe the interaction between the Russian culture and the cultures introduced by the expatriates.

In the past two decades at least, the interaction of the Russian culture with Western cultures has moved to the micro level, the level of companies. It has become part of the production process involving specific business practices rather than general romanticized values, forcing people to overcome daily their long-term habits and stereotypes, because the company's performance is at stake, and, respectively, the assessment of their own input. This type of interaction identifies the culture's genuine properties—in particular, its integrability with other cultures, its flexibility, its periphery and sustainable core, i.e., the set of properties underlying the achievement of business objectives. An analysis of this experience enables, first, to overcome the impact of stereotypes and identify the authentic characteristics of the national business culture, and second, to assess its stability (ability to maintain core properties) and variability (ability to absorb new sociocultural patterns).

---

196 Huntington S. *The Clash of Civilizations*. M.: OOO Izdatel'stvo AST, 2003. pp. 107–108; Huntington S. *The Clash of Civilization and the Remarking of World Order.* N.Y., 1996. p. 75.

Fig. 8.1. Typology of society development scenarios in the "Modernization—Westernization" axes.

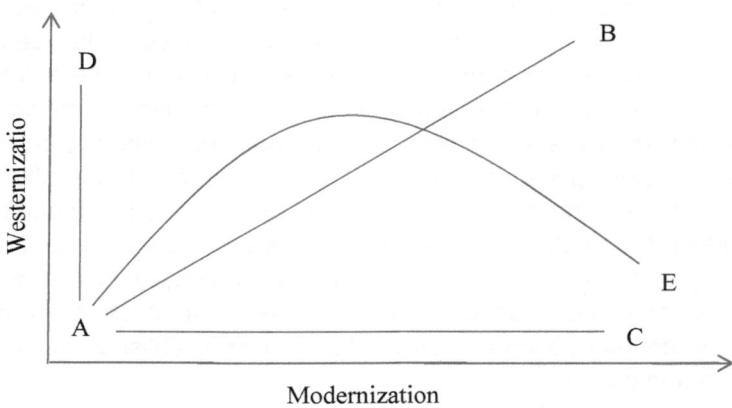

Designations: **A** -rejection of modernization, **A-B** -modernization through Westernization ("Kemalism"), **A-C** -modernization without Westernization ("Reformism"), **A-D** - Westernization without modernization (modernization failure), **A-E** -modernization with revival (catch-up development)
Source: Huntington S. *The Clash of Civilization and the Remarking of World Order*. N. Y., 1996. p. 75.

As for Russia, the issue of transferring foreign (generally, "Western") sociocultural patterns to Russian soil has always been under close scrutiny. The accumulated experience of modernization attempts (both successful and failed ones) reveals a path dependence (Alexander Auzan coined the term "track" effect), which any Russian modernization attempt systematically encounters and which keeps the country on a certain path of development.[197]

Thus, some studies show that reproduction of adopted foreign socio-cultural patterns in Russia requires that their individual bearer be "protected" from the influence of the local culture and institutions by a high-level status or a specific social environment. "Only those who hold more or less advanced positions in business or are engaged in interna-

---

197 Auzan A.A. *The "Track" of Russian Modernization* // Obshchestvennye Nauki i Sovremennost'. 2007. No. 6. pp. 54–60.

tional cooperation succeed in reproducing this ("western"—authors' note) model in practice."[198]

In this respect a classic question arises—what comes first in what we call "modernization": culture, which preserves archaic principles and therefore has to be "overcome", or work with institutions that can be designed to "serve" the core of the national business culture ensuring its most efficient use. In the second case, modernization is not limited to adopting and transferring "Western" sociocultural patterns, but also includes developing special institutions that work properly with the cultural core. In fact, the thesis of the German historical school formulated by Friedrich List is almost classic. List expressed the idea that special temporary institutions promoting accelerated development of the national economy are needed. Moreover, these institutions differ from country to country depending on the historically established economic traditions and culture.[199]

We support the relevance of this principle but would like to mention that today one cannot be certain that a sustainable benchmark for comparing the success of cultures exists. V.G. Fedotova pointed out some time ago that currently modernization cannot be achieved by applying the strategy of "...adopting and imitating the existing structures of the western society, which themselves are starting to undergo change."[200]

At the same time, the issue remains open whether the concept of a national business culture has "pass-through" features permeating all social strata and groups. In today's global economy, the focus is on social groups with high human capital—professionals. Professionals are the driving force of modernization processes, and the path that modernization takes depends primarily on them. Business practices implemented by representatives of these strata are more important than their personal attitudes, because they demonstrate to what extent the professionals are able to change the environment and transform institutions.

---

198 Konstantinovskiy D., Voznesenskaya E., Cherednichenko G. *Russians in Western Countries: The Effect of Long-Term Sojourn* / In: Yadov V.A. (ed.). Impact of Western Socio-Cultural Patterns on Russian Social Practices. M.: TAUS, 2009. p. 187.
199 List F. *The National System of Political Economy*. SPb., 1891. p. 235.
200 Fedotova V.G. *Modernization of the Other Europe*. M.: IF RAN, 1997. Chapter I, §3.

Our analysis focuses precisely on the most advanced stratum of professionals in this respect—the stratum directly engaged in cross-cultural interaction on the micro-level, the level of companies. As these professionals are directly involved in interaction with representatives of other cultures, with the effectiveness of such interaction immediately influencing personal professional success, hypothetically they should be the best at assimilating "Western" sociocultural patterns and reproducing respective practices. But is that the case?

The answer to this question indicates to what extent Russian culture allows for copying other cultures. A study focused on identifying the attitudes of this group of professionals could actually produce a result evidencing a more "Western" trend in their mentality. However, such a study would not be immune from "aberration",[201] since in their self-assessment, these professionals would tend to exaggerate the importance of actually minor changes in their mentality, because these changes occur rapidly and in extremely close contact with another culture. In this sense, the picture is more adequate when foreign professionals evaluate the work practices of their Russian colleagues and vice versa.

Such research was always of considerable interest. In the late 1980s, Vladimir Gaskov, a Russian specialist on inter-cultural contacts and interaction of workers from different countries in multinational corporations, studied mutual stereotype perceptions of Soviet (actually Russian) and Mongolian workers occupied at the Erdenet joint venture. Following is a summary of his findings (see Table 8.1).[202]

---

[201] Here we apply the term "aberration" in the sense used by Lev Gumilev to indicate distortions of reality that may arise when assessing processes in which the observer is included, or when performing a comparative analysis of recent and distant historical events due to psychologically overestimating the significance of the former and underestimating that of the latter. See: Gumilev L.N. *Ethnogenesis and the Biosphere of Earth*. M.: Tanais DI-DIC, 1994. pp. 49–53, 605. We believe that when studying changes in culture and mentality, similar distortions of reality can occur if researchers focus on how representatives of the studied culture assess themselves.

[202] Gaskov V.M. *Social Problems Related to Exchanging Industrial Experiences in CMEA Member Countries*. Abstract of the dissertation for a doctoral degree in economic sciences. M., 1989. p. 25.

Table 8.1. Mutual stereotype perceptions of Russian and Mongolian workers occupied at a joint venture

Stereotype perceptions of Russian workers by Mongolian specialists (N=220)		Stereotype perceptions of Mongolian workers by Russian specialists (N=230)	
Russian workers **to a greater degree** than the Mongolians:	Russian workers **to a lesser degree** than the Mongolians:	Mongolian workers **to a greater degree** than the Russians:	Mongolian workers **to a lesser degree** than the Russians:
Seek promotion Seek a prestigious job Wish to participate in decision-making Seek high wages and recognition for good performance Strive to improve their skills	Want to contribute to the team performance Seek cooperation in the team Use the opportunity to help team members	Seek high wages and recognition for good performance Seek promotion Seek to improve and use their skills at work	Want to have an important job Seek to work independently Wish to participate in decision-making Seek to help other team members Want to have clear and specific job requirements

As we see, the Mongolian employees perceived the Russians as representing European work mentality.

The following reflections of Japanese professor Shigeki Hakamada continue the topic of how oriental people perceive Russians. In the late 1990s, he made a comparative analysis of the socio-psychological make-up of Japanese and Russians and came to quite unusual conclusions.[203]

The starting point of his reasoning was the thesis that "natural human feelings and desires have been traditionally suppressed in both countries", however, this phenomenon has resulted in the emergence of fundamentally different (in their inner essence) Japanese and Russian societies. Hakamada explains that "social or socio-psychological suppression of natural feelings, desires, and selfish motives" in Japan was caused by "limited natural resources and a social system where it was impossible to hide from 'prying eyes'." He believes "this has served to form such national features as respect for order and trust-based rela-

---

[203] See: Hakamada S. *Self-Organization and Spontaneity: A Comparative Social and Psychological Analysis of Japan and Russia* // Sotsiologicheskie issledovaniia. 1999. No. 4.

tions between people, diligence and punctuality, which are a prerequisite for the existence of modern civilization and a market economy."

In Russia, by contrast, a seemingly similar repressive system rested on a completely different national genotype and consequently triggered a completely different result, which crystallized in a counterproductive attitude to work, if we speak about Russians as a people in general. Stressing this point, he associates himself with the observations made by Jules Legras in his book *L'ame russe* (1934), "The majority of Russians believe that professional diligence and conscience are unnecessary. Everybody thinks that the population of the Russian North is hardworking; however, the inhabitants of Arkhangelsk are extremely lazy." Or: "Once started, the Russians can perform a task with great enthusiasm; when commanded, they can put an office or a house in exemplary order. But in general they are lazy, work carelessly, and work for them is no more than external coercion; left without control, they neglect work. For that reason, under autocracy soldiers and peasants were whipped. The absolutist regime destroyed their mind, intelligence and morality, and only fear made the people work."[204]

However, there is also a reverse side to the issue, which Hakamada clearly articulates. A completely different type of mentality was widespread in certain social strata of the Russian society. Hakamada's following statement precisely expresses its essence—in many cases Russians "worked diligently, because their 'soul protested against' careless work." Hakamada links this specific phenomenon with the variational imprint of the Orthodox "spirit" on the specific Russian genotype, which "was able to produce the original national character, great writers and artists." According to him, this did not happen in Japan. On the contrary, due to the mechanism of psychological suppression and restrictions, "nonconformity, originality, and elitism have become an exception to the rule in Japanese society; therefore, it is difficult to engage in business ventures or lead a creative life here."[205]

It is certainly impossible to ignore the classic comparison of the professional and business images that Russians and representatives of the Western European civilization have. In this respect, we should men-

---

204   Cit. ex: Hakamada S. Same work. pp. 16, 17.
205   Here and above quotes from the same work of S. Hakamada. pp. 9–10, 14, 16 17, and 18.

tion the studies of Richard D. Lewis, a prominent expert in comparative management.

Among factors determining the core features of the Russian character he names many centuries of "ruthless authoritarian rule", "incalculable vastness of the Russian land", and "the unvarying harshness of its climate". According to Lewis, each of these factors had affected the work behavior in its own way. Thus, due to the harsh climate, the people became accustomed to work irregularly but frantically. He emphasizes that "both Czarist and Soviet rule took advantage of the collective, submissive, self-sacrificial, enduring...subjects under their sway."[206]

Comparing Russians and Americans Lewis writes, "Both peoples distrust aristocrats and are uncomfortable, even today, with the smooth eloquence of some Europeans. Bluntness wins friends both in Wichita and Kazan. Both nations think big and consider they have an important role to play—a 'mission' in world affairs."[207] According to Lewis, other traits common for Russians and Americans include bluntness of speech, expansionism, hospitality, rejection of aristocracies, sense of being a great power, and a "frontier spirit".

At the same time, there are significant differences related to the historical roots of the two cultures: Russian caution as opposed to American risk-taking, emotions as opposed to pragmatism, optimism versus pessimism, freedom of action versus centralized authority, and others.

Lewis's vision of Russians is neither negative, nor positive. The author concludes that Americans may quite well deal with Russians, subject to finding the key to their character, "Russian values are deeply humane, their heroes are universally authentic, their external manifestations are full of artistry and aesthetics. To succeed in relations with Russians, one should clearly keep in mind these traits rather than pay too much attention to the mysterious and paradoxical aspects of their behavior and current attitudes."[208]

Catherine J. Baker adds her own observations resulting from long-term experience to Lewis's judgments. She believes that "there are certain key distinctions in the approach of many Americans and Russians

---

206 Lewis R.D. *When Cultures Collide. Managing Successfully Across Cultures*. M. Izd-vo Delo, 1999, p. 317.
207 Ibid. p. 320.
208 Ibid. p. 326.

to relationships. Americans are inclined to be very open and trusting in new relationships—until the other person does something disappointing or betrays their trust. The Russians tend to be more cautious and evaluate each step until they are sure they can fully rely on the other person. Americans are inclined to base their business relationships on practicability: what is most convenient, who has the necessary skills, contacts and resources, who can participate in the project. Russians tend to strike up a friendship based on shared principles, values, and attitudes, as well as interpersonal comfort. Under the Soviet system, ability to reach an agreement with the authorities and find an approach to them were more important for business relations than competence. Now, of course, the Russian society is in a state of constant change demonstrating numerous variations in work relationships."[209]

All the research findings we have described pertain to the 1990s, when Russia, re-opening to the world after long decades, was attracting unprecedented interest. What can we say about the Russians' business culture today—more than two decades later?

Russian and foreign professionals in business communication. The findings herein result from a survey of a selection of European and US expatriates with ongoing experience of working relations with Russians, and of Russian employees with ongoing experience of working relations with European and US expatriates (the sample is described in Chapter VII). Both parties were asked to evaluate the usefulness of business contacts with their partners by responding to a number of questions. Selected survey findings are consolidated in Table 8.2.

---

[209] Baker C.J. *Building Working Relationships* // Znanie - Sila. January 1996, pp. 8–10.

Table 8.2. Selected indicators characterizing the interaction between Russian and foreign professionals working together in Russia

Question wording and answer options [1]	Share, % [2]	
	Russians (N=71)	Expats (N=78)
Mutual understanding		
To what extent are you satisfied with the level of understanding between you and your foreign (/**Russian**) colleagues? (1 -absolutely not satisfied, 5 -completely satisfied)	90.4%	87.0%
Professional exchange		
When working together with foreigners (/ **with Russian colleagues**), did you acquire any fundamentally new professional knowledge from them or did your cooperation help you develop any new occupational skills?		
I did not learn anything new that would be useful in my work	15.1%	17.9%
I learned a number of new things, but they serve only to adapt to working with foreign (/**Russian**) colleagues in my work team	30.1%	34.6%
I have acquired certain new knowledge and skills, which will in any case be useful in my further professional activities	54.8%	47.4%
Transplanting foreign experience to Russia		
Should Russia adopt the organizational and management experience accumulated in other countries? (1 -definitely not, 5 -definitely yes)	83.6%	83.1%
Attitude to Russia as a place to live and work		
Are you considering the option of taking up permanent residence abroad (/**leaving Russia**) in the next 2–3 years? (shows the percentage of those who answered "Yes")	31.5%	41.0%
Do you think it would be better for your children to live and work abroad rather than in Russia (/**Would you like your children to live and work in Russia**)? (1 -definitely no, 5 -definitely yes)	42.5%	8.9%

Notes to the table:

[1] The provided wording is taken from questionnaires for Russian respondents (the bold text in brackets indicates differences, if any, in the wording of the questions drafted for foreign respondents).

[2] Shows the percentage of respondents who gave an affirmative answer to the question (in the event of a 5-point scale -the total percentage of respondents whose answer was 4 or 5 points; in the event of a 3-point scale -the percentage of respondents whose answer was 3 points).

In general, the cooperation of Russian professionals and expatriates can be regarded as quite effective. The overwhelming majority of both Russians and expatriates are satisfied by the level of understanding with their foreign colleagues. About 90.4 percent of Russians and 87.0 percent of expatriates gave an affirmative answer to this question. According to their self-assessment, the ongoing professional exchange is quite effective—54.8 percent of Russians and 47.4 percent of expatriates indicated that cooperation with colleagues representing an opposite culture helped them acquire fundamentally new knowledge and skills important for their professional activities.

Over 83 percent of professionals consider that Russia should adopt the organizational and management experience accumulated in other countries.

At the same time, it is impossible to ignore the rather skeptic attitude to Russia as a place to live and work demonstrated by professionals who have extensive contacts with representatives of other cultures. Thus, over a third of surveyed Russian professionals intend to take up permanent residence abroad in the next two to three years. Foreign professionals working in Russia do not want to stay here long—over 40% of them are planning to return home in the next two to three years. The question "Do you think it would be better for your children to live and work abroad rather than in Russia" emphasizes this attitude even more—42.5 percent of Russian respondents answered "yes" and "rather yes". On the contrary, less than 9 percent of the surveyed expatriates believe their children would be better off living and working in Russia rather than in their home country.

As part of the same survey, foreign professionals were asked to name the business attitudes of their Russian colleagues that promote or, conversely, hamper the effective/coordinated work of the team. Further, foreign professionals were asked whether they had acquired any new business skills in the course of working together with Russian colleagues, and which of them they were likely to retain upon returning home. Similar questions were posed to the Russians. Typical responses are provided in Table 8.3.

Analysis revealed the dualism of cross-cultural interaction in large companies. The area of cultural incompatibility is generally clearly expressed, however, the existing differences are not insurmountable. However, there is also an extensive area where the cultures are complementary and where a productive exchange of values occurs.

Most identified differences (see Table 8.3, row 1) are instrumental and do not affect basic values. Example: *"Poor time management"* (something expatriates typically accuse Russians of) vs. *"Excessively punctual, meticulous, and thorough"* (something Russians typically accuse expatriates of). Or, typical of Russians: "*Formal means of communication...bureaucracy, process driven*" vs. typical of expatriates: "*Excessive attention to positioning themselves and the results of their work.*" Generally, such differences can be easily overcome.

According to Russian professionals, template thinking typical of foreigners, when Russian specifics are ignored, is the most serious difference negatively affecting team performance. Following are some critical judgments made by Russians about the business attitudes of their foreign colleagues: "*some of them (expatriates—authors' note) believe that they know better and do not take into account that Russia has its own specifics—in terms of culture and mentality*"; "*(it is typical of expatriates—authors' note) to impose their views when discussing current issues without really understanding the existing situation*"; "*(the expatriates—authors' note) have no knowledge of Russia, they mostly rely on foreign experience*"; "*a false impression of being right in everything (is typical of expatriates—authors' note)*"; "*in general, the expatriates are very formal; there are exceptions with broad views, however, in general, they tend to think in categories that are inapplicable here (in Russia—authors' note)*", etc.

These quite common accusations that Russian professionals make against their foreign colleagues reflect an interesting phenomenon—the public legitimacy of the "Western" type of consciousness and system of values as a universal guide in life has disappeared in Russia. This situation is fundamentally different from the orthodox perception of "Western" values and "Western" experience as universal and absolute categories—a trend that had formed in Russian culture back in the 1990s.

In contrast, exchange of values today no longer involves automatic replication of foreign recipes and patterns; it is based on adopting only those features of "Western" culture that had proven their appeal and effectiveness. Skills promoting team performance, as mutually assessed by Russian and foreign professionals, include many textbook examples (see Table 8.3, row 2). However, it is interesting to focus on two groups of skills—"**universal**" and "**local**". Professionals assess the former to be useful independent of the cultural environment, whereas the latter makes sense only for representatives of different cultures to find common ground (compare rows 2 and 3 of Table 8.3).

Table 8.3. The mutual evaluation of each other's business qualities by Russian and foreign professionals

Relation between qualities and performance	Selected answers by foreign professionals (N= 78)	Selected answers by Russian professionals (N= 71)
1. Qualities hampering the effective work of the team or the enterprise in general	Lack motivation, don't take initiative, are lazy, unreliable, seek easy ways, resist change Satisfied with the status quo, prefer to leave everything as it is Poor time management. Russians are not timely and put things off until the last minute Desire to determine guilt rather than resolve an issue Lack of willingness to take responsibility They require more formal means of communication, loads of paperwork which is a bit ineffective at times. Bureaucracy.	Lack understanding of the Russian market and consumers. Tend to think in categories that are inapplicable here. False impression of being right in everything. Excessively punctual. Meticulous. Thorough. Impersonal attitude to work. Not always willing to work with difficult clients that require an individual approach. Process-driven *(tend to act "properly", follow the "letter" rather than the "spirit" of the rules.—authors' note)* Excessive attention to positioning themselves and the results of their work.
2. Qualities promoting the effective work of the team or the enterprise in general	Creative, innovative, think out of the 'template' box. Can find workaround solutions, get around restrictive rules, and plough through bureaucracy. Can quickly navigate the situation and adapt to a changing environment. Stress resistant; steadfast in the face of adversity; no high drama. Ambitious, aim career growth, goal-oriented, dedicated. Diligent (hardworking) and enthusiastic to progress. Patient, outgoing, respectful.	Positive attitude. Belief in success. Accuracy, adherence to routine. Exceptionally well-organized. Courtesy and tact. Diplomacy. Political correctness. Friendly, likable, polite. Open for communication with subordinates. Strong inter-personal skills. Negotiation skills. Ability to explain the issue clearly and patiently. Ability to assume responsibility. Focus on results. Desire to win—work for result. Fully committed to work. High motivation. Ready to go into details. Competence. High level of professionalism.

	Qualities assessed by foreign professionals as useful even upon return to their home country	Qualities estimated as useful even when not working in close contact with foreigners
3. Qualities that were not common for foreign/Russian professionals but emerged in the process of working together with Russian/foreign colleagues (self-assessment)	Perspective in understanding people with different history and priorities. Skills in leading a diverse team. Adaptable to extreme situations, flexible to any significant change in plans—open and prepared to any change within two minutes. Think outside the box. I learned to be more patient, developed the ability to reach reasonable compromises. Having a "plan B" *(back-up plan of action—authors' note)* **Qualities not necessarily useful upon return of the foreign professionals to their home country** Ability to work with people I do not trust. Ability to plough through bureaucracy, acquiescence to bureaucratic obstacles. Documentation skills (a lot of paperwork in Russia!). Understanding complex regulatory rules.	Strong inter-personal skills. Negotiation skills. Ability to win people, to find common ground in dealing with business issues. Presentation skills, ability to position oneself in the company. Greater degree of self-organization. Ability to take decisions. A system, diplomatic approach to building relations with senior management. Impersonal attitude to work. Structured approach. Time management. Ability to focus on the task. Focus on the result/profit. Development of strategic thinking. Professional integrity. **Qualities not necessarily useful when not working in close contact with foreigners** Working against tight deadlines. Meeting deadlines. Restraint in estimates and judgments. Skills of independent work without supervision.

According to the expatriates, the "universal" qualities worth adopting from Russians most often include the ability to think outside the box, work in extreme conditions, always have a plan B, and apply an individual (as opposed to "impersonal") approach to teamwork. According to the Russian professionals, the "universal" qualities worth adopting from expatriates include firm faith in success (as opposed to skepticism and pessimism), good time management, diplomacy (even in the most routine working issues), high involvement in work, and "professional integrity" (as opposed to oriental "professional cunning").

Finally, examples of "local" business skills that lose value beyond the "Russian reality" are very indicative. For foreigners, they include the ability to plough through bureaucracy and work with people they do not trust, for Russians—skills of independent work without supervision and the ability to work against tight deadlines. Foreigners generally consider such "local" skills and qualities useless outside Russia, whereas Russians consider them useless when not working in close contact with foreigners.

Is there something that is not subject to influence—an invariant core of the Russian business culture?[210] Among others, our study was based on the prerequisite that people representing other cultures can evaluate the strengths and reveal the weaknesses of their "host" culture by "marking" the features they do not encounter in similar business interactions in their home countries.

Many judgments voiced by foreigners (independent of their class or nationality) about the business qualities of Russians are consistent with the results obtained from studies of the Russian national character dating 10–30 years back, as well as from much earlier observations of the "average" Russian worker. This allows advancing a hypothesis that the Russian work culture has a sustainable core "resistant to modernization".

A passive attitude and indifference to corporate affairs is one such example often mentioned by foreigners working in Russia. This is very close to what Nikolay Lossky once termed as **indifference to the "middle area" of culture.** "…Material culture in Russia is at a low level. The Russian people have still not developed the vast territory of their state <…> even… in places favorable for life, the Russians have done little to facilitate their everyday existence <…> to a large extent, poverty is a result of the people having little interest in material culture.".[211]

> "We tried to increase energy in the organization, because they [the people] were very passive." (UK, advisor to the chairman of the board of a bank)
> "If a client of ours is late, I am always prepared to stay and wait for him. He is bringing money—so there is no problem to wait for half an hour or an hour. But what is surprising—nothing of the sort was ever practiced before my arrival! At 5:45 p.m. … everyone went home, they couldn't care less—'see you tomorrow'." (Middle East, director of sales in a trading company)
> "What immediately catches the eye is probably the lack of punctuality in Russia. We even joke back home (in Germany—authors' note), 'Will you be in for dinner by 7 p.m.?—7 p.m. Russian style or German style?'" (Germany, top manager of a recruiting agency)

---

210   This section is based on the results of the qualitative analysis of in-depth interviews with foreign and Russian professionals. The interviews are described in Chapter VI.
211   Lossky N.O. *Absolute Good*. M.: Republic, 1991. p. 56.

"The middle area of culture" is that part of the life space that lies between the threshold of one's home and "sovereign" affairs, problems of national importance, the scope of Messianic ideas. This includes everything that is no longer important personally and not yet significant nationally. This is the area of "small things", basic household needs, addressing which the West has reached its modern level of comfort.

Russian mentality is specific precisely by the fact that for an "average" Russian the value of success in this "middle" area is minimal. Saving the nation is one thing and diligently repairing roads or serving customers—quite another. The familiar popular phrase "work starts with a coffee break" pertains exactly to this kind of activity. Here is how famous writer Anatoly Rybakov commented in his time such "failures" of the Russian civilization, "By their mentality, the Russian people are very hardworking. All the talk that they do not know how to work is nonsense! I am eighty-six years old. I have lived all my life in Russia and I have seen—oh, yes, they can! And they know how to fight. I went through the entire war. However, Russian people do not want to live in luxury."[212]

In Russia, the desire "to live in luxury" had never been promoted economically; it had never become a culturally emphasized goal for ordinary people. The thinking was different. Following is a typical judgment of the outstanding Russian scientist Dmitri Mendeleev. In his program memorandum *On the Foremost Need of the Russian Industry*, he wrote to Emperor Alexander III, "The people who have colonized unprecedentedly vast territories have enough enterprise needed in industrial affairs."[213] The style of the reasoning is indicative—"colonized unprecedentedly vast territories". This argument may have been used for more vividness or probably because there were no other arguments besides "colonization"? Success in "expanding frontiers", success in "gathering lands"—can that be the only kind of success achieved based on Russian values?

Indeed, throughout Russian history, the society had no social institutions that could shape the economic culture of the "middle" area. Potentially, religion could have become such an institution. However, as

---

212 Interview with Anatoly Rybakov // Izvestia. 13 January 2001.
213 Mendeleev D. *Issues of the Economic Development of Russia*. M.: Sotsecgiz, 1960. p. 69.

we have attempted to show in Chapter III, Orthodoxy was not interested in economic practice and did not seek to streamline it by developing relevant cultural and ethical attitudes. The state could have been another such institution, but it was preoccupied primarily with macro issues and cultivated the prestige and significance only of areas of national importance; the area of ordinary economic everyday life was of no interest to it. Consequently, the "middle" area of culture remained not articulated—derelict, so to say.

Another familiar feature is the **"ethics of idleness"**.[214] Following are some traits that expatriates observe in the Russians of today:

> "Oh, yeah, it's a normal issue—people (in Russia—authors' note) getting late to work and leaving earlier. People go on vacation for four weeks, whereas people in the US wouldn't go on vacation at all. Russians are more relaxed towards work." (USA, analyst, financial department of a bank)
> "Now Germans, for example, come to the office at 9 a.m. and leave at 5 p.m. and they do their work ... No one will spend a whole hour lunching or chat with colleagues about their private affairs. They do their job, then they go home and relax with the family. Maybe in our business it is not the same as in other companies, but I see that in general the attitude to work is a bit different here. Labor productivity is lower than in other countries. Personally, I know that the performance of our colleagues in London or in Germany is twice as high." (Germany, top manager of a recruiting agency)
> "Every other day somebody has a birthday. The entire office gathers to celebrate, but it is unacceptable to spend a whole hour for this. I forbade such celebrations in my office." (Germany, top manager of a recruiting agency)
> "Vacations here are incredibly long. So, here you could ask a question and won't be having an answer for three weeks because somebody is on vacation. In the US that would be impossible, because we don't get that much vacation, and people are checking their e-mails even when they are out of the office. Here, no." (USA, technology manager, FMCG company)
> "Russians couldn't care less about time. They have no time management; being late is an absolutely common affair for them." (Sweden, economist in a Russian financial company)

Russians themselves confirm this judgment passed by the expatriates; however, they note that this trait is also largely common for some (especially southern) European nations:

---

214 Mironov B.N. *Attitude to Work in Pre-revolutionary Russia //* Sotsiologicheskie issledovaniia. 2001. No. 10.

> "The Russian people are more relaxed in their schedules. When they say five minutes, this may mean they will arrive in half an hour <…> there are foreigners from Protestant countries where the culture is more punctual and demanding, but there are also foreigners from southern European countries where the attitude to time is rather relaxed." (Russian, CEO of an investment company)

"Ethics of idleness" is a system of values based on the tradition not to regard time as one of the most valuable assets, which can generate income. The respective set of values was firmly adopted by the Russian business culture, which, according to Boris Mironov's shrewd remark, replaced the well-known American imperative "time is money" with an alternative approach—"time is holiday".[215]

As we wrote earlier, historically Russian idleness had exclusively objective reasons related to the harsh climate—bad weather was the cause of most non-working days in Russia. However, we see that even today foreigners attribute such qualities to Russian workers (representing by no means the peasant estate, but a highly professional stratum), which are at first glance firmly associated with and resulting from the ethics of idleness, namely, **"unreliability", "laziness", "lack of motivation", "unwillingness to take responsibility and initiative":**

> "There are issues that a particular person in the company must deal with. However, in Russia people very often delegate their duties to three other colleagues and wait for someone to perform. …I have repeatedly encountered this and not only in this company, in many companies." (Eastern Europe, top manager of an engineering and construction company)
>
> "I once asked a question of one of my managers. He was busy and forwarded it to another colleague: Oleg will give you an answer. Oleg also forwarded my question further—to Igor, Igor to somebody else, and in the end I never got an answer. I was furious." (USA, owner of a transport company)
>
> "So, the other thing that I noticed here is people in the company. Generally, they don't take initiative, they want to be told very, very, very precisely what they are supposed to do, and they do it and then stop. If you tell them to do A, B, and C, they will not think as well to do D and E. For example, my marketing manager in the soft company is like this…" (UK, advisor to the chairman of the board of a bank)
>
> "I am from Northern Italy where the work culture is robust. People want to work, to do something, whereas here I rarely encounter such an attitude." (Italy, deputy director of a company engaged in the cultural and social sphere)
>
> "One other thing (I don't know whether it's just in my company or typical for Russia in general) is that a lot of pieces of information are very often scattered among dif-

---

215 Mironov B.N. *Attitude to Work in Pre-revolutionary Russia //* Sotsiologicheskie issledovaniia. 2001. No. 10, p. 106.

ferent people. And I have a problem putting it all together. So, whereas, I don't know, in some others countries, I just think like you could go to one person and he would collect all the information for you. Here you have to go to a lot of people to find one piece of information ... It's like the organization here is very weak and does not promote cooperation. Like 'this is my department and I don't need to know or do anything else'." (USA, technology manager, FMCG company)

"Boys in Russia are brought up in such a way that they don't want to do anything. My wife and I even had arguments about bringing up our son. Suppose, we are sitting home lunching and some product runs out. I call our son and tell him to go out and buy whatever is needed. He replies he has other things to do and my wife also takes his side. But I demand that he do what I am asking. Children should serve the family, in the first place." (USA, owner of a transport company)

However, when we speak about the ethics of idleness, indifference or unreliability, we should make at least four reservations to evaluate correctly the role of these features in the general attitudes and behavioral practices of the Russian people.

First, Russians believe that the significance of an extremely formal, meticulous, and thorough attitude to work common for Western Europeans is currently overemphasized. As a result, the reverse (quite questionable) side of these qualities may escape attention—namely, accuracy and involvement in work are the reverse side of lack of passion for what one is doing:

"It seems to me that the expatriates on average had a more casual attitude to life and to work in particular. They didn't make any "tragedy" out of work. <...> I had the feeling I was more emotionally engaged, because for me the project was more personal than for them. < ... > I am not sure that I was more involved, but my involvement was somehow more intimate." (Russian, software developer in an IT company)

Second, Russians note that indifference to work is quite common for Europeans as well:

"The French and the Portuguese, for example, are real slackers ... they try to slip away (from work—authors' note) early or idle away the time. Relaxed guys. Italians are also relaxed." Or "All Europeans have a very formal attitude to work. If he is supposed to work until six, he will stand up at six and go home... The Italians don't even try to finish their work today in order to leave at six. They just stand up and go. The Germans will try to have everything done in time, but they will also leave at six." (Russian, engineer in a company producing and distributing medical equipment).

These cross-evaluations by expatriates and Russians are a good illustration of the conclusion we made in Chapter VII—every culture has "marginal" groups representing values not typical for their culture, but demonstrating similarities with the mentality of most representatives of the opposite culture. We believe this is a more precise wording of the currently widespread "all people are different" statement.

Third, and we believe this point is extremely important for understanding—the problem of the Russian work culture is by no means inefficiency of its entire layers (if that were true, Russia would not have become Russia), but the fact that the arsenal of its features cannot be used equally effectively in all aspects of economic development. Svetlana Lurie, an expert in culture studies, correctly noted, "... it is widely accepted that Germans like order and Russians do not. I think this statement cannot be proven. A survey will show that the same social strata, both in Germany and in Russia, appreciate order more or less the same way. The question is which spheres of life the people choose to organize."[216]

We can say that the Russian work culture is not "isotropic" in the space of economic development objectives. Indeed, Russia usually achieved "super results" in several selected fields, which were declared areas of priority (generally, they included major nation-building tasks); all other areas stagnated over the life of entire generations. The essence in this case is not so much which areas of activity are funded and which are not, as which of them are articulated by culture and which leave the people indifferent. Russian laziness is not some general feature of the national character—it is just an attitude to those spheres of life that leave the Russian person indifferent (compare with the above notion of "indifference to the 'middle' area of culture").

And, finally, fourth, we would like to emphasize that the classic Russian unreliability and laziness are not stand-alone qualities. They are just one projection of the more complex phenomenon of Russian mentality revealed in the following contradiction: along with a lack of initiative and lack of responsibility, foreign professionals clearly state that Russians are **hardworking and capable of superhuman efforts** (almost opposite qualities):

---

216 Lurie S.V. *Anthropologists on the Lookout* // Znanie - Sila. 1994. No. 3. p. 53.

"Russians are super hardworking people!" (USA, manager, research and development department, FMCG company)
"You can entrust Russians with any work." (Czech Republic, a programmer in an automotive company)
"It was bizarre for me that particularly Russians work a lot. They can put in long hours. They can come in early. They can work weekends. For us, this is not customary. In summer, as far as I know, people back home even work shorter hours—till 3 p.m." (North Africa, leading engineer in a construction company)
"Some of them (Russian workers—authors' note) can work long, long hours. We work long hours too, but not to that extent. Some (Russians—authors' note) will stay until midnight. I don't feel the need to stay until 12 o'clock at night! But that's just because I respect the work-life boundaries." (USA, editor of research in a Russian bank)
"In my own case, the difference is that people (Russian employees—authors' note) can stay at work very late and it's not a problem for them! Employees in France like to work just 35 hours per week and not more. After 6 o'clock they go home and enjoy their life. They are more relaxed than Russians..." (France, co-owner of an IT company)

The answer explaining this apparent contradiction is simple. Suffice it to note that in most cases the respective qualities are attributed to Russian employees only in a very particular context. Almost always diligence is meant not as a day-to-day observable virtue, but only as the ability to exert maximum efforts in order to perform the work in a short time (*"at the last moment"*). Diligence as a quality manifests itself in short periods of mobilization (indeed, it is apparent that something is always "at stake" in Russia—plan, report, quarterly indicators, etc.). Lack of initiative and laziness coexisting with the immense ability to mobilize are some of the most vibrant ambivalent features of the Russian employee.

Over centuries, this has particularity manifested itself in virtually all sectors of the Russian society and is well known as the Russian **emergency "all hands on board" manner of work.** Vasily Klyuchevsky wrote, "No other people in Europe is capable of such short-term overexertion; but it seems that nowhere in Europe can we find such a lack of habit for regular, moderate, and continuous labor as in the same Great Russia."[217] Russian physiologist Ivan Pavlov noted the same qualities specific of Russians, "...For us, recommending features are not focus, but pressure, speed, charge. This is what we obviously re-

---

217 Klyuchevsky V.O. *Writings in eight volumes*. M.: Gospolitizdat, 1956–1959. V. 1. pp. 313–314.

gard as an indication of talent. Diligence and patience for us fit poorly with the notion of giftedness."[218] Foreign professionals taking up jobs in Russia today say exactly the same thing, noting that this quality lies on the border between efficiency and inefficiency:

> "They (Russians—authors' note) are drivers for results. If you give them a task, they will have it done. They are dedicated. At 11 p.m. Friday night people would be at work. One day I went to a game and left my bag here; I came back and they were still running work. There are two options: either you are completely inefficient or you are dedicated to your job." (USA, manager, research and development department, FMCG company)

Russians themselves confirm this psychological feature:

> "The Russian style of management is tough, pressing, not collaborative, inconsistent—unlike what Europeans and Americans advocate. <...> They do everything in advance, and we are always facing situations when everything has to be accomplished in a day." (Russian, marketing manager, FMCG company)

Here we would like to mention an error common for reformers when they try to eradicate qualities indigenous for a national culture and introduce instead some "proper" qualities, generally, of "western" origin. Indeed, our familiar "emergency" (*avral*) style of work has an almost entirely negative connotation, whereas its opposite—regular orderly work—is considered to be ideal, even though practice almost always shows that it is impracticable on Russian soil. In this sense, the reverse strategy would have been more effective—to align the institutions with basic features inherent in a culture without radically changing these features. It is interesting that foreign managers working in Russia often come precisely to this conclusion in an attempt to raise the performance of their companies or branches employing Russians:

> "If you want to put a stop to late arrivals, be the first to come to the office. You must set a personal example. But see how it often is, 'I am the boss, I have privileges, I do what I want, but you have to come on time.' You can introduce penalties. But the system of penalties is also useless. ...We partially resolved the issue of late arrivals only when we switched to flexible working hours—you come to the office when you want, but the job has to be done." (Germany, top manager of a recruiting agency)

---

218   Pavlov I.P. *On the Russian Mind* // Literaturnaya Gazeta. 1991. No. 30.

This principle (*to change working arrangements rather than the employee*) is reflected in well-known theoretical constructs. Thus, the *"power-culture"* concept developed by American sociologist Jeffrey Hass (discussed in Chapter II herein) deserves special attention.[219] His studies demonstrated that a firm intention and available relevant resources were by themselves not enough to ensure effective management. Introducing change based on adequate understanding of the employees' "mentality" as a given factor shaped in other circumstances produces better results at lower costs.

It is also impossible to ignore the core theme of Russian culture— **the attitude towards authority**. One of the expatriates characterized Russian employees as people who *"are willing to do what they are told, are prepared to act upon orders."* Many foreigners working in Russia emphasize this feature of Russian mentality in different manifestations:

> "And the sense I sometimes get here is that people take what somebody tells them as a fact and they don't challenge back, because culturally (in Russia—authors' note) it's not acceptable to challenge (what the superior says—authors' note)." (USA, manager, research and development department, FMCG company)
>
> "Russians highly appreciate relations with superiors: everything the superiors say is indisputable and must be accomplished accurately, without discussion." (Japan, head of a department in an international trading company)
>
> "With Russians, all decisions are taken by the leader and very quickly (during negotiations—authors' note). After the leader decides, they stop listening; they are no longer interested to negotiate, and it is very difficult to make them change their mind." (Japan, head of a department in an international trading company)
>
> "Russians tend to establish some "vertical of power", a hierarchy... When somebody is the boss, he will always also have a boss, you know. And it's like boss is Boss—all-knowing and never making mistakes." (USA, web-based media editor)
>
> "As for people, when I go to a shop or restaurant and I want to ask something or have a discount, the shop assistants always need to ask their supervisor. Even when it concerns a small issue. They can't solve it, they go and ask their supervisor. So they don't take responsibility!" (Japan, advisor in an audit and consulting company)
>
> "To be honest, I am even slightly annoyed, because it seems that everyone lives according to instructions. As if the slightest deviation may result in a death penalty. Of course, there are sometimes situations when you can get around the rules but in Russia this rarely happens. Take, for example, a waiter or a shop assistant—the shop is closed, the cash register is switched off, that's it. 'I cannot issue a sales check for you.' But for us this is nonsense! You have a client, a buyer who has

---

[219] Hass J. *Power, Culture and Economic Change in Russia: to the Undiscovered Country of Post-Socialism*, 1988–2008. Routledge, 2012.

brought you money, and you are telling him, 'get out, goodbye'?! We have nothing of the sort. In our country (especially if it's a small town), you can simply knock on the shop owner's door at any time; he will get up and sell you whatever you need." (Middle East, director of sales in a trading company)

"The most efficient form of influence here in Russia is the order of a senior. Nothing here is safe until the senior agrees." (Germany, engineer at an industrial enterprise)

"Russians are very bad managers because they don't know how to motivate people. They think they can motivate people being rude." (Colombia, client manager in an oil and gas company)

"I personally find it easier to convince foreign management. They pay attention to my opinion, and if they believe I am right, they acknowledge it. When I am wrong, they gently persuade me. Whatever matters we handled, everything was done very delicately, without being rude to each other... Well, among Russians we used to have improper behavior." (Russian, process engineer at an industrial enterprise)

Several respondents noted the effectiveness of what we traditionally call a "**strong hand**". Judgments of foreign professionals show that a "strong hand" is not an abstract macro-social or political concept, but a tool that works in everyday practice at the micro level:

"If they (the Russians—authors' note) fear you, they will do it, but if you just ask them, they will think that you are weak." (UK, advisor to the chairman of the board of a bank)

"When you ask Russians politely, it doesn't work, so you need to ask twice and maybe you have to shout at another manager, but the person would not be offended, he will understand and do what is needed." (France, key account manager in a French-Russian newspaper)

Another indicative aspect of the attitude towards authority is that Russians generally do not like authority in its particular embodiment, but on the contrary, they respect authority as a generalized phenomenon and **appreciate involvement in it**. The following observation of a foreign professional is illustrative:

"Here (in Russia—authors' note) it is very important how your position in the company sounds. People really care about the title. Like in the lower level, you also have 'managers'! Nothing like it in the US. Even in my business card—I don't really care what it even says. But they (Russian colleagues—authors' note) said, 'We are going to make sure that your title sounds important.' In English, it's only three words, but in Russian it looks really fancy! And I don't even know what it really says..." (USA, manager, research and development department, FMCG company)

However, similar to such opposite qualities as laziness and diligence, the Russian person also demonstrates a dual attitude to authority—**desire for a strong hand and love for freedom at the same time:**

> "Part of the Russian culture is to disobey rules that you do not agree with. <...> Russians are enthusiastic, but this enthusiasm sometimes seems like aggression when they are defending their views." (USA, researcher at a Russian university employed under an international contract)
>
> "A Russian businessman can perceive a contract as a kind of general line of activity where it is impossible to foresee everything; he sees there will be numerous deviations, which will give him a certain freedom of action." (Russian, CEO of an investment company)

Thus, **duality, the ability to combine polar qualities** is, perhaps, an independent and long observed sustainable feature of the Russian culture:

> "At the early stage of communication, a Russian person expresses no emotions, and this is very difficult for foreigners (especially for passionate and emotional Italians) to get used to. Why is it that the person you are talking to fails to react, responds monotonously, and demonstrates no enthusiasm?" (Italy, university lecturer)

Compare:

> "Russians have a very emotional way of communicating...it can be very warm and close—close to Brazilians. Often, people speak very loudly to each other and with a tone that I do not recognize normal, but this absolutely does not mean that my Russian colleagues are fighting." (Brazil, researcher at a Russian university employed under an international contract)

Or:

> "When we were discussing some technical matter with a Russian colleague, a nearby expat (who spoke no Russian) asked why we were yelling at each other. And we were just standing and discussing something in a friendly manner..." (Russian, software developer in an IT company)
>
> "Russians are emotional and disorganized fatalists. <...> You must spend a lot of time with Russians to understand what is going on in their minds. It seems that Russians are open, but then it turns out that they are keeping something to themselves." (Italy, deputy director of a company engaged in the cultural and social sphere)

Compare:

> "Russia is this fusion of West and Asia. It has a kind of Western veneer, but deep down inside it's something very Asian, something absolutely non-Western. And that's deep inside of psychology of every single person I've met here. And that translates itself into every little detail, like driving the road, for instance. Traffic jams, your 'probki' here. And it's not because there are too few roads, it's because of the psychology of the people. And a thousand tiny other little things, which combined make Russia completely different from the West." (USA, editor of research in a Russian bank)

In this respect, a mid-1994 study *On the Russian National Character* conducted by Ksenia Kasyanova is quite interesting. Using the MMPI methodology to compare Russians and Americans, she demonstrates the Russians' ability to combine high self-control (high scores on the *Repression* scale) with its opposite feature—emotional immaturity (similarly named scale of this methodology). The difference in scores between Russians and Americans on the self-control scale is 20% along the entire scale, with Russians scoring higher. At the same time, Russians score markedly higher on the emotional immaturity scale than the Americans, exceeding their indicators by approximately 13.5% of the scale.[220]

In conclusion, we would like to note that the contradictory judgments made by foreigners about the specific traits of Russian professionals fit into a coherent and consistent logic, if we keep in mind the most important property of the Russian work culture—**the ambivalence** of its main features. Indeed, it is impossible to distinguish purely negative or purely positive features of the Russian work culture—they all have a "shadow" side. The reverse side of the ethics of idleness is the high effectiveness of flexible working hours; the emergency-style manner of work is compensated by the ability for extreme concentration and exertion; and the pronounced power distance results in a high mobilization potential.

---

[220] Kasyanova K. *On the Russian National Character*. M.: Institute for national economic model, 1994.

Conclusion

The society's transformation potential and its possible scenarios largely depend on the existing type of culture, on the extent to which it is resistant to external cultural influences, and on what cultural code proves to be stronger—the national one reproducible by the system or the one proposed in exchange in the form of alternative sociocultural patterns that had demonstrated their effectiveness in other countries. In this case, *the national work culture,* which serves as a basic element of civilizational breakthroughs, is one of culture's key segments.

Summarizing the conceptual approaches prevailing in literature, we have identified the following factors, which created the "core" of the Russian work culture: *civilizational and economic, geo-climatic, ethno-environmental, and ethno-religious*. An important finding of our study is that originally the Russian work culture is a global phenomenon, as it was shaped not only by domestic circumstances, but was largely a response to the external geo-cultural and geopolitical challenges and threats typical for Russian history. In an ironic twist of fate, these challenges and treats are still relevant today, and this means that the Russian work culture has not lost its unique potential in the current political, economic, and cultural configuration of the world.

Foreign influence on shaping the Russian work culture as a totality of personal attitudes to labor and sustainable work practices is not a random or situational factor. The "milestones" indicating the dramatic expansion of areas of influence of foreign ideas and foreign specialists (foreigners in government, science, industry, and the army) are clearly traceable in Russian history. Assimilating and "digesting" foreign (mostly "Western") values became a sustainable pattern of Russian development. It runs like a golden thread through Russian history, not interrupting even with the emergence of the USSR sealed off from the rest of the world by an "iron curtain". Then, in a slightly modified form, it became an instrument used by superpowers in their global technological rivalry in the military field.

At the end of the 1980s and in the 1990s, Russian culture withstood a massive expansion of western values, when everything foreign unconditionally triumphed over anything domestic. However, at that time

Russia observed the "West" from afar, and therefore its perception was idealized and far from reality. The situation started changing radically in the early 2000s. Owing to the increasing presence of multinational corporations, the interaction of the Russian culture with foreign cultures moved to the micro level, the level of companies. Communication with representatives of other cultures became part of the production process involving *specific business practices rather than abstract romanticized values, forcing people to overcome daily their long-term habits and stereotypes, because the company's performance was at stake, and, respectively, the assessment of their own input.*

In this context, we should consider the role of foreign professionals (expatriates) as a relatively new and understudied driver of sociocultural and socio-economic modernization. Our study focuses on highly skilled foreign specialists working alongside Russian professionals. As compared to monocultural entities, multinational companies may have certain advantages generated by a more extensive exchange of experience, knowledge, and ideas within the work team. However, the key issue in this case is the compatibility of cultures, which would make this exchange possible. There are studies demonstrating failures of such multicultural teams, with foreign specialists and managers often terminating their contracts early and returning to their home countries, thus inflicting significant losses on the company. These phenomena are largely caused by the "culture shock", when foreigners are unable to bridge the gap with the host culture in close daily contact with it in the course of business interactions.

Judging by the numbers employed, the expat community in Russia is not very numerous. A review of the Russian Federal Migration Service statistics provides the following figures of employed expatriates from non-CIS countries: slightly over 16,000 in executive positions of all levels; about 8,000 highly skilled specialists in engineering and natural sciences; and 7,000 in the financial and economic, administrative, and social spheres. However, their role in the economy should not be underestimated. *Foreign professionals and executives are economic agents who, on the one hand, participate in strategic decision-making in the largest companies and, accordingly, are potentially very influential, and, on the other hand, are bearers of a fundamentally different worldview and system of values.*

An analysis of current trends in the market for highly skilled workforce in Russia provides a mixed picture. On the one hand, foreign companies and investors demonstrated an increasing interest in Russia until 2008–2009. As a result, the number of foreign professionals and executives working in Russia sharply grew. However, *at the end of 2008—beginning of 2009, the trend changed, and since then, the number of foreign professionals from the EU and the United States has been shrinking.*

The departure of expatriates from Russia and the role of this phenomenon for Russia's future development is a point of discussion herein. We propose addressing this issue by considering *the need of structural change in the composition of expatriates employed in Russia.* Special focus should be made on those expatriates who do not distance themselves from Russia, who work for Russia rather than just in Russia, who create capital and technology under the Russian brand rather than just manage imported capital and technology.

The expatriates' social and ethno-national structure, their perception of Russian capitalism and Russian society in general directly determine the role this social stratum can play at the current stage in the development of the Russian society. Analysis shows that by these features the expat community is quite heterogeneous and under different circumstances can have a negative as well as a positive impact on the host Russian culture.

We have proposed *two basic criteria underlying the social structure of foreign professionals with different "utility" for Russian companies.* The first criterion is *the nature of integration of foreign professionals into the Russian society.* Here, two polar and one intermediate stratum are clearly distinguishable. One extreme is the stratum of professionals whose attitude is not to be integrated into the Russian society (staying "out of society"). In many cases, this is not just an attitude but a contractual provision paid for by the employer. The other extreme are professionals significantly influenced by Russian culture or culturally fully assimilated. In-between are the professionals whose mission is to find common ground with the Russian business culture and design fundamentally new "culture-centric" efficient business models on that basis.

The second criterion determining the role of Russian-based foreign professionals as agents of influence is their *vision or perception of the*

Russian society. Our research has revealed at least three basic ways in which foreign professionals perceive the Russian society. We have tentatively classified these perception types into the following categories: *"Cold War-style"*, *"rationally pragmatic"*, and *"allowing for modernization"*.

Segmentation of foreign professionals based on the above two criteria allows distinguishing at least *six typological groups, the representatives of which play fundamentally different roles in the development of Russian entities*. In some cases, organizational effectiveness is improved "top-down" by enhancing the isomorphism of Russian companies with "Western" organizational standards through rigid implementation of relevant sociocultural patterns. In other cases, organizational effectiveness is provided using the "bottom-up" approach based on enhancing group performance, which implies finding a balance between core features of the interacting cultures and building mixed development models. These two approaches compete; however, the approach involving implementation of "Western" interaction and work patterns that are presented as reference has a weak consolidation effect due to sometimes insufficient social legitimacy of the introduced "standards". On the other hand, the approach based on managing group efficiency should take into account the availability and nature of areas where the cultures are complementary and where a mutually beneficial exchange of values is possible.

An analysis using this tool has revealed a disturbing trend—a growing entirely negative or largely skeptical perception of the Russian society and the Russian socio-economic system. This triggers if not a repulsive, but in many respects a consumer, functional attitude to Russia and Russians. At the same time, there is a rather extensive group of foreign professionals whose attitude to Russia can be described as "perception, allowing for modernization". This type of perception is the most productive in terms of positive culture change, since, for one thing, it implicitly contains no aggression or excessive skepticism and, for another thing, it does not consider Russia as a static system.

Expat activities also influence the transformation of the Russian work culture indirectly—*foreign professionals deal with the unique task of "marking" those properties of the host culture that they do not encounter under similar circumstances in their home countries, and this creates a fundamental basis for national introspection.* Foreign professionals serve as a "mirror" of the national culture.

Our analysis of the way foreign professionals working long in Russia and able to observe it from within perceive the Russian work culture revealed *an invariant set of characteristics, a certain core of the Russian work culture "resistant to modernization". In general, we cannot say that the features of the Russian work culture are becoming more isomorphic with the core properties of Western cultures.*

In particular, we identified a range of judgments made by foreigners (independent of their class or nationality) working long in Russia about the features of Russians that are consistent with the results obtained from studies of the Russian national mentality dating back 10–30 years, as well as from much earlier observations of the "average" Russian worker. Such features still constituting the core of the work culture of today's Russian professionals include *the ethics of idleness, indifference to the "middle" area of culture, an emergency-style manner of work, and love of the "strong hand".*

Finally, the essential characteristic of the Russian professionals' work culture is the ambivalence of its core features. Analysis shows that it is impossible to distinguish purely negative or purely positive features of the Russian work culture—they all have a "shadow" side. For example, the reverse side of the "ethics of idleness" is the high effectiveness of flexible working hours; the emergency-style manner of work is compensated by the ability for extreme concentration and exertion; and the pronounced power distance often results in a high mobilization potential.

Our analysis also focused on *the mutual evaluation of each other's business skills by Russian and foreign professionals working in multinational teams and the cross-cultural adoptions resulting from such joint work.* This enabled us to assess which features of the Russian work culture are "local" and which are "universal", i.e., to determine which of its qualities are effective only in a local Russian institutional context, and which ones make it competitive globally. We also evaluated the openness of the Russian professionals' work culture to change, as well as its capacity to influence and enrich other cultures.

The area of tension between Russian and foreign professionals working together emerges along the axis "initiative—responsibility—

attitude to corporate standards—time-management—degree of impersonality when dealing with business issues." Indeed, the expatriates often note that their Russian colleagues lack motivation, are unwilling to take initiative and responsibility, have poor self-organization (poor time management), and demonstrate a skeptical attitude to corporate events (purely formal attendance of Russian colleagues at various corporate trainings often served as an example in this context). The desire to determine guilt rather than resolve an issue is another feature often mentioned.

In turn, Russians criticize their foreign colleagues mostly for such features as "template thinking along with the impression of being right in everything", excessive thoroughness in routine work, and being unreasonably process-driven even if it is impracticable. A frequent item of criticism is such quality of the foreign professionals as an "impersonal" attitude to work, their unwillingness to consider various "personal circumstances", as well as "personalities" when dealing with business issues.

According to Russian professionals, template thinking typical of foreigners, when Russian specifics are ignored, is the most serious difference negatively affecting team performance in companies. These quite common accusations that Russian professionals make against their foreign colleagues reflect an interesting phenomenon—*the social legitimacy of the "Western" type of consciousness and system of values as a universal guide in life exists in Russia no more. This situation is fundamentally different from the orthodox perception of "Western" values and "Western" experience as universal and absolute categories—a trend that had formed in Russian culture back in the 1990s.* In contrast, exchange of values today no longer involves automatic replication of foreign recipes and patterns; it is based on adopting only those features of "Western" culture that have proven their appeal and effectiveness.

Nowadays, the Russian society has quite seriously changed its attitude to "Western" culture and to foreign influence in general, especially if we compare today with the late 1980s—first half of the 1990s. This is largely due to Russians having accumulated fundamentally new experience of cross-cultural interaction on the corporate level. The abstract and idealized perception of "Western" mentality has been replaced by a purely pragmatic approach in evaluating foreigners and their role in the development of the Russian society and economy.

In the meantime, *both parties mutually evaluate many of each other's business qualities as positive and worth adopting.* According to how foreign employees judge their Russian colleagues, two groups of positively assessed qualities are distinguishable. The first group includes a certain "average Russian set": forgiving nature, innovative approach, ability to think out of the "template" box, steadfastness in the face of adversity, diligence and hard work. The second group of qualities that foreigners positively evaluate in Russians reflect a toolkit required to adapt to the realities of life: ability to plough through bureaucracy, get around restrictive rules, no high drama, as well as stress resistance and patience.

Qualities that the expatriates have adopted from Russians and which they consider useful not only for work in Russia but also for their further activities include adaptability to extreme situations, flexibility to any significant change in plans, having a "plan B" (back-up plan of action), individual (as opposed to "impersonal") approach to teamwork, the ability to reach compromise, caution, thinking out of the template box. Foreigners also adopt from Russians certain qualities, which they consider useless anywhere outside Russia. Besides quite predictable features (such as "acquiescence to bureaucratic obstacles" or "documentation skills due to lots of paperwork and understanding of complex regulatory rules"), they also include rather unexpected ones (an illustrative example is "ability to work with people I do not trust").

Russian professionals acknowledge a broader area of business skills of their foreign colleagues: faith in success (as opposed to skepticism and pessimism), exceptionally good organization and time management, diplomacy and political correctness (even in the most routine business issues), focus on results and profit, high involvement in work (as opposed to regarding work as an inevitable "burden"), high professionalism, and "professional integrity" (as opposed to oriental "professional cunning").

Among qualities adopted from expatriates, Russian specialists most often refer to the ability to focus on the task, structured and consistent approach, capacity for self-organization, ability to assume responsibility, "professional integrity", ability to position oneself in the company, a system, diplomatic approach to building relations with senior management.

Finally, we have obtained interesting results from using the *CVSCALE international methodology* to analyze cultural differences and cultural dynamics in groups of Russian and foreign professionals working together. The methodology is based on measuring five complex dimensions—power distance, uncertainty avoidance, collectivism, masculinity, and long-term orientation.

Analysis revealed that *in spite of effective professional exchange, Russian and foreign professionals are separated by a certain cultural distance, which manifests itself in different attitudes to authority, risk, and group interests.*

Thus, *expatriates employed in Russia are practically unaffected by the Russian sociocultural environment and reproduce their traditional cultural profiles virtually unchanged.* The only exception is the set of properties included in collectivism. Its excessive (as compared to the "benchmark") score for expatriates working in Russia may be a reaction to staying in an unfamiliar sociocultural environment, which promotes solidarity.

In the meantime, Russians working with expatriates actually represent an extremely "Western"-focused group of employees. Russian professionals differ from the Europeans by lower levels of uncertainty avoidance and collectivism, while having comparable long-term orientation scores. This contrasts with the traditional perception of the Russian nature as per G. Hofstede (high levels of uncertainty avoidance and collectivism with low-level long-term orientation).

The power distance is the main (and only) dimension demonstrating that the cultural profile of Russian professionals has features linking them with the traditional portrait of a Russian worker—a high level of acceptance of the authoritarian nature of power. The fact that a Russian employee combines high power distance, on the one hand, with low uncertainty avoidance (and, therefore, low value of instructions, rules, and regulations), on the other hand, fits well into the logic of the classic Russian rule that "the stringency of Russian laws is offset by their non-observance".

This particular combination of work culture features can be described as a specific "Russian type". *The aggregate national portrait of a Russian professional represents a specific combination of radicalized Western European cultural features and oriental features that continue to coexist with traits typical of the European image.*

Another interesting result is the *low level of collectivism specific of Russians*. This feature in Russian culture clearly stands apart. The issue of whether a Russian person is more inclined to collectivism or individualism remains open. Indeed, collectivism in Russia has always been a forced measure, which made survival possible. However, precisely this forced and essentially artificial rapprochement of the people generated a directly opposite feature of culture—inner denial of collectivist values on the backdrop of the externally imposed need to abide by them. Collectivism has become a functional and intrinsically syncretic feature of culture having produced its antithesis—extreme individualism, which manifests itself whenever the external threat requiring cohesion disappears.

An analysis of cultural diversity within each nationality yields some important results. *The aggregate national cultural profile of both Russians and expatriates results from a combination of properties of two polar subgroups existing "within" each culture—"core" and marginal ("dissident").* The "core" group includes most respondents of the given nationality and represents the set of values characteristic of the majority of this nationality; the "marginal" group includes the minority of respondents of the same nationality who by their attitudes are closer to the majority of people representing the other culture.

The most apparent difference between the "core" and marginal groups is observed in the power distance dimension (for Russians it is much higher in the core group, and for expatriates—in the marginal one). High power distance is the classic characteristic of Russian and most oriental cultures.

The emergence of "marginal" groups within each culture is generally not associated with the duration of joint work with representatives of the other culture. A marginal group exists in the culture originally.

Interestingly, *despite the expectation that the duration of collaboration and frequency of contacts of representatives of contrasting cultures should be strong drivers of cultural transformation, analysis shows that cultural transformation caused by these factors provides no clear result.* In the case of Russians, the joint work duration factor has an unsustainable effect. In the case of expatriates, however, an extended stay in Russia has a certain (although not pronounced) impact on their cultural profile, shifting it toward "Russification". At the same time, we captured the culture resistance effect in the surveyed expat sample. The expatriates who work in close contact with Russians or in companies with Russian top management are more likely to demonstrate qualities specific of the "core" group of their culture than those expatriates whose contacts are less frequent.

***

Close cross-cultural interaction is a typical phenomenon in contemporary societies. The cultural distance between the interacting parties, internal diversity and sustainability of culture types are the key elements, which help understanding what is good for each culture, what needs to be done to unlock its potential to the utmost, and what path leads it to success.

Selected bibliography

Аузан А.А. *«Колея» российской модернизации* // Общественные науки и современность. 2007. № 6.

    Auzan A.A. *The "Track" of Russian Modernization* // Obshchestvennye Nauki i Sovremennost'. 2007. No. 6.

Афанасьев Э. *О некоторых православных принципах формирования рыночной экономики* // Вопросы экономики. 1993, №8.

    Afanasiev E. *On Some Orthodox Principles for the Development of a Market Economy* // Voprosy Ekonomiki. 1993, No. 8.

Ахиезер А.С. *Россия: критика исторического опыта*. Тт. I-III. М: Философское общество СССР, 1991.

    Akhiezer A.S. *Russia: A Critique of Historical Experience*. Volumes I-III. M: Philosophical Society of the USSR, 1991.

Ахиезер А.С. *Эмиграция как индикатор состояния российского общества* // Мир России. 1999, N4.

    Akhiezer A.S. *Emigration as a Status Indicator in Russian Society* // Mir Rossii. 1999, No. 4.

Бейкер Кэтрин Дж. *Как устроить работающие взаимоотношения* // Знание -сила.1996, №1.

    Baker C.J. *Building Working Relationships* // Znanie -Sila. 1996, No. 1.

Бердяев Н. *Философия неравенства*. М.: ИМА-ПРЕСС, 1990.

    Berdyaev N. *The Philosophy of Inequality*. M.: IMA-PRESS, 1990.

Березной А.В., Панкин С.М., Славинский В.А. и др. *Производство выходит за национальные границы*. М., 1991.

    Bereznoy A.V., Pankin S.M., Slavinsky V.A. et al. *Production Crosses National Borders*. M., 1991.

Биллингтон Дж. *Икона и топор. Опыт истолкования истории русской культуры*. М.: Рудомино, 2001.

    Billington J. *The Icon and the Axe. An Interpretive History of Russian Culture*. M.: Rudomino, 2001.

Васильев Л.С. *История Востока*. М.: Высшая школа, 1994.

    Vasiliev L.S. *The History of the Orient*. M.: Vysshaya shkola, 1994.

Вебер М. *Протестантская этика и дух капитализма* / М. Вебер. Избранные произведения. М.: Прогресс, 1990.

Weber M. *The Protestant Ethic and the Spirit of Capitalism* / M. Weber. Selected works. M.: Progress, 1990.

Вебер М. *Хозяйственная этика мировых религий. Попытка сравнительного исследования в области социологии религий* / Макс Вебер. Избранное. Образ общества. М.: Юрист, 1994.

Weber M. *Economic Ethics of World Religions. A Comparative Study of the Sociology of Religion* / Max Weber. Selected works. The Image of Society. M.: Jurist, 1994.

Вишневский А., Зайончковская Ж. *Волны миграции. Новая ситуация* // Свободная мысль. 1992, N 12.

Vishnevsky A., Zayonchkovskaya Zh. *Migration Waves. The New Situation* // Svobodnaya Mysl'. 1992, No. 12.

Вишневский А., Зайончковская Ж. *Четвертый вал эмиграции* // Московские новости. 1992, 9 февраля.

Vishnevsky A., Zayonchkovskaya Zh. *The Fourth Wave of Emigration* // Moskovskiye Novosti. 1992, 9 February.

Гайдар Е.Т. *Государство и эволюция*. М.: Евразия, 1995.

Gaidar Ye.T. *State and Evolution*. M.: Eurasia, 1995.

Гаськов В.М. *Социальные аспекты международного обмена производственным опытом*. М.: МНИИПУ, 1988.

Gaskov V.M. *Social Aspects of International Exchange of Industrial Experience*. M.: MNIIPU, 1988.

Гаськов В.М. *Социальные проблемы обмена производственным опытом в странах -членов СЭВ*. Автореферат диссертации на соискание ученой степени доктора экономических наук. М., 1989.

Gaskov V.M. *Social Problems Related to Exchanging Industrial Experiences in CMEA Member Countries*. Abstract of the dissertation for a doctoral degree in economic sciences. M., 1989.

Гловели Г. *Цивилизационный опыт России: необходимость уточнения* // Вопросы экономики. 1993. №8.

Gloveli G. *Russia's Civilizational Experience: The Need to Clarify* // Voprosy Ekonomiki. 1993. No. 8.

Горичева Л. *Экономические проблемы и национальное самосознание* // Вопросы экономики.1993. №8.

    Goricheva L. *Economic Issues and the National Identity* // Voprosy Ekonomiki. 1993. No. 8.

Гохберг Л.М., Некипелова Е.Ф. *Статистическая оценка эмиграции научных кадров* // Интеллектуальная миграция в России / Под общ. ред. С.А. Кугеля. СПб, 1993.

    Gokhberg L.M., Nekipelova E.F. *Emigration of Scientists: Statistical Estimate* // Intellectual Migration in Russia / General editor S.A. Kugel. SPb, 1993.

Гранин Ю. *Меняем «бусы» на нефть. Модернизация по-российски: имитация и формализм* // Свободная мысль, 2014. №1.

    Granin Yu. *Exchanging "Necklaces" for Oil. Russian-Style Modernization: Simulation and Formalism* // Svobodnaya Mysl', 2014. No. 1.

Гумилев Л.Н. *От Руси к России. Очерки этнической истории.* М.: Экопрос, 1994.

    Gumilev L.N. *From Rus' to Russia. Essays on Ethnic History.* M.: Ecopros, 1994.

Гумилев Л.Н. *Этногенез и биосфера Земли.* М.: Танаис ДИ-ДИК, 1994.

    Gumilev L.N. *Ethnogenesis and the Biosphere of Earth.* M.: Tanais DI-DIC, 1994.

Данилевский Н.Я. *Россия и Европа: Взгляд на культурные и политические отношения Славянского мира к Германо-Романскому.* 6-е изд. Спб: Изд-во СпбГУ: Глаголъ, 1995.

    Danilevski N.Ya. *Russia and Europe: An Inquiry into the Cultural and Political Relations of the Slavic World to the Romano-Germanic World.* Sixth edition. SPb: Izd-vo SPbGU: Glagol, 1995.

Данилова Е., Тарарухина М. *Российская производственная культура в параметрах Г. Хофштеда* // Мониторинг общественного мнения. 2003. №3(65).

    Danilova E., Tararukhina M. *The Russian Industrial Culture in Hofstede's Dimensions* // Public Opinion Monitoring. 2003. No. 3(65).

Долгих Е. *Почему уезжают ученые* // Московские новости. 1993, 4 апреля.

    Dolgikh E. *Why are Scientists Leaving* // Moskovskiye Novosti. 1993, 4 April.

Емельянов Ю.В. *Рождение и гибель цивилизаций.* М.: Изд-во «Вече», 1999.

    Yemelyanov Yu.V. *The Birth and Death of Civilizations.* M.: Izd-vo Veche, 1999.

Жижко Е.В. *Российская трудовая этика в социально-психологическом контексте экономической реформы* // Российское общество на рубеже веков: штрихи к портрету / Отв. Ред. Бутенко И.А. М.: МОНФ, 2000.

    Zhizhko E.V. *The Russian Work Ethics in the Socio-psychological Context of Economic Reform* // Russian Society at the Turn of the Century: Touches to the Portrait / Publishing editor Butenko I.A. M.: MONF, 2000.

Жунин М.М. *Просвещенный купец -украшение старой веры* // Мир России. 1998. №3.

    Zhunin M.M. *An Enlightened Merchant is Pride of the Old Belief* // Mir Rossii. 1998. No. 3.

Зарубина Н.Н. *Модернизационный вызов современности и российские альтернативы. Материалы круглого стола* // Мир России. 2001. №4.

    Zarubina N.N. *The Current Modernization Challenge and Russian Alternatives. Round table proceedings* // Mir Rossii. 2001. No. 4.

Зарубина Н.Н. *Православный предприниматель в зеркале русской культуры* // Общественные науки и современность. 2001, №5.

    Zarubina N.N. *The Orthodox Entrepreneur in the Mirror of the Russian Culture* // Obshchestvennye Nauki i Sovremennost'. 2001, №5.

Иваницкий В. *Архетипы успеха и русская сказка* // Знание –сила. 1997. №8-10.

    Ivanitsky V. *Archetypes of Success and the Russian Fairy Tale* // Znanie – Sila. 1997. №8–10.

Ильин В.В., Ахиезер А.С. *Российская цивилизация: содержание, границы, возможности.* М.: Изд-во МГУ, 2000.

    Ilyin V.V., Akhiezer A.S. *The Russian Civilization: Essence, Boundaries, Potential.* M.: Izd-vo MGU, 2000.

Инновации – это не полеты на Марс. Готова ли Россия к «высокотехнологичным санкциям»? // Деловая Москва, 15 сентября 2014, №42 (141).

    Innovations are not flights to Mars. Is Russia ready for "high-tech sanctions"? // Delovaya Moskva, 15 September 2014, No.42 (141).

Интервью с Анатолием Рыбаковым // Известия. 13.01.01.

    Interview with Anatoly Rybakov // Izvestia. 13 January 2001.

Интервью с К. Касьяновой // Знание -сила. 1992, №1.

    Interview with K. Kasyanova // Znanie -Sila. 1992, No. 1.

Кабалина В. И. *Трудовая мобильность: организационные, институциональные и социально-структурные факторы* // Социологический журнал. 1999, №3-4.

    Kabalina V.I. *Labor mobility: organizational, institutional and socio-structural factors* // Sotsiologicheskiy zhurnal. 1999, No. 3–4.

Карамзин Н. М. *Предания веков*. М.: Изд-во «Правда», 1988.

    Karamzin N.M. *The Tradition of Centuries*. M.: Izd-vo Pravda, 1988.

Карачаровский В.В. *О восприятии России иностранными специалистами* // Экономист. 2014. №7.

    Karacharovskiy V.V. *Perception of Russia by Foreign Specialists* // Economist. 2014. No. 7.

Карачаровский В.В., Ястребов Г.А. *Иностранные профессионалы в России как агенты модернизации* // Общество и экономика. 2013. №11-12.

    Karacharovskiy V.V., Yastrebov G.A. *Foreign Professionals in Russia as Agents of Modernization* // Obshchestvo i Ekonomika. 2013. No. 11–12.

Карачаровский В.В., Шкаратан О.И., Ястребов Г.А. *Культура и модернизация в зеркале взаимодействия российских и иностранных профессионалов в мультинациональных трудовых коллективах в России* // Социологические исследования. 2014. №8.

    Karacharovskiy V.V., Shkaratan O.I., Yastrebov G.A. *Culture and Modernization in the Mirror of Interaction Between Russian and Foreign Professionals in Multinational Work Teams in Russia* // Sotsiologicheskiye Issledovaniya. 2014. No. 8.

Карсавин Л. П. *Монашество в средние века.* М., 1992.

Karsavin L.P. *Monasticism in the Middle Ages.* M., 1992.

Кастельс М. *Глобализация и глобальная экономика* // Экономические стратегии. 2000. Май-июнь, июль-август.

Castells M. *Globalization and the Global Economy* // Ekonomicheskiye Strategii. 2000. May-June, July-August.

Кастельс М., Киселева Э. *Россия и сетевое общество* // Мир России. 2000, №1.

Castells M., Kiselyova E. *Russia and the Network Society* // Mir Rossii. 2000, No. 1.

Касьянова К. *О русском национальном характере.* М.: Институт национальной модели экономики, 1994.

Kasyanova K. *On the Russian National Character.* M.: Institute for National-al Economic Model, 1994.

Кива А.В. *"Экономика -язык -культура" через призму виртуальной реальности* // Общественные науки и современность. 2001. №4. С. 46.

Kiva A.V. *"Economy -Language -Culture" Through the Prism of Virtual Reality* // Obshchestvennye Nauki i Sovremennost'. 2001. No. 4. p. 46.

Китахара А. *Реальность и идеальный образ общины (Япония и Таиланд)* // Философские науки.1996, №1-6.

Kitahara A. *The Reality and the Community's Ideal Image (Japan and Thailand)* // Philosofskiye nauki. 1996, No. 1–6.

Ключевский В.О. *Сочинения в 8-ми томах.* М.: Госполитиздат, 1956-1959.

Klyuchevsky V.O. *Writings in eight volumes.* M.: Gospolitizdat, 1956–1959.

Клямкин И.М., Лапкин В.В. *Русский вопрос в России* // Полис. 1995, №5.

Klyamkin I.M., Lapkin V.V. *The Russian Question in Russia* // Polis. 1995, No. 5.

Коваль Т.Б. *"Духовные христиане": религиозное своеобразие и этика труда* // Мир России. 1993, № 1.

Koval T.B. *"The Spiritual Christians": Religious Distinctness and Work Ethics* // Mir Rossii. 1993, No. 1.

Коваль Т.Б. *Православная этика труда* // Мир России. 1994, №2.

Koval T.B. *Orthodox Work Ethics* // Mir Rossii. 1994, No. 2.

Коваль Т.Б. *"Тяжкое благо". Христианская этика труда. Православие. Католицизм. Протестантизм.* М.: Институт этнологии и антропологии РАН, 1994.

Koval T.B. *"Back-Breaking Benefit". Christian Work Ethics. Orthodoxy. Catholicism. Protestantism.* M.: Institut Etnologii i Antropologii RAN, 1994.

Колесникова Л., Перекрестов В. *Организационные структуры и культура предпринимательства* // Вопросы экономики. 2000. № 8.

Kolesnikova L., Perekryostov V. *Organizational Structures and Business Culture* // Voprosy Ekonomiki. 2000. No. 8.

Константиновский Д., Вознесенская Е., Чередниченко Г. *Эффект длительного пребывания россиян в странах Запада* / В кн.: Ядов В.А. (ред.). Воздействие западных социокультурных образцов на социальные практики в России. М.: ТАУС, 2009. С.187.

Konstantinovskiy D., Voznesenskaya E., Cherednichenko G. *Russians in Western Countries: The Effect of Long-Term Sojourn* / In: Yadov V.A. (ed.). Impact of Western Socio-Cultural Patterns on Russian Social Practices. M.: TAUS, 2009. p. 187.

Лапин Н.И. *Социокультурный подход и социетально-функциональные структуры* // СОЦИС. 2000, №7.

Lapin N.I. *Sociocultural Approach and Societal Functional Structures.* // Sotsiologicheskie issledovaniia. 2000, No. 7.

Латова Н.В., Латов Ю.В. *Российская экономическая ментальность на мировом фоне* // Общественные науки и современность. 2001.№4.

Latova N.V., Latov Yu.V. *Russian Economic Mentality in the World Context* // Obshchestvennye Nauki i Sovremennost'. 2001. No. 4.

Латов Ю.В., Латова Н.В. *Открытия и парадоксы этнометрического анализа российской хозяйственной культуры по методике Г. Хофстеда* // Мир России. 2007. № 4. С. 52-53.

Latov Yu.V., Latova N.V. *Findings and Paradoxes of Ethnometric Analysis of Russia's Economic Culture According to Hofstede* // Mir Rossii. 2007. No. 4. pp. 52–53.

Латуха М., Цуканова Т. *Талантливые сотрудники в российских и зарубежных компаниях* // Вопросы экономики, 2013 №1

    Latukha M., Tsukanova T. *Talented Employees in Russian and Foreign Companies* // Voprosy Ekonomiki, 2013, No. 1.

Левада Ю. *Ищем человека. Социологические очерки. 2000-2005.* М.: Новое издательство, 2006.

    Levada Yu. *Searching for Man. Essays in Sociology. 2000–2005.* M.: Novoye Izdatel'stvo, 2006.

Лист Ф. *Национальная система политической экономии.* СПб., 1891. С. 235.

    List F. *The National System of Political Economy.* SPb, 1891. p. 235.

Лосский Н.О. *Условия абсолютного добра.* М.: Республика, 1991.

    Lossky N.O. *Absolute Good.* M.: Republic, 1991.

Лотман Ю. *Труды по знаковым системам.* Тарту, 1972. Вып.15.

    Lotman Yu. *Writings on landmark systems.* Tartu, 1972. Issue 15.

Лурье С. *Антропологи ищут* // Знание -сила. 1994, №3.

    Lurie S. *Anthropologists on the Lookout* // Znanie -Sila. 1994, No. 3.

Льюис Р. *Деловые культуры в международном бизнесе. От столкновения к взаимопониманию. Перевод с английского.* М.: Изд-во "Дело", 1999.

    Lewis R. *When Cultures Collide. Managing Successfully Across Cultures.* Translation from English. M.: Izd-vo Delo, 1999.

Лэйн Д. *Преобразование государственного социализма в России: от "хаотической" экономики к кооперативному капитализму, координируемому государством?* // Мир России. 2000, №1.

    Lane D. *The Transformation of State Socialism in Russia. From a "Chaotic" Economy to Cooperative Capitalism Coordinated by the State?* // Mir Rossii. 2000, No. 1.

Магун В.С., Руднев М.Г. *Базовые ценности россиян в европейском контакте* // Общественные науки и современность, 2010, №4, С.16.

    Magun V.S., Rudnev M.G. *The Russian's Fundamental Values in the European Contact* // Obshchestvennye Nauki i Sovremennost', 2010, No. 4, p. 16.

Мальцев А. *К вопросу о несовместимости автаркии и модернизации. Российское подтверждение общемировой закономерности* // Свободная мысль, №2. 2010

> Maltsev A. *On the Incompatibility of Autarchy and Modernization. The Russian Confirmation of Global Patterns* // Svobodnaya Mysl', No. 2. 2010.

Мартин Л. *Чего не хватает российскому менеджменту?* // Проблемы теории и практики управления. 2000, №4.

> Martin L. *What is Russian Management Lacking?* // Problemy Teorii i Praktiki Upravleniya. 2000, No. 4.

Мартьянов В.С. *Инволюция элиты в обществе модерна* // Политическая экспертиза, том 6 №3. 2010.

> Martianov V.S. *Involution of the Elite in the Modern Society* // Politica Expertise, Vol. 6, No. 3. 2010.

Материалы круглого стола *"Экономика-язык-культура"* // Общественные науки и современность. 2000. №6.

> Proceedings of the round table *Economy-Language-Culture* // Obshchestvennye Nauki i Sovremennost'. 2000. №6.

Межуев В. *Традиция самовластия в современной России* // Свободная мысль. 2000. N 4.

> Mezhuev V. *The Tradition of Autocracy in Contemporary Russia* // Svobodnaya Mysl'. 2000. No. 4.

Межуев В.М. *Российская цивилизация -утопия или реальность* / Постиндустриальный мир и Россия. Отв. ред.: Хорос В.Г., Красильщиков В.А. М.: Эдиториал, УРСС, 2001.

> Mezhuev V.M. *The Russian Civilization—Utopia or Reality* / The Post-Industrial World and Russia. Publishing editors: Khoros V.G., Krasilshchikov V.A. M.: Editorial, URSS, 2001.

Мельников-Печерский П.И. *В лесах.* Кн.1. Горький, 1956.

> Melnikov-Pechersky P.I. *In the Forests.* Book 1. Gorky, 1956.

Менделеев Д. *Проблемы экономического развития России.* М.: Соцэкгиз, 1960.

> Mendeleev D. *Issues of the Economic Development of Russia.* M.: Sotsecgiz, 1960.

Миронов Б.Н. *Отношение к труду в дореволюционной России* // СОЦИС. 2001, №10.

    Mironov B.N. Attitude to Work in Pre-Revolutionary Russia // Sotsiologicheskie issledovaniia. 2001, No. 10.

Миронов Б.Н. *Социальная история России периода империи. XYIII - начало XX в.: Генезис личности, демократической семьи, гражданского общества правового государства. Тт.1-2. 2-е изд.* Спб.: Дмитрий Булавин, 2000.

    Mironov B.N. The Social History of Russia at the Times of the Empire (18th-early 20th Centuries): Genesis of the Individual, Democratic Family, Civil Society and the Rule of Law. Volumes 1–2. Second edition. SPb.: Dmitry Bulavin, 2000.

Моисеев Н.Н. *Судьба цивилизации. Путь Разума.* М.: МНЭПУ, 1998.

    Moiseev N.N. The Fate of Civilization. The Path of Reason. М.: MNEPU, 1998.

Моритани М. *Современная технология и экономическое развитие Японии.* М., 1986.

    Moritani M. Advanced Technology and the Japanese Contribution. M., 1986.

Мясникова Л. *Российский менталитет и управление* // Вопросы экономики. 2000, №8.

    Myasnikova L. Russian Mentality and Management // Voprosy Ekonomiki. 2000, No. 8.

Наумов А. *Хофстидово измерение России: влияние национальной культуры на управление бизнесом* // Менеджмент. 1996, N3.

    Naumov A. Hofstede's Dimension of Russia: Influence of the National Culture on Business Management // Management. 1996, No. 3.

Наумова Т. *Научная эмиграция из России* // Свободная мысль. 2004. №3.

    Naumova T. Science Emigration from Russia // Svobodnaya Mysl'. 2004. No. 3.

НТР и национальные процессы / Под ред. О. И. Шкаратана. М.: Наука, 1987.

    The Scientific-Technical Revolution and National Processes / Edited by O.I. Shkaratan. M.: Nauka, 1987.

Нуреев Р.М. *Экономический строй докапиталистических формаций.* Душанбе: "Дониш", 1989.

 Nureev R.M. *The Economic System of Pre-Capitalist Formations.* Dushanbe: Donish, 1989.

Орлова И.Б. *Современные цивилизации и Россия.* М., 2000.

 Orlova I.B. *Modern Civilizations and Russia.* M., 2000.

Павленко Ю.В. *Раннеклассовые общества: генезис и пути развития.* Киев, 1989.

 Pavlenko Yu.V. *Early Class Societies: Genesis and Ways of Development.* Kiev, 1989.

Павлов И.П. *О русском уме* // Литературная газета. 1991. №30.

 Pavlov I.P. *On the Russian Mind* // Literaturnaya Gazeta. 1991. No. 30.

Павлюткин В. *"Мышеловка" для академиков* // Мир за неделю. N12. 1999, 13-20 ноября.

 Pavlyutkin V. *"Mousetrap" for Academics* // Mir za Nedelyu. No. 12. 1999, 13–20 November.

Пайпс Р. *Собственность и свобода.* М.: Московская школа политических исследований, 2000.

 Pipes R. *Property and Freedom.* M.: Moscow School of Political Studies, 2000.

Паршев А.П. *Почему Россия не Америка. Книга для тех, кто остается здесь.* М.: Форум, 2001.

 Parshev A.P. *Why Russia is not America. A Book for Those Who Remain Here.* M.: Forum, 2001.

Пастухов В.Б. *Посткоммунизм как логическая фаза развития евразийской цивилизации* // Полис. 1992. №5-6.

 Pastukhov V.B. *Post-communism as a Logical Eurasian Civilization Development Phase* // Polis. 1992. No. 5–6.

Перепелкин Л.С. *Русский рабочий и современное производство* // Мир России. 1994, №2.

 Perepyolkin L.S. *The Russian Worker and Modern Production* // Mir Rossii. 1994, No. 2.

Перепелкин Л.С., Шкаратан О.И. *Экономический рост и национальное развитие* // Экономика и организация промышленного производства. 1988, №10.

    Perepyolkin L.S., Shkaratan O.I. *Economic Growth and National Development* // Economy and Industrial Production. 1988, No. 10.

Пивоваров Ю., Фурсов А. *Русская власть, русская система, русская история* / Красные холмы. Альманах. 1999. М.: Издательский дом "Городская собственность", 1999.

    Pivovarov Yu., Fursov A. *Russian Power, the Russian system, Russian History* / Krasnye Kholmy. Anthology. 1999. M.: Publishing house Gorodskaya Sobstvennost', 1999.

Пивоваров Ю., Фурсов А. *Русская Система и реформы* // Pro et Contra. Т.4, 1999, № 4.

    Pivovarov Yu., Fursov A. *The Russian System and Reforms* // Pro et Contra. V. 4, 1999, No. 4.

Пивоваров Ю.С. *Николай Данилевский: в русской культуре и в мировой науке* // Мир России, 1992, №1.

    Pivovarov Yu.S. *Nikolay Danilevsky: in Russian Culture and in World Science* // Mir Rossii, 1992, No. 1.

Пивоваров Ю.С., Фурсов А.И. *«Русская система» как попытка понимания русской истории* // ПОЛИС. 2001. №4.

    Pivovarov Yu.S., Fursov A.I. *"The Russian System" as an Attempt to Understand Russian History* // POLIS. 2001. No. 4.

Пименов А.В. *Дряхлый Восток и светлое будущее* // Мир России. 1999. N 1-2.

    Pimenov A.V. *The Decrepit Orient and the Bright Future* // Mir Rossii. 1999. No. 1–2.

Платонов О.А. *Русская цивилизация*. М.: "Рада", 1992.

    Platonov O.A. *The Russian Civilization*. M.: Rada, 1992.

Пронников В.А., Ладанов И.Д. *Японцы*. М.: Наука,1983.

    Pronnikov V.A., Ladanov I.D. *The Japanese*. M.: Nauka,1983.

Рашин А.Г. *Формирование рабочего класса России.* Москва: Соцэкгиз, 1958, Сс. 360-361.

Rashin A.G. *The Emergence of the Working Class in Russia.* Moscow: Sotsecgiz, 1958, pp. 360–361.

Рих А. *Хозяйственная этика.* Перевод с немецкого. М.: Посев, 1996.

Rich A. *Business Ethics.* Translation form German. M.: Posev, 1996.

Русские. Этнографические очерки / Отв. Ред.: Александров В.А., Власова И.В., Полищук Н.С. М.: Наука, 1999.

The Russians. Ethnographic Essays / Publishing editors: Alexandrov V.A., Vlasova I.V., Polishchuk N.S. M.: Nauka, 1999.

Русский узел евразийства: Восток в русской мысли. Сб. трудов евразийцев. М.: Беловодье, 1997.

The Russian knot of Eurasianism: The Orient in Russian thought. Collected studies of Eurasianists. M: Belovod'ye, 1997.

Сакаия Т. *Что такое Япония?* М.: Партнер Ко Лтд., 1992.

Sakaiya T. *What is Japan?* M.: Partner Co. Ltd., 1992.

Санто Б. *Инновация как средство экономического развития.* М.: Прогресс, 1990.

Santo B. *Innovation as a Tool for Economic Development.* M.: Progress, 1990.

Семенова А. *Проблемы инновационной системы России* // Вопросы экономики, 2005, №11.

Semyonova A. *The Problems of Russia's Innovation System* // Voprosy Ekonomiki, 2005, No. 11.

Собчик Л.Н. *Введение в психологию индивидуальности.* М., 1997.

Sobchik L.N. *Introduction to Personality Psychology.* M., 1997.

Супян В.Б. *Эволюция рабочей силы: качественные характеристики* // США: экономика, политика, идеология. 1990, №5.

Supyan V.B. *The Evolution of Labor Force: Qualitative Characteristics* // USA: Economy, Politics, Ideology. 1990, No. 5.

Сусоколов А.А. *Культура и обмен. Введение в экономическую антропологию.* М.: SPSL-«Русская панорама», 2006.

Susokolov A.A. *Culture and Exchange. Introduction to Economic Anthropology.* M.: SPSL-Russkaya Panorama, 2006.

Сусоколов А.А. *Русский этнос в XX веке: этапы кризиса экстенсивной культуры* // Мир России. 1994, №2.

    Susokolov A.A. *The Russian Ethnos in the Twentieth Century: Extensive Culture Crisis Stages* // Mir Rossii. 1994, No. 2.

Тойнби А. *Постижение истории.* М.: Прогресс, 1991.

    Toynbee A. *A Study of History.* M.: Progress, 1991.

Тойнби А. *Цивилизация перед судом истории.* Сборник. Спб: ЮВЕНТА, 1995.

    Toynbee A. *Civilization on Trial.* Collected works. SPb.: JUVENTA, 1995.

Трубецкой Н.С. *Наследие Чингисхана. Взгляд на русскую историю не с Запада, а с Востока.* М.: ЭКСМО, 2012.

    Trubetskoy N.S. *The Legacy of Genghis Khan. View of the Russian History from the East Rather than from the West.* M.: EXMO, 2012.

Урманов И. *Синергические связи как новая модель организации производства* // Мировая экономика и международные отношения. 2000, №3.

    Urmanov I. *Synergies as a New Model of Production Organization* // Mirovaya Ekonomika i Mezhdunarodnye Otnosheniya. 2000, No. 3.

Фальцман В. *Российское предпринимательство с позиций христианской морали* // Вопросы экономики. 2000, №8.

    Faltsman V. *Russian Business from the Perspective of Christian Morality* // Voprosy Ekonomiki. 2000, No. 8.

Федотова В.Г. *Модернизация другой Европы.* М.: ИФ РАН, 1997.

    Fedotova V.G. *Modernization of the Other Europe.* M.: IF RAN, 1997.

Фукуяма Ф. *Конец истории?* // Вопросы философии. 1990, №3.

    Fukuyama F. *The End of History?* // Voprosy Philosophii. 1990, No. 3.

Хакамада С. *Самоорганизация и стихийность: опыт сравнительного социально-психологического анализа Японии и России* // СОЦИС. 1999, №4.

    Hakamada S. *Self-Organization and Spontaneity: A Comparative Social and Psychological Analysis of Japan and Russia* // Sotsiologicheskie issledovaniia. 1999, No. 4.

Хантингтон С. *Столкновение цивилизаций и Россия* // Московские новости. 1995, №5, 22-29 января 1995г. С.5.

Huntington S. *The Clash of Civilizations and Russia* // Moscow News. 1995, No. 5, 22–29 January 1995. p. 5.

Хантингтон С. *Столкновение цивилизаций*. М.: ООО «Издательство АСТ», 2003.

Huntington S. *The Clash of Civilizations*. M.: OOO Izd-vo AST, 2003.

Хантингтон С. *Столкновение цивилизаций?* // ПОЛИС. 1994, №1.

Huntington S. *The Clash of Civilizations?* // POLIS. 1994, No. 1.

Харичев И. *Российская наука: быть или не быть?* // Знание – сила. 2005. №6. С. 32.

Kharichev I. *Russian Science: to be or not to be?* // Znanie – Sila. 2005. No. 6. p. 32.

Чубайс И. *Россия в поисках себя*. М.: Изд-во НОК "Музей бумаги", 1998.

Chubais I. *Russia in Search of Itself*. M.: Izd-vo NOK Muzei Bumagi, 1998.

Шкаратан О.И. и коллектив. *Социально-экономическое неравенство и его воспроизводство в современной России*. М.: ОЛМА МЕДИА ГРУПП, 2009

Shkaratan O.I. et al. *Socio-Economic Inequality and its Reproduction in Contemporary Russia*. M.: OLMA Media Group, 2009.

Шкаратан О.И. *Тип общества, тип социальных отношений. О современной России* // Мир России. 2000, №2.

Shkaratan O.I. *Type of Society, Type of Social Relations. On Contemporary Russia* // Mir Rossii. 2000, No. 2.

Шкаратан О.И., Карачаровский В.В. *Русская трудовая и управленческая культура: опыт исследования в контексте перспектив экономического развития* // Мир России. 2002. Т.11. №1.

Shkaratan O.I., Karacharovskiy V.V. *The Russian Work and Management Culture: A study in the Context of Economic Development Prospects* // Mir Rossii. 2002. V. 11. No. 1.

Шпенглер О. *Закат Европы. Очерки морфологии мировой истории*. Т.1. Гештальт и действительность. М.: Мысль, 1993.

Spengler O. *The Decline of the West. Essays on the Morphology of World History*. V. 1. Gestalt and Reality. M.: Mysl', 1993.

Юревич А. *Умные, но бедные: ученые в современной России.* М.: МОНФ, 1998.

Yurevich A. *Clever but Poor: Scientists in Modern Russia.* M.: MONF, 1998.

Юревич А., Цапенко И., Прихидько А. *Сколько и как зарабатывают наши ученые?* // Науковедение. 2004. №1.

Yurevich A., Tsapenko I., Prikhodko A. *How and How Much do our Scientists Earn?* // Naukovedeniye. 2004. No. 1.

Ядов В.А. (ред.). *Воздействие западных социокультурных образцов на социальные практики в России.* М.: ТАУС, 2009.

Yadov V.A. (ed.). *Impact of Western Socio-Cultural Patterns on Russian Social Practices.* M.: TAUS, 2009.

Яковенко И. *В чем ошибся Хантингтон? Монолог культуролога* // Знание-сила.2002, №1.

Yakovenko I. *What was Huntington's mistake? Monologue of a Cultural Studies Scholar* // Znanie-Sila. 2002, No. 1.

Berger C.R., Calabrese R.J. *Some Explorations in Initial Interaction and Beyond: Toward a Developmental Theory of Interpersonal Communication* // Human Communication Research. №1. 1975.

Berry J.W., Kim U., Minde T., Mok D. *Comparative Studies of Acculturative Stress* // International Migration Review. Vol.21. No.3. 1987;

Bhagat R.S. *Effects of Stressful Life Events on Individual Performance Effectiveness and Work Adjustment Processes within Organizational Settings: A Research Model* // Academy of Management Review. №8. 1983.

Black J.S. *Work Role Transitions: A Study of American Expatriate Managers in Japan* // Journal of International Business Studies. №19. 1988.

Black J.S., Gregersen H.B. *The Right Way to Manage Expats* // Harvard Business Review. Vol.77. No.2. 1999;

Black J.S., Mendenhall M. *Crosscultural Training Effectiveness: A Review and a Theoretical Framework for Future Research* // Academy of Management Review. №15. 1990;

Black J.S., Mendenhall M. *The U-Curve Adjustment Hypothesis Revisited: A Review and Theoretical Framework* // Journal of International Business Studies. №22. 1991;

Bochner S. *Cultures in Contact. Studies in Cross-Cultural Interaction.* Oxford: Pergamon Press, 1982;

Boonghee Yoo, Naveen Donthu, Tomasz Lenartowicz. *Measuring Hofstede's Five Dimentions of Cultural Values at the Individual Level: Development and Validation of CVSCALE* // Journal of International Consumer Marketing, 23: 193–210, 2011.

Caligiuri P., Phillips J., Lazarova M., Tarique I., Burgi P. *The Theory of Met Expectations Applied to Expatriate Adjustment: The Role of Cross-Cultural Training* // International Journal of Human Resource Management. Vol.12. No.3. 2001.

Caligiuri P.M. *Assessing Expatriate Success: Beyond Just "Being There"* / Saunders D.M., Aycan Z. (Eds.) New Approaches to Employment Management. Volume 4. Greenwich, CT: JAI Press, 1997;

Campbell R.W. *Soviet and post-Soviet Telecommunications: An Industry under Reform.* Boulder, Colorado. 1995.

Castells M. *The Information Age: Economy, Society and Culture. Volume I. The Rise of the Network Society.* Oxford: Blackwell Publishers, 1996, reprinted 1997.

Castells M. *The Information Age: Economy, Society and Culture. Vol. II. The Power of Identity.* Oxford: Blackwell Publishers, 1997.

Castells M. *The Information Age: Economy, Society and Culture. Vol. III. End of Millennium.* Oxford: Blackwell Publishers, 1998.

Cox T.H. *Cultural Diversity in Organizations: Theory, Research and Practice.* San Francisco: Berrett-Koehler, 1993.

Dabic M., Gonzalez-Loureiro M., Harvey M. *Evolving Research on Expatriates: What is 'Known' after Four Decades (1970–2012)* // The International Journal of Human Resource Management. 2013.

Fukuyama F. *The End of History and the Last Man.* L.-N.Y., 1992.

Fukuyama F. Trust. *The Social Virtues and the Creation of Prosperity.* N.Y.: Free Press, 1996.

Furnham A., Bochner S. *Culture Shock. Psychological Reactions to Unfamiliar Environments.* – London, New York: Methuen, 1986.

Hailey J. *The Expatriate Myth: Cross-Cultural Perceptions of Expatriate Managers* // International Executive. Vol.38. No.2. 1996.

Hall E.T. *The Hidden Dimension.* New York: Doubleday, 1966.

Huntington S. *The Clash of Civilization and the Remarking of World Order.* N.Y., 1996.

Hass J. *Power, Culture and Economic Change in Russia: to the Undiscovered Country of Post-Socialism, 1988–2008.* Routledge, 2012.

Hofstede G. *Culture's Consequences: Comparing Values, Behaviors, Institutions, and Organizations Across Nations.* Second Edition, Thousand Oaks CA: Sage Publications, 2001.

Hofstede G. *Culture's Consequences: International Differences in Work-Related Values.* Beverly Hills, CA: Sage Publications, 1980.

Holtbruegge D. (Ed.) *Cultural Adjustment of Expatriates. Theoretical Concepts and Empirical Studies.* Rainer Hampp Verlag, 2008.

Inkeles A. & Diamond L. *Personal Development and National Development: A Cross-National Perspective* // Quality of Life: Comparative Studies. Ed. By Szalai A. & Andrews F.M. L.: Sage Publications, 1980.

Inkeles A. & Smith D.M. *Becoming Modern: Individual Change in Six Developing Countries.* 3rd ed. Cambridge, MA.: Harvard University Press, 1982.

Inkeles A. *National Differences in Individual Modernity* // Comparative Studies in Sociology -Vol. 1. JAI Press, Inc., 1978.

Janssens M. *Intercultural Interaction: A Burden on International Managers?* // Journal of Organizational Behavior. Vol.16. 1995.

Kealey D.J., Protheroe D.R. *The Effectiveness of Cross-Cultural Training for Expatriates: An Assessment of the Literature on the Issue* // International Journal of Intercultural Relations. №2. 1996.

Kirchmeyer C., McLellan J. *Capitalizing on Ethnic Diversity: An Approach to Managing the Diverse Work Groups of the 1990s* // Canadian Journal of Administrative Sciences. №8. 1991;

Kraimer M.L., Wayne S.J., Jaworski R.A. *Sources of Support and Expatriate Performance: The Mediating Role of Expatriate Adjustment* // Personnel Psychology. №54. 2001;

Marquardt M.J., Horvath L. *Global Teams: How Top Multinationals Span Boundaries and Cultures with High-speed Teamwork.* Palo Alto, CA: Davies-Black, 2001.

Maznevski M.L. *Understanding our Differences: Performance in Decision-making Groups with Diverse Members* // Human Relations №47. 1994

McClelland D.C., Winter D.G. *Motivating Economic Achievement. Accelerating Economic Development through Psychological Training.* N.Y., 1960.

McEvoy G.M., Buller P.F. *Research for Practice: The Management of Expatriates* // Thunderbird International Business Review. Vol. 55. No.2. 2013.

Mendenhall G., Oddou G. *The Dimensions of Expatriate Acculturation: A Review* // Academy of Management Review. Vol. 10. 1985.

Merriam-Webster's Collegiate Dictionary. 11th Ed. Encyclopedia Britannica Company, 2004.

Merritt A. *Culture in the Cockpit: Do Hofstede's Dimensions Replicate?* // Journal of Cross-Cultural Psychology, Thousand Oaks; May 2000; Vol. 31.

Mol S., Born M., Willemsen M., Van der Molen H. *Predicting Expatriate Job Performance for Selection Purposes: A Quantitative Review* // Journal of Cross-Cultural Psychology. Vol. 36. No.5. 2005.

Mowshowitz A. *Virtual Organization* // Communication ACM. №40. 1997;

Murphy W.H. *Hofstede's National Culture as a Guide for Sales Practices Across Countries: The Case of a MNC's Sales Practices in Australia and New Zealand* // Australian Journal of Management, Sydney; Jun 1999; Vol. 24.

Ng E.S.W., Tung R.L. *Ethnocultural Diversity and Organizational Effectiveness: A Field Study* // The International Journal of Human Resource Management. №9. 1998.

Nicholson N. *A Theory of Work Role Transitions* // Administrative Science Quarterly. 1984. №29.

Oberg K. *Cultural Shock: Adjustment to New Cultural Environments* // Practical Anthropology. №7. 1960.

Parker B., McEvoy G. *Initial Examination of a Model of Intercultural Adjustment* // International Journal of Intercultural Relations. №17. 1993.

Porter M. E. *The Competitive Advantage of Nations.* N.Y., 1990.

Post-Fordism. A Reader / Ed. by Ash Amin. Oxford, 1994.

Saks A.M., Ashforth B.E. *Organizational Socialization: Making Sense of the Past and Present as a Prologue for the Future* // Journal of Vocational Behavior. №51. 1997.

Salk J.E. *National Culture, Networks, and Individual Influence in a Multinational Management Team* // Academy of Management Journal, Mississippi State; Apr 2000; Vol. 43.

Schumann J.H., Wangenheim F.v., Stringfellow A., Yang Zh., Blazevic V., Praxmarer S., Shainesh G., Komor M., Shannon R.M., Jiménez F.R. *Cross-Cultural Differences in the Effect of Received Word-of-Mouth Referral in Relational Service Exchange* // Journal of International Marketing. 2010.Vol. 18. № 3.

Selmer J. *To Train or Not to Train? European Expatriate Managers in China* // International Journal of Cross-Cultural Management. №2. 2002.

Shaiken H., Herzenberg S. *Automation and Global Production. Automobile Engine Production in Mexico, the United States and Canada.* San Diego, 1987.

Shamir B., Melnik Y. *Boundary Permeability as a Cultural Dimension. A Study of Cross Cultural Working Relations between Americans and Israelis in High-Tech Organizations* // International Journal of Cross-Cultural Management. №2. 2002.

Shay J.P., Baack S. *An Empirical Investigation of the Relationships between Modes and Degree of Expatriate Adjustment and Multiple Measures of Performance* // International Journal of Cross-Cultural Management. №6. 2006.

Snow C.C., Snell S.A., Davison S.C., Hambrick D.C. *Use Transnational Teams to Globalize your Company* // Organizational Dynamics. №32. 1996.

Sorokin P. *Social Philosophies of an Age of Crisis.* Boston, 1951.

Spence L.J., Petrick J.A. *Multinational Interview Decisions: Integrity Capacity and Competing Values* // Human Resource Management Journal, L., 2000. Vol. 10

The Political Economy of Japan: The Domestic Transformation / Ed. by Yamamura Kozo, Jasuba Yasukichi. Stanford, 1987. Vol.1.

Triandis H.C. *Culture and Social Behavior.* New York: McGraw-Hill. 1994.

Trompenaars F. *Riding the Waves of Culture: Understanding Diversity in Global Business.* New York: Irwin, 1994.

Tung R.L. *Managing Cross-National and Intra-National Diversity* // Human Resource Management. №32. 1993.

Tung R.L. *Selecting and Training of Personnel for Overseas Assignments* // Columbia Journal of World Business. №16. 1981;

Tung R.L. *Selection and Training Procedures of U.S., European, and Japanese Multinationals* // California Management Review. Vol.25. 1982.

Ulijn J. *Innovation, Corporate Strategy, and Cultural Context: What is the Mission for International Business Communication?* //The Journal of Business Communication, Urbana; Jul 2000; Vol. 37.

Veiga J. *Measuring Organizational Culture Clashes: A Two-Nation Post-Hoc Analysis of a Cultural Compatibility Index* // Human Relations, New York; Apr 2000, Vol. 53.

Ward C., Bochner S., Furnham A. *The Psychology of Culture Shock.* 2nd Edition. Philadelphia, PA: Routledge, 2001.

Watson W.E., Kumar K., Michaelson L.K. Cultural Diversity's Impact on Interaction Process and Performance: Comparing Homogeneous and Diverse Task Groups // Academy of Management Journal. №36. 1993.

Zimmerman A., Holman D., Sparrow P. *Unravelling Adjustment Mechanisms: Adjustment of German Expatriates to Intercultural Interactions, Work, and Living Conditions in the People's Republic of China* // International Journal of Cross-Cultural Management. Vol.3. No.1. 2003.

Information about the authors

Vladimir V. Karacharovskiy, PhD (candidate of sciences) in Economics, associate professor, deputy head of the Laboratory for Comparative Analysis of Development in Post-Socialist Countries, National Research University Higher School of Economics. Author and co-author of studies on the national model of technological modernization, social efficiency of business activities, and the national culture as a factor of economic development. Publications include: Business Communications and Cultural Distance Between Russian and Foreign Professionals (2015), Culture and Modernization in the Mirror of Interaction Between Russian and Foreign Professionals in Multinational Work Teams in Russia (2014), Social Efficiency of Technological Modernization in Russia (2013), The Effect of Innovations in the Russian Economy at the Macro and Meso Level (2012), Economic Motivation and Innovative Processes (2011), The Actor of Technological Modernization in Russia: Private Business Interests vs. Strategic Economic Objectives (2009), Capital Concentration and Technological Modernization of the Russian Economy (2006), The Russian Work and Management Culture: A Study in the Context of Economic Development Prospects (2002), High-Tech Development and the Liberal Paradigm (2003), The Russian High-Tech Industrial Complex: Political and Economic Imperatives and Development Safety and Security (2001), and others.

Ovsey I. Shkaratan, Doctor of History, tenured professor, head of the Laboratory for Comparative Analysis of Development in Post-Socialist Countries, National Research University Higher School of Economics; Honored Scholar of the Russian Federation; has been awarded the Order of Friendship. One of the founders of the Russian school of research in industrial sociology and social stratification, author of the concept that the Russian society is a late etacratic society. Founder and first Editor-in-Chief (1992–2013) of the prestigious Russian academic journal *Mir Rossii*. Author, co-author, and editor of the following books: Russia as a Civilization: Information for Reflection (2015); Sociology of Inequality. Theory and Reality (2012); Socio-Economic Inequality and its Reproduction in Contemporary Russia

(2009); Social Stratification in Russian and Eastern Europe (2006), The Russian Order: Vector of Change (2004), The State Social Policy and the Strategy for the Survival of Households (2003), Work and Welfare in the New Russia (2000), Ethno-Social Problems of the City (1986); The Worker and the Engineer. Social Factors of Labor Performance (1985); Industrial Enterprise. Sociological Essays (1978); The Scientific-Technical Revolution, the Working Class, and the Intelligentsia (1973), and others. Scientific papers have been translated into English, German, Italian, Japanese, Chinese, Polish, Bulgarian, and other languages.

Gordey A. Yastrebov, PhD (candidate of sciences) in Sociology, senior research fellow at the Laboratory for Comparative Analysis of Development in Post-Socialist Countries, National Research University Higher School of Economics; deputy Editor-in-Chief of the *Mir Rossii* journal. Author and co-author of several studies on social inequality and social mobility. Publications include: Russia as a Civilization: Information for Reflection (2015), Social Mobility in Post-Soviet Russia: A New Perspective (2014), The Socio-Economic Status of Families and School as Competing Factors of Educational Opportunities: The Situation in Russia (2014); Socio-Economic Inequality and its Reproduction in Contemporary Russia (2009), and others.

Appendix 1.
Qualitative research tools [221]

1A. Interview guide for interviewing Russian professionals working together with foreign professionals (expatriates) in multinational teams

I. INTRODUCTION MODULE

Before proceeding to the main part of the interview, let me ask you a few biographical questions. What education have you received and where? Please say a few words about your previous work experience? Were you born in Russia or elsewhere? What is your ethnic origin? Who do you consider yourself to be ethnically? What city were you born in? What was your occupation before you joined a multinational company? Is this your first employment experience in a multinational company or not? Do you have experience working abroad?

II. SOCIALIZATION MODULE

In general, do you easily find common language with your foreign colleagues—expatriates? In your opinion, to what extent is the distinction in everyday communication and behavior (outside of work) between Russian and western colleagues discernible? Do you hang out together (eat out or picnic together, etc.)? If yes, how often? If no, why not? Is it because the Russians have no desire for such socializing or, on the contrary, the expatriates are wary of it? Or is it because neither the ones nor the others have any common interests outside of work?

Imagine that as of tomorrow there will be no more expatriates in your team. Will you be relieved or, on the contrary, you will feel that something familiar and dear has disappeared? Can you say that you have become friends with any of your foreign colleagues?

In general, as people, outside of the office, how different are Russians and the foreigners you know? Maybe there are no essential dif-

---

[221] The interview guides have been developed by the team of the NRU HSE Laboratory for Comparative Analysis of Post-Socialist Development – O.I. Shkaratan, V.V. Karacharovskiy, G.A. Yastrebov, A.N. Krasilova, and S.A. Korotaev.

ferences and all modern people are alike? Or is there something fundamentally different—in the approach to life, to leisure, maybe, in political views, in the attitude to certain socially significant matters (charity, concern for one's homeland, attitude towards the authorities, towards other people, etc.)?

Going back to the time when you still had no experience working abroad or any extended experience of joint work with foreigners in Russia, can you say that since then, interaction with foreign colleagues has changed you as a person and as a personality? For example, have your habits or beliefs changed? Your attitude to Russia, to foreigners, and to the people around in general? What specifically has changed and how, and what do you believe is the underlying reason? Can you say that you have become slightly more like your foreign colleagues? If yes, that in what?

III. BUSINESS MODULE

Let us now focus on your current job. What is your role in the company? What is your field of responsibility? What do you do? Do you have subordinates? Do you have superiors? What is the approximate percentage of western professionals in your company? At what levels of the organizational hierarchy are they mostly concentrated? What are their roles and functions? How are responsibilities split between Russians and foreigners in your company? Who do you believe "sets the tone" in the daily work of your team—Russians or foreigners?

Is your direct superior a foreigner (expatriate) or a Russian? Can you compare the management styles of Russians with that of foreigners working in Russia? What is the difference? Please provide some examples from your company, from your personal experience—something you have participated in or witnessed?

How would you generally characterize the attitude of your foreign colleagues towards yourself? Do they show you sufficient respect? Can you say that you are an authority for them, that they consider you as a "senior" and in some respects more experienced colleague? Does this sometimes trigger a negative attitude towards you?

Who do you most often interact with—Russians or your foreign colleagues? How direct is such interaction—you work in the same room, communicate via e-mails or other means of communication? What language do you usually communicate in, exchange assignments and ideas? Do you think language is a serious barrier to communication, to finding common ground? Did you experience any situations when language was the cause of any incidents, errors or misunderstandings?

Is it sometimes difficult to convey the sense of certain assignments and recommendations to your foreign colleagues? Can you in principle influence the approach of your foreign colleagues to their job, and how often does this need arise? How adequately do foreign colleagues take your requests, advice or tasks that you assign them? Have you ever managed to convince your foreign colleagues of something they initially did not agree with, and what should have been done otherwise according to their opinion or experience? Please describe such cases in detail. The key issue is how you managed to convince your foreign colleagues? How often do you have to inform your superiors in such situations and involve them in resolving such problems? Has positive settlement of these conflict situations ever resulted in any substantial improvements in the overall performance (for example, higher efficiency, meeting project deadlines, etc.)? Was it possible to say in such situations that your colleagues had "learned their lesson" and henceforth acted in line with the rules and procedures outlined by you or the executive management?

Does lack of understanding between Russian and foreign colleagues often trigger conflicts? Can you provide examples of such conflicts from your personal experience and tell a little more about them? What do you think, to what extent the misunderstanding was caused by personal features of the people involved and to what—by their belonging to different cultures?

Can you say that your foreign colleagues have certain common features? Please specify! In your opinion, what is positive in these features and what is negative? Do any of them ever irritate you? Are there any spheres of activity or situations where foreign employees cope better with their tasks and assignments than their Russian colleagues? Can you provide some examples and tell us more about them? What tasks, do you think, should never be assigned to Russians? For what reason? Is it because of their education, experience or some other factors?

To summarize, can you name the main business qualities of your foreign colleagues that you believe hamper the effective/coordinated work of the team or the enterprise in general? Conversely, which features of your foreign colleagues promote effective/coordinated work?

In general, can you say that you manage your time more efficiently than your foreign colleagues or, vice versa, foreigners are often more efficient than Russians? If yes, please explain why (please specify what you mean by "efficiency"). Does it have to do with how Russians and foreigners organize their work?

What advantages do you see in working in a multicultural team, when Russians and foreigners work side by side? For you personally? For your department? For the entire company? What do you think, would the activity of your company, its internal functioning and general competitiveness change, if it were to employ only Russians? And if it were to consist entirely of representatives of the western culture? Would you feel significantly more at ease working in such a company?

Can you say that joint work with foreigners changes the Russians or changes the foreigners themselves? In your opinion, do foreigners employed in Russia become more "Russian" in terms of their approach to work, their work behavior, and manner in dealing with business issues? Or, vice versa, are the Russians more likely to change under the influence of foreign professionals with whom they have to work side by side many years? Please provide examples from your personal experience!

Has work with foreigners changed you personally in any way? Please name two or three major business qualities that were not characteristic of you and which you acquired while working with your foreign colleagues? If such qualities exist, to what extent are they forced and to what—natural, meaning how useful are these qualities for you professionally, regardless of working in this specific team or entity? Would you maintain the acquired business qualities if you were to continue working in Russia but ceased interacting with expatriates?

IV. CREATIVITY MODULE

Do you consider your work creative, innovative? What do you mean by that?

How often do you come up with creative, unusual solutions for certain tasks assigned to you under various projects? Can you provide examples of such solutions or innovative proposals? In your opinion, how radical, how innovative were these solutions and how did they affect the outcome (e.g., resulted in higher sales revenues, contributed to cost-cutting, etc.)? Were these solutions spontaneous, i.e., initiated by you, or the task assigned to you initially implied such an innovative, creative approach?

Can you describe situations or circumstances that triggered creative solutions (e.g., brainstorming with a colleague, contemplating the issue by yourself, by chance over a glass of beer in a bar, etc.)? Tell us about such situations focusing on details that you believe facilitated or hampered the emergence of such solutions. How do Russians and expatriates behave in such situations? In general, how often do your colleagues (Russians and expatriates) come up with creative solutions? Could you please recall such situations and tell us more about them? How often are such solutions *implemented*? Your own? Those of your colleagues?

How favorable is your corporate environment for realizing your creative potential? What hurdles do you see? How do the executives and colleagues take your ideas and proposals? For executives—how often do your subordinates come up with such proposals? Can you recall such cases? Do you encourage such behavior? In what way?

V.   PROJECTIONS MODULE

What are your plans for the nearest future? Do you plan to work in Russia some time longer or do you intend to leave? If you intend to leave, what is the reason? Under otherwise equal conditions, would you accept a foreign assignment, if you were offered one? Maybe you are already considering the option of going to work and live abroad n the next two to three years? If yes, then why? What does not suit you in Russia? If not, this is also interesting. You never wanted to work abroad, you think it is unnatural, or you simply feel no urge to go there? Do you have a feeling that you cannot fully realize yourself in Russia, that you would be able to achieve more abroad? Would you prefer your children to work in Russia or abroad? What is the key argument for you in this matter?

THANK YOU!

1B. Interview guide for interviewing foreign professionals (expatriates) working together with Russian professionals in multinational teams

I. BIOGRAPHY AND MOTIVATIONS MODULE

Basic biographical information.
Take note of the respondent's *age, sex, home country, history of education, history of earlier employment* (prior to assignment in Russia), *earlier assignments in other countries* (expat experience).
Record milestone events only (devote no longer than 10 minutes to this part of the interview)

Length of stay and arrival motives.
How long have you been working in Russia?
Have you chosen to come here or have you been assigned?
Why have you chosen to come here? Why is working in Russia so attractive? [*the main motive—salary, professional experience, career prospects, curiosity, etc.*]
Have you had any connections with Russia before you came here? [*friends, past experience, curiosity, etc.*]
Have you ever been to Russia before your current assignment? [*as a tourist or for business purposes*]
Is your work mostly *seasonal* (you come here occasionally) or you stay here *all the time*?

II. SOCIALIZATION MODULE

Expectations and stereotypes, special training.
Have you gone through any kind of special training before you came to Russia? [*by special training we mean certain things making it easier for you to adapt to your current roles and life in a new country*]
Can you explain what this training was about?
What did you learn or were taught?
How useful and necessary do you find this training?

Have you had any *stereotypes* or *expectations* about living and working in Russia before you came here? [*what problems and attitudes did you expect to come across?*]
Have any of them changed upon your arrival here? Which ones? How?
Do you have any *strong impressions* about Russia? Please state positive and negative ones [*e.g. people being unfriendly in the streets; traffic being weirdly organized, etc.*]

Family.
Do you have a family? Do they live with you here, in Russia?
What is their attitude towards your decision to work in Russia?

Integration into the local environment.
In general, how well do you consider yourself integrated into the local environment? Do you generally feel comfortable living here? Is something lacking compared to the lifestyle you had in your home country?
Who helped you get around and settle different everyday problems? [problems like *finding an apartment to rent, getting medical treatment, settling various legal issues concerning your stay, etc.*] You, your friends, colleagues, your company?
Does it ever grow uncomfortable to the point that you want to leave?

Daily interactions.
Do you have Russian friends? How many?
How often do you communicate or hang out together?
How do you usually spend your free time here? How do you socialize? Does it help you adapt better?
Maybe you prefer associating with other foreign colleagues (expatriates) like yourself?
Is it easier to find common language with other expatriates or with Russians?
In your opinion, to what extent is the distinction in everyday communication and behavior between "Russians" and "Westerners" [*or others if appropriate*] discernible?

Attitudes.
How would you characterize your attitude towards Russia and its people in general?
What about Russian authorities (the interview is strictly confidential!)?
To how life is organized here? To political issues? Do you consider yourself a part of what is happening here (recall recent meetings and demonstrations) or do you prefer to keep a distance?

Change.
Has anything changed in your attitudes, habits or perceptions since you came to Russia for your assignment? Can you tell us a little bit about these changes?
Have you become more "Russian"? What do you mean by that?

III. BUSINESS MODULE

Let us now focus on your current job.
What is your role in the company? What is your field of responsibility? What do you do?
Do you have subordinates? How many?
Do you have superiors?
How many other highly skilled foreign professionals (expatriates) work in your company?
At what levels of the organizational hierarchy are they mostly concentrated?
What are their roles and functions? Do they differ from yours?

The attitude of Russian colleagues.
How would you generally characterize the attitude of your Russian colleagues towards yourself? [is it *respectful / suspicious / neutral / indifferent / hostile?*]
Are you an authority for them?
Do they consider you as somewhat more experienced and knowledgeable than themselves?
Do they often ask your advice?

Work interactions.
Who do you most often interact with—Russians or other foreign colleagues?
How direct is such interaction—you work in the same room, communicate via e-mails or other means of communication?

Language and understanding.
What language do you usually communicate in? [*to convey ideas and assignments to others in your company*]
Is insufficient knowledge of a common (English?) language a serious problem in finding common ground between colleagues? Can you recall some problematic or, perhaps, embarrassing situations when language was the cause? Can you give an example?
Is it difficult to make other people in the company understand what you want from them?
Do they often get the correct sense of your assignments, or do you have to be very careful and precise in explaining what you want?
There must be cases when you and your Russian colleagues misunderstand each other. Has this ever grown into a *conflict*? Can you recall such examples and tell us about them? To what extent, do you think, the conflict was triggered by "cultural" or "personal" reasons? Why?

Wrongdoings.
If you see a Russian colleague doing something wrong or inefficiently, can you persuade him or her to do it otherwise?
How often does it happen and how do you succeed?
How adequately do Russians react to your critique and suggestions?
Do you often bring such issues to your seniors when it becomes a real problem? How efficient is that?
What forms of influence do you consider most efficient? What incentives do you provide?

Compliance with corporate standards.
How well do you think Russians comply with organizational standards and corporate ethics in your company?
What about you? Are these standards and ethics in any away different from those typical in your country?

Qualities of Russians.
Is it possible to say that some qualities or traits are typical of Russians? Which ones? [*e.g. sense of responsibility, approach to time management, work etc.*]
In your opinion, what is positive in these qualities and what is negative? Do any of them ever irritate you?

Time attitudes and efficiency.
Can you say that you manage your time more efficiently than your Russian colleagues? Explain why.
What, in your case, do you mean by "more efficiently"?
Does it have to do with how you organize your work? Or is it because you are more experienced/have better education/are more capable/whatever?
Can you recall situations when Russians did better than their foreign colleagues in their *tasks and assignments*?
What where those *tasks and situations*?
What tasks, do you think, should never be assigned to Russians? For what reason? Is it because of their education, experience or some other factors?

Perceptions about general performance.
What advantages do you see in working in a multicultural team, when Russians and foreigners work side by side?
Can you distinguish between personal advantages (special experience, etc.) and advantages for the company?
What do you think, how would your company and its competitiveness change if it were monocultural (i.e. if there were only Russians or foreigners working in it)?
Would you feel more comfortable if it were that way?

Change.
Now let's go back to the beginning of your assignment here, in Russia.
Can you remember any crucial turns and changes since then in your professional life?
Were there any promotions? Have you gained some vital experience? Have you become better adjusted to the local environment?

Do you now find more understanding among Russians in general, and your Russian colleagues in particular?
Has your attitude towards work, career, and company changed since then?
What was the cause of this change?
Can you say that something has changed in your company (or in your team) due to your influence?
If you were asked about the major results and achievements of your work in Russia, which ones would you name (two or three most important ones)?

IV. CREATIVITY MODULE

Do you consider your work requires such qualities as creativity? If yes, what do you mean by that?
Is there any particular way in which you or your company stimulate creativity in your staff?
Is your company/department suited for creative workers? Why? Do you see any problems?
Do you implement in Russia any of the strategies or practices common in your home country, but lacking here? Does it count as innovations?
Can you describe situations or circumstances that triggered creative solutions? [*e.g., brainstorming with colleagues, thinking about it alone by yourself, during informal communications, etc.*] Tell us about such situations focusing on details, which you believe facilitated or hampered the emergence of such solutions.
How do Russians and expatriates behave in such situations?
How often, in general, do Russians and expatriates come up with creative solutions to their tasks and assignments?
How often are such solutions implemented (i.e., find understanding among other colleagues and seniors)? How are they appreciated?

V. PROJECTIONS MODULE

What are your plans for the nearest future?
Do you plan to work in Russia a little longer or do you intend to leave soon? How soon?
If you intend to leave, what is the reason? Is it because of your contract or your own considerations? Other factors?

Would you return to your home country, if you were offered the same rewards and prospects that you have here? Why?

Where do you feel you (your skills and experience) are most required (and valued)—here or back in your home country?

Are you going back to your home country or taking an assignment somewhere else?

Have you ever considered staying in Russia "for good", i.e. buying a house, opening your own business?

Is there anything that keeps you from doing so? Personal reasons?

Is there anything in Russia that could be attractive to your compatriots?

THANK YOU! [Ask for another potential interviewee, if appropriate]

Appendix 2.
CVSCALE methodology in the original and translated into Russian

2A. Scale items in the original [222]

POWER DISTANCE

To what extent do you agree or disagree with the following statements? *Please rate the statements from 1 to 5, where 1 corresponds to a strong disagreement and 5 corresponds to your full agreement with the statement.*

	Strongly disagree	Disagree	Neutral	Agree	Strongly agree
1. People in higher positions should make most decisions without consulting people in lower positions	1	2	3	4	5
2. People in higher positions should not ask the opinions of people in lower positions too frequently	1	2	3	4	5
3. People in higher positions should avoid social interaction with people in lower positions	1	2	3	4	5
4. People in lower positions should not disagree with decisions by people in higher positions	1	2	3	4	5
5. People in higher positions should not delegate important tasks to people in lower positions	1	2	3	4	5

---

[222] The scale is provided from: Boonghee Yoo, Naveen Donthu, Tomasz Lenartowicz. *Measuring Hofstede's Five Dimensions of Cultural Values at the Individual Level: Development and Validation of CVSCALE //* Journal of International Consumer Marketing, 23: 193–210, 2011.

UNCERTAINTY AVOIDANCE

To what extent do you agree or disagree with the following statements? *Please rate the statements from 1 to 5, where 1 corresponds to a strong disagreement and 5 corresponds to your full agreement with the statement.*

	Strongly disagree	Disagree	Neutral	Agree	Strongly agree
1. It is important to have instructions spelled out in detail so that I always know what I'm expected to do	1	2	3	4	5
2. It is important to closely follow instructions and procedures	1	2	3	4	5
3. Rules and regulations are important because they inform me of what is expected of me	1	2	3	4	5
4. Standardized work procedures are helpful	1	2	3	4	5
5. Instructions for operations are important	1	2	3	4	5

COLLECTIVISM

To what extent do you agree or disagree with the following statements? *Please rate the statements from 1 to 5, where 1 corresponds to a strong disagreement and 5 corresponds to your full agreement with the statement.*

	Strongly disagree	Disagree	Neutral	Agree	Strongly agree
1. Individuals should sacrifice self-interest for the group (either at school or the work place)	1	2	3	4	5
2. Individuals should stick with the group even through difficulties	1	2	3	4	5

3. Group welfare is more important than individual rewards	1	2	3	4	5
4. Group success is more important than individual success	1	2	3	4	5
5. Individuals should only pursue their goals after considering the welfare of the group	1	2	3	4	5
6. Group loyalty should be encouraged even if individual goals suffer	1	2	3	4	5

MASCULINITY

To what extent do you agree or disagree with the following statements? *Please rate the statements from 1 to 5, where 1 corresponds to a strong disagreement and 5 corresponds to your full agreement with the statement.*

	Strongly disagree	Disagree	Neutral	Agree	Strongly agree
1. It is more important for men to have a professional career than it is for women	1	2	3	4	5
2. Men usually solve problems with logical analysis; women usually solve problems with intuition	1	2	3	4	5
3. Solving difficult problems usually requires an active, forcible approach, which is typical of men	1	2	3	4	5
4. There are some jobs that a man can always do better than a woman	1	2	3	4	5

LONG TERM ORIENTATION

To what extent do you consider the following values as important or unimportant to yourself? *Please rate the statements from 1 to 5, where 1 corresponds to "very unimportant" and 5 corresponds to "very important".*

	Very unimportant	Unimportant	No opinion	Important	Very important
1. Careful management of money (Thrift)	1	2	3	4	5
2. Going on resolutely in spite of opposition (Persistence)	1	2	3	4	5
3. Personal steadiness and stability	1	2	3	4	5
4. Long-term planning	1	2	3	4	5
5. Giving up today's fun for success in the future	1	2	3	4	5
6. Working hard for success in the future	1	2	3	4	5

2B. Russian translation of scale items

ШКАЛА «ДИСТАНЦИЯ ВЛАСТИ» / POWER DISTANCE

Насколько Вы согласны со следующими утверждениями?
Оцените каждое суждение по шкале от 1 до 5, где 1 – «Абсолютно не согласен», 5 – «Абсолютно согласен».

	Абсолютно не согласен	Скорее не согласен	Может быть да, может быть нет	Скорее согласен	Абсолютно согласен
1. Большую часть решений руководители должны принимать, не консультируясь с подчиненными	1	2	3	4	5
2. Руководители не должны слишком часто интересоваться мнением подчиненных	1	2	3	4	5
3. Руководителям следует избегать сближения с подчиненными	1	2	3	4	5
4. Подчиненным не следует подвергать сомнению решения руководителей	1	2	3	4	5
5. Руководители не должны поручать ответственные задачи подчиненным	1	2	3	4	5

ШКАЛА «ИЗБЕГАНИЕ НЕОПРЕДЕЛЕННОСТИ» / UNCERTAINTY AVOIDANCE

Насколько Вы согласны со следующими утверждениями? *Оцените каждое суждение по шкале от 1 до 5, где 1 – «Абсолютно не согласен», 5 – «Абсолютно согласен».*

	Абсолютно не согласен	Скорее не согласен	Может быть да, может быть нет	Скорее согласен	Абсолютно согласен
1. Для меня важно, чтобы инструкции были предельно четкими, чтобы я точно знал, чего от меня хотят	1	2	3	4	5
2. Во всем необходимо четко следовать инструкциям и процедурам	1	2	3	4	5
3. Правила и установленные нормы очень важны, потому что по ним я могу сориентироваться, чего от меня ждут	1	2	3	4	5
4. Стандартизация труда полезна	1	2	3	4	5
5. В работе важны инструкции	1	2	3	4	5

ШКАЛА «КОЛЛЕКТИВИЗМ» / COLLECTIVISM

Насколько Вы согласны со следующими утверждениями?
Оцените каждое суждение по шкале от 1 до 5, где 1 – «Абсолютно не согласен», 5 – «Абсолютно согласен».

	Абсолютно не согласен	Скорее не согласен	Может быть да, может быть нет	Скорее согласен	Абсолютно согласен
1. Люди должны жертвовать собственными интересами ради групповых/коллективных интересов	1	2	3	4	5
2. Люди не должны отделять себя от коллектива как бы ни было трудно	1	2	3	4	5
3. Благополучие группы/коллектива важнее индивидуального благополучия	1	2	3	4	5
4. Групповой/коллективный успех гораздо важнее индивидуального успеха	1	2	3	4	5
5. Люди могут преследовать собственные цели только тогда, когда достигнуты групповые/коллективные цели	1	2	3	4	5
6. Верность групповым/коллективным интересам должна поощряться даже в ущерб индивидуальным интересам	1	2	3	4	5

ШКАЛА «МАСКУЛИННОСТЬ» / MASCULINITY

Насколько Вы согласны со следующими утверждениями? *Оцените каждое суждение по шкале от 1 до 5, где 1 – «Абсолютно не согласен», 5 – «Абсолютно согласен».*

	Абсолютно не согласен	Скорее не согласен	Может быть да, может быть нет	Скорее согласен	Абсолютно согласен
1. Для мужчин профессиональная карьера важнее, чем для женщин	1	2	3	4	5
2. Мужчины обычно решают проблемы, руководствуясь логикой; женщины обычно решают проблемы, руководствуясь интуицией	1	2	3	4	5
3. Решение серьезных проблем обычно требует активного, силового подхода, который типичен для мужчин	1	2	3	4	5
4. Есть виды работ, которые мужчина всегда сделает лучше, чем женщина	1	2	3	4	5

ШКАЛА «ДОЛГОСРОЧНАЯ ОРИЕНТАЦИЯ» / LONG TERM ORIENTATION

Оцените нижеследующие установки/качества по степени их важности с Вашей точки зрения. *Используйте шкалу от 1 до 5, где 5 – «Очень важно», 1 – «Совершенно не важно».*

	Совершенно не важно	Неважно	Ни то, чтобы важно, ни то, чтобы не важно	Важно	Очень важно
1. Бережливость (по отношению к деньгам), экономность	1	2	3	4	5
2. Оставаться твердым и решительным, несмотря на противодействие (Стойкость)	1	2	3	4	5
3. Уравновешенность, постоянство характера	1	2	3	4	5
4. Планировать, ориентируясь на долгосрочную перспективу	1	2	3	4	5
5. Отказ от сегодняшних удовольствий ради успеха в будущем	1	2	3	4	5
6. Упорный труд ради успеха в будущем	1	2	3	4	5

SOVIET AND POST-SOVIET POLITICS AND SOCIETY

Edited by Dr. Andreas Umland

ISSN 1614-3515

1   Андреас Умланд (ред.)
    Воплощение Европейской
    конвенции по правам человека в
    России
    Философские, юридические и
    эмпирические исследования
    ISBN 3-89821-387-0

2   Christian Wipperfürth
    Russland – ein vertrauenswürdiger
    Partner?
    Grundlagen, Hintergründe und Praxis
    gegenwärtiger russischer Außenpolitik
    Mit einem Vorwort von Heinz Timmermann
    ISBN 3-89821-401-X

3   Manja Hussner
    Die Übernahme internationalen Rechts
    in die russische und deutsche
    Rechtsordnung
    Eine vergleichende Analyse zur
    Völkerrechtsfreundlichkeit der Verfassungen
    der Russländischen Föderation und der
    Bundesrepublik Deutschland
    Mit einem Vorwort von Rainer Arnold
    ISBN 3-89821-438-9

4   Matthew Tejada
    Bulgaria's Democratic Consolidation
    and the Kozloduy Nuclear Power Plant
    (KNPP)
    The Unattainability of Closure
    With a foreword by Richard J. Crampton
    ISBN 3-89821-439-7

5   Марк Григорьевич Меерович
    Квадратные метры, определяющие
    сознание
    Государственная жилищная политика в
    СССР. 1921 – 1941 гг
    ISBN 3-89821-474-5

6   Andrei P. Tsygankov, Pavel
    A.Tsygankov (Eds.)
    New Directions in Russian
    International Studies
    ISBN 3-89821-422-2

7   Марк Григорьевич Меерович
    Как власть народ к труду приучала
    Жилище в СССР – средство управления
    людьми. 1917 – 1941 гг.
    С предисловием Елены Осокиной
    ISBN 3-89821-495-8

8   David J. Galbreath
    Nation-Building and Minority Politics
    in Post-Socialist States
    Interests, Influence and Identities in Estonia
    and Latvia
    With a foreword by David J. Smith
    ISBN 3-89821-467-2

9   Алексей Юрьевич Безугольный
    Народы Кавказа в Вооруженных
    силах СССР в годы Великой
    Отечественной войны 1941-1945 гг.
    С предисловием Николая Бугая
    ISBN 3-89821-475-3

10 Вячеслав Лихачев и Владимир
    Прибыловский (ред.)
    Русское Национальное Единство,
    1990-2000. В 2-х томах
    ISBN 3-89821-523-7

11 Николай Бугай (ред.)
    Народы стран Балтии в условиях
    сталинизма (1940-е – 1950-е годы)
    Документированная история
    ISBN 3-89821-525-3

12 Ingmar Bredies (Hrsg.)
    Zur Anatomie der Orange Revolution
    in der Ukraine
    Wechsel des Elitenregimes oder Triumph des
    Parlamentarismus?
    ISBN 3-89821-524-5

13 Anastasia V. Mitrofanova
    The Politicization of Russian
    Orthodoxy
    Actors and Ideas
    With a foreword by William C. Gay
    ISBN 3-89821-481-8

14 Nathan D. Larson
Alexander Solzhenitsyn and the
Russo-Jewish Question
ISBN 3-89821-483-4

15 Guido Houben
Kulturpolitik und Ethnizität
Staatliche Kunstförderung im Russland der
neunziger Jahre
Mit einem Vorwort von Gert Weisskirchen
ISBN 3-89821-542-3

16 Leonid Luks
Der russische „Sonderweg"?
Aufsätze zur neuesten Geschichte Russlands
im europäischen Kontext
ISBN 3-89821-496-6

17 Евгений Мороз
История «Мёртвой воды» – от
страшной сказки к большой
политике
Политическое неоязычество в
постсоветской России
ISBN 3-89821-551-2

18 Александр Верховский и Галина
Кожевникова (ред.)
Этническая и религиозная
интолерантность в российских СМИ
Результаты мониторинга 2001-2004 гг.
ISBN 3-89821-569-5

19 Christian Ganzer
Sowjetisches Erbe und ukrainische
Nation
Das Museum der Geschichte des Zaporoger
Kosakentums auf der Insel Chortycja
Mit einem Vorwort von Frank Golczewski
ISBN 3-89821-504-0

20 Эльза-Баир Гучинова
Помнить нельзя забыть
Антропология депортационной травмы
калмыков
С предисловием Кэролайн Хамфри
ISBN 3-89821-506-7

21 Юлия Лидерман
Мотивы «проверки» и «испытания»
в постсоветской культуре
Советское прошлое в российском
кинематографе 1990-х годов
С предисловием Евгения Марголита
ISBN 3-89821-511-3

22 Tanya Lokshina, Ray Thomas, Mary
Mayer (Eds.)
The Imposition of a Fake Political
Settlement in the Northern Caucasus
The 2003 Chechen Presidential Election
ISBN 3-89821-436-2

23 Timothy McCajor Hall, Rosie Read
(Eds.)
Changes in the Heart of Europe
Recent Ethnographies of Czechs, Slovaks,
Roma, and Sorbs
With an afterword by Zdeněk Salzmann
ISBN 3-89821-606-3

24 Christian Autengruber
Die politischen Parteien in Bulgarien
und Rumänien
Eine vergleichende Analyse seit Beginn der
90er Jahre
Mit einem Vorwort von Dorothée de Nève
ISBN 3-89821-476-1

25 Annette Freyberg-Inan with Radu
Cristescu
The Ghosts in Our Classrooms, or:
John Dewey Meets Ceauşescu
The Promise and the Failures of Civic
Education in Romania
ISBN 3-89821-416-8

26 John B. Dunlop
The 2002 Dubrovka and 2004 Beslan
Hostage Crises
A Critique of Russian Counter-Terrorism
With a foreword by Donald N. Jensen
ISBN 3-89821-608-X

27 Peter Koller
Das touristische Potenzial von
Kam''janec'–Podil's'kyj
Eine fremdenverkehrsgeographische
Untersuchung der Zukunftsperspektiven und
Maßnahmenplanung zur
Destinationsentwicklung des „ukrainischen
Rothenburg"
Mit einem Vorwort von Kristiane Klemm
ISBN 3-89821-640-3

28 Françoise Daucé, Elisabeth Sieca-
Kozlowski (Eds.)
Dedovshchina in the Post-Soviet
Military
Hazing of Russian Army Conscripts in a
Comparative Perspective
With a foreword by Dale Herspring
ISBN 3-89821-616-0

29 Florian Strasser
Zivilgesellschaftliche Einflüsse auf die Orange Revolution
Die gewaltlose Massenbewegung und die ukrainische Wahlkrise 2004
Mit einem Vorwort von Egbert Jahn
ISBN 3-89821-648-9

30 Rebecca S. Katz
The Georgian Regime Crisis of 2003-2004
A Case Study in Post-Soviet Media Representation of Politics, Crime and Corruption
ISBN 3-89821-413-3

31 Vladimir Kantor
Willkür oder Freiheit
Beiträge zur russischen Geschichtsphilosophie
Ediert von Dagmar Herrmann sowie mit einem Vorwort versehen von Leonid Luks
ISBN 3-89821-589-X

32 Laura A. Victoir
The Russian Land Estate Today
A Case Study of Cultural Politics in Post-Soviet Russia
With a foreword by Priscilla Roosevelt
ISBN 3-89821-426-5

33 Ivan Katchanovski
Cleft Countries
Regional Political Divisions and Cultures in Post-Soviet Ukraine and Moldova
With a foreword by Francis Fukuyama
ISBN 3-89821-558-X

34 Florian Mühlfried
Postsowjetische Feiern
Das Georgische Bankett im Wandel
Mit einem Vorwort von Kevin Tuite
ISBN 3-89821-601-2

35 Roger Griffin, Werner Loh, Andreas Umland (Eds.)
Fascism Past and Present, West and East
An International Debate on Concepts and Cases in the Comparative Study of the Extreme Right
With an afterword by Walter Laqueur
ISBN 3-89821-674-8

36 Sebastian Schlegel
Der „Weiße Archipel"
Sowjetische Atomstädte 1945-1991
Mit einem Geleitwort von Thomas Bohn
ISBN 3-89821-679-9

37 Vyacheslav Likhachev
Political Anti-Semitism in Post-Soviet Russia
Actors and Ideas in 1991-2003
Edited and translated from Russian by Eugene Veklerov
ISBN 3-89821-529-6

38 Josette Baer (Ed.)
Preparing Liberty in Central Europe
Political Texts from the Spring of Nations 1848 to the Spring of Prague 1968
With a foreword by Zdeněk V. David
ISBN 3-89821-546-6

39 Михаил Лукьянов
Российский консерватизм и реформа, 1907-1914
С предисловием Марка Д. Стейнберга
ISBN 3-89821-503-2

40 Nicola Melloni
Market Without Economy
The 1998 Russian Financial Crisis
With a foreword by Eiji Furukawa
ISBN 3-89821-407-9

41 Dmitrij Chmelnizki
Die Architektur Stalins
Bd. 1: Studien zu Ideologie und Stil
Bd. 2: Bilddokumentation
Mit einem Vorwort von Bruno Flierl
ISBN 3-89821-515-6

42 Katja Yafimava
Post-Soviet Russian-Belarussian Relationships
The Role of Gas Transit Pipelines
With a foreword by Jonathan P. Stern
ISBN 3-89821-655-1

43 Boris Chavkin
Verflechtungen der deutschen und russischen Zeitgeschichte
Aufsätze und Archivfunde zu den Beziehungen Deutschlands und der Sowjetunion von 1917 bis 1991
Ediert von Markus Edlinger sowie mit einem Vorwort versehen von Leonid Luks
ISBN 3-89821-756-6

44   Anastasija Grynenko in
     Zusammenarbeit mit Claudia Dathe
     Die Terminologie des Gerichtswesens
     der Ukraine und Deutschlands im
     Vergleich
     Eine übersetzungswissenschaftliche Analyse
     juristischer Fachbegriffe im Deutschen,
     Ukrainischen und Russischen
     Mit einem Vorwort von Ulrich Hartmann
     ISBN 3-89821-691-8

45   Anton Burkov
     The Impact of the European
     Convention on Human Rights on
     Russian Law
     Legislation and Application in 1996-2006
     With a foreword by Françoise Hampson
     ISBN 978-3-89821-639-5

46   Stina Torjesen, Indra Overland (Eds.)
     International Election Observers in
     Post-Soviet Azerbaijan
     Geopolitical Pawns or Agents of Change?
     ISBN 978-3-89821-743-9

47   Taras Kuzio
     Ukraine – Crimea – Russia
     Triangle of Conflict
     ISBN 978-3-89821-761-3

48   Claudia Šabić
     "Ich erinnere mich nicht, aber L'viv!"
     Zur Funktion kultureller Faktoren für die
     Institutionalisierung und Entwicklung einer
     ukrainischen Region
     Mit einem Vorwort von Melanie Tatur
     ISBN 978-3-89821-752-1

49   Marlies Bilz
     Tatarstan in der Transformation
     Nationaler Diskurs und Politische Praxis
     1988-1994
     Mit einem Vorwort von Frank Golczewski
     ISBN 978-3-89821-722-4

50   Марлен Ларюэль (ред.)
     Современные интерпретации
     русского национализма
     ISBN 978-3-89821-795-8

51   Sonja Schüler
     Die ethnische Dimension der Armut
     Roma im postsozialistischen Rumänien
     Mit einem Vorwort von Anton Sterbling
     ISBN 978-3-89821-776-7

52   Галина Кожевникова
     Радикальный национализм в России
     и противодействие ему
     Сборник докладов Центра «Сова» за 2004-
     2007 гг.
     С предисловием Александра Верховского
     ISBN 978-3-89821-721-7

53   Галина Кожевникова и Владимир
     Прибыловский
     Российская власть в биографиях I
     Высшие должностные лица РФ в 2004 г.
     ISBN 978-3-89821-796-5

54   Галина Кожевникова и Владимир
     Прибыловский
     Российская власть в биографиях II
     Члены Правительства РФ в 2004 г.
     ISBN 978-3-89821-797-2

55   Галина Кожевникова и Владимир
     Прибыловский
     Российская власть в биографиях III
     Руководители федеральных служб и
     агентств РФ в 2004 г.
     ISBN 978-3-89821-798-9

56   Ileana Petroniu
     Privatisierung in
     Transformationsökonomien
     Determinanten der Restrukturierungs-
     Bereitschaft am Beispiel Polens, Rumäniens
     und der Ukraine
     Mit einem Vorwort von Rainer W. Schäfer
     ISBN 978-3-89821-790-3

57   Christian Wipperfürth
     Russland und seine GUS-Nachbarn
     Hintergründe, aktuelle Entwicklungen und
     Konflikte in einer ressourcenreichen Region
     ISBN 978-3-89821-801-6

58   Togzhan Kassenova
     From Antagonism to Partnership
     The Uneasy Path of the U.S.-Russian
     Cooperative Threat Reduction
     With a foreword by Christoph Bluth
     ISBN 978-3-89821-707-1

59   Alexander Höllwerth
     Das sakrale eurasische Imperium des
     Aleksandr Dugin
     Eine Diskursanalyse zum postsowjetischen
     russischen Rechtsextremismus
     Mit einem Vorwort von Dirk Uffelmann
     ISBN 978-3-89821-813-9

60 Олег Рябов
«Россия-Матушка»
Национализм, гендер и война в России XX века
С предисловием Елены Гощило
ISBN 978-3-89821-487-2

61 Ivan Maistrenko
Borot'bism
A Chapter in the History of the Ukrainian Revolution
With a new introduction by Chris Ford
Translated by George S. N. Luckyj with the assistance of Ivan L. Rudnytsky
ISBN 978-3-89821-697-5

62 Maryna Romanets
Anamorphosic Texts and Reconfigured Visions
Improvised Traditions in Contemporary Ukrainian and Irish Literature
ISBN 978-3-89821-576-3

63 Paul D'Anieri and Taras Kuzio (Eds.)
Aspects of the Orange Revolution I
Democratization and Elections in Post-Communist Ukraine
ISBN 978-3-89821-698-2

64 Bohdan Harasymiw in collaboration with Oleh S. Ilnytzkyj (Eds.)
Aspects of the Orange Revolution II
Information and Manipulation Strategies in the 2004 Ukrainian Presidential Elections
ISBN 978-3-89821-699-9

65 Ingmar Bredies, Andreas Umland and Valentin Yakushik (Eds.)
Aspects of the Orange Revolution III
The Context and Dynamics of the 2004 Ukrainian Presidential Elections
ISBN 978-3-89821-803-0

66 Ingmar Bredies, Andreas Umland and Valentin Yakushik (Eds.)
Aspects of the Orange Revolution IV
Foreign Assistance and Civic Action in the 2004 Ukrainian Presidential Elections
ISBN 978-3-89821-808-5

67 Ingmar Bredies, Andreas Umland and Valentin Yakushik (Eds.)
Aspects of the Orange Revolution V
Institutional Observation Reports on the 2004 Ukrainian Presidential Elections
ISBN 978-3-89821-809-2

68 Taras Kuzio (Ed.)
Aspects of the Orange Revolution VI
Post-Communist Democratic Revolutions in Comparative Perspective
ISBN 978-3-89821-820-7

69 Tim Bohse
Autoritarismus statt Selbstverwaltung
Die Transformation der kommunalen Politik in der Stadt Kaliningrad 1990-2005
Mit einem Geleitwort von Stefan Troebst
ISBN 978-3-89821-782-8

70 David Rupp
Die Rußländische Föderation und die russischsprachige Minderheit in Lettland
Eine Fallstudie zur Anwaltspolitik Moskaus gegenüber den russophonen Minderheiten im „Nahen Ausland" von 1991 bis 2002
Mit einem Vorwort von Helmut Wagner
ISBN 978-3-89821-778-1

71 Taras Kuzio
Theoretical and Comparative Perspectives on Nationalism
New Directions in Cross-Cultural and Post-Communist Studies
With a foreword by Paul Robert Magocsi
ISBN 978-3-89821-815-3

72 Christine Teichmann
Die Hochschultransformation im heutigen Osteuropa
Kontinuität und Wandel bei der Entwicklung des postkommunistischen Universitätswesens
Mit einem Vorwort von Oskar Anweiler
ISBN 978-3-89821-842-9

73 Julia Kusznir
Der politische Einfluss von Wirtschaftseliten in russischen Regionen
Eine Analyse am Beispiel der Erdöl- und Erdgasindustrie, 1992-2005
Mit einem Vorwort von Wolfgang Eichwede
ISBN 978-3-89821-821-4

74 Alena Vysotskaya
Russland, Belarus und die EU-Osterweiterung
Zur Minderheitenfrage und zum Problem der Freizügigkeit des Personenverkehrs
Mit einem Vorwort von Katlijn Malfliet
ISBN 978-3-89821-822-1

75 Heiko Pleines (Hrsg.)
Corporate Governance in postsozialistischen Volkswirtschaften
ISBN 978-3-89821-766-8

76 Stefan Ihrig
Wer sind die Moldawier?
Rumänismus versus Moldowanismus in Historiographie und Schulbüchern der Republik Moldova, 1991-2006
Mit einem Vorwort von Holm Sundhaussen
ISBN 978-3-89821-466-7

77 Galina Kozhevnikova in collaboration with Alexander Verkhovsky and Eugene Veklerov
Ultra-Nationalism and Hate Crimes in Contemporary Russia
The 2004-2006 Annual Reports of Moscow's SOVA Center
With a foreword by Stephen D. Shenfield
ISBN 978-3-89821-868-9

78 Florian Küchler
The Role of the European Union in Moldova's Transnistria Conflict
With a foreword by Christopher Hill
ISBN 978-3-89821-850-4

79 Bernd Rechel
The Long Way Back to Europe
Minority Protection in Bulgaria
With a foreword by Richard Crampton
ISBN 978-3-89821-863-4

80 Peter W. Rodgers
Nation, Region and History in Post-Communist Transitions
Identity Politics in Ukraine, 1991-2006
With a foreword by Vera Tolz
ISBN 978-3-89821-903-7

81 Stephanie Solywoda
The Life and Work of Semen L. Frank
A Study of Russian Religious Philosophy
With a foreword by Philip Walters
ISBN 978-3-89821-457-5

82 Vera Sokolova
Cultural Politics of Ethnicity
Discourses on Roma in Communist Czechoslovakia
ISBN 978-3-89821-864-1

83 Natalya Shevchik Ketenci
Kazakhstani Enterprises in Transition
The Role of Historical Regional Development in Kazakhstan's Post-Soviet Economic Transformation
ISBN 978-3-89821-831-3

84 Martin Malek, Anna Schor-Tschudnowskaja (Hrsg.)
Europa im Tschetschenienkrieg
Zwischen politischer Ohnmacht und Gleichgültigkeit
Mit einem Vorwort von Lipchan Basajewa
ISBN 978-3-89821-676-0

85 Stefan Meister
Das postsowjetische Universitätswesen zwischen nationalem und internationalem Wandel
Die Entwicklung der regionalen Hochschule in Russland als Gradmesser der Systemtransformation
Mit einem Vorwort von Joan DeBardeleben
ISBN 978-3-89821-891-7

86 Konstantin Sheiko in collaboration with Stephen Brown
Nationalist Imaginings of the Russian Past
Anatolii Fomenko and the Rise of Alternative History in Post-Communist Russia
With a foreword by Donald Ostrowski
ISBN 978-3-89821-915-0

87 Sabine Jenni
Wie stark ist das „Einige Russland"?
Zur Parteibindung der Eliten und zum Wahlerfolg der Machtpartei im Dezember 2007
Mit einem Vorwort von Klaus Armingeon
ISBN 978-3-89821-961-7

88 Thomas Borén
Meeting-Places of Transformation
Urban Identity, Spatial Representations and Local Politics in Post-Soviet St Petersburg
ISBN 978-3-89821-739-2

89 Aygul Ashirova
Stalinismus und Stalin-Kult in Zentralasien
Turkmenistan 1924-1953
Mit einem Vorwort von Leonid Luks
ISBN 978-3-89821-987-7

90 Leonid Luks
    Freiheit oder imperiale Größe?
    Essays zu einem russischen Dilemma
    ISBN 978-3-8382-0011-8

91 Christopher Gilley
    The 'Change of Signposts' in the
    Ukrainian Emigration
    A Contribution to the History of
    Sovietophilism in the 1920s
    With a foreword by Frank Golczewski
    ISBN 978-3-89821-965-5

92 Philipp Casula, Jeronim Perovic
    (Eds.)
    Identities and Politics
    During the Putin Presidency
    The Discursive Foundations of Russia's
    Stability
    With a foreword by Heiko Haumann
    ISBN 978-3-8382-0015-6

93 Marcel Viëtor
    Europa und die Frage
    nach seinen Grenzen im Osten
    Zur Konstruktion ‚europäischer Identität' in
    Geschichte und Gegenwart
    Mit einem Vorwort von Albrecht Lehmann
    ISBN 978-3-8382-0045-3

94 Ben Hellman, Andrei Rogachevskii
    Filming the Unfilmable
    Casper Wrede's 'One Day in the Life
    of Ivan Denisovich'
    Second, Revised and Expanded Edition
    ISBN 978-3-8382-0044-6

95 Eva Fuchslocher
    Vaterland, Sprache, Glaube
    Orthodoxie und Nationenbildung
    am Beispiel Georgiens
    Mit einem Vorwort von Christina von Braun
    ISBN 978-3-89821-884-9

96 Vladimir Kantor
    Das Westlertum und der Weg
    Russlands
    Zur Entwicklung der russischen Literatur und
    Philosophie
    Ediert von Dagmar Herrmann
    Mit einem Beitrag von Nikolaus Lobkowicz
    ISBN 978-3-8382-0102-3

97 Kamran Musayev
    Die postsowjetische Transformation
    im Baltikum und Südkaukasus
    Eine vergleichende Untersuchung der
    politischen Entwicklung Lettlands und
    Aserbaidschans 1985-2009
    Mit einem Vorwort von Leonid Luks
    Ediert von Sandro Henschel
    ISBN 978-3-8382-0103-0

98 Tatiana Zhurzhenko
    Borderlands into Bordered Lands
    Geopolitics of Identity in Post-Soviet Ukraine
    With a foreword by Dieter Segert
    ISBN 978-3-8382-0042-2

99 Кирилл Галушко, Лидия Смола
    (ред.)
    Пределы падения – варианты
    украинского будущего
    Аналитико-прогностические исследования
    ISBN 978-3-8382-0148-1

100 Michael Minkenberg (ed.)
    Historical Legacies and the Radical
    Right in Post-Cold War Central and
    Eastern Europe
    With an afterword by Sabrina P. Ramet
    ISBN 978-3-8382-0124-5

101 David-Emil Wickström
    Rocking St. Petersburg
    Transcultural Flows and Identity Politics in
    the St. Petersburg Popular Music Scene
    With a foreword by Yngvar B. Steinholt
    Second, Revised and Expanded Edition
    ISBN 978-3-8382-0100-9

102 Eva Zabka
    Eine neue „Zeit der Wirren"?
    Der spät- und postsowjetische Systemwandel
    1985-2000 im Spiegel russischer
    gesellschaftspolitischer Diskurse
    Mit einem Vorwort von Margareta Mommsen
    ISBN 978-3-8382-0161-0

103 Ulrike Ziemer
    Ethnic Belonging, Gender and
    Cultural Practices
    Youth Identitites in Contemporary Russia
    With a foreword by Anoop Nayak
    ISBN 978-3-8382-0152-8

104 **Ksenia Chepikova**
,Einiges Russland' - eine zweite KPdSU?
Aspekte der Identitätskonstruktion einer postsowjetischen „Partei der Macht"
Mit einem Vorwort von Torsten Oppelland
ISBN 978-3-8382-0311-9

105 **Леонид Люкс**
Западничество или евразийство? Демократия или идеократия?
Сборник статей об исторических дилеммах России
С предисловием Владимира Кантора
ISBN 978-3-8382-0211-2

106 **Anna Dost**
Das russische Verfassungsrecht auf dem Weg zum Föderalismus und zurück
Zum Konflikt von Rechtsnormen und -wirklichkeit in der Russländischen Föderation von 1991 bis 2009
Mit einem Vorwort von Alexander Blankenagel
ISBN 978-3-8382-0292-1

107 **Philipp Herzog**
Sozialistische Völkerfreundschaft, nationaler Widerstand oder harmloser Zeitvertreib?
Zur politischen Funktion der Volkskunst im sowjetischen Estland
Mit einem Vorwort von Andreas Kappeler
ISBN 978-3-8382-0216-7

108 **Marlène Laruelle (ed.)**
Russian Nationalism, Foreign Policy, and Identity Debates in Putin's Russia
New Ideological Patterns after the Orange Revolution
ISBN 978-3-8382-0325-6

109 **Michail Logvinov**
Russlands Kampf gegen den internationalen Terrorismus
Eine kritische Bestandsaufnahme des Bekämpfungsansatzes
Mit einem Geleitwort von Hans-Henning Schröder
und einem Vorwort von Eckhard Jesse
ISBN 978-3-8382-0329-4

110 **John B. Dunlop**
The Moscow Bombings of September 1999
Examinations of Russian Terrorist Attacks at the Onset of Vladimir Putin's Rule
Second, Revised and Expanded Edition
ISBN 978-3-8382-0388-1

111 **Андрей А. Ковалёв**
Свидетельство из-за кулис российской политики I
Можно ли делать добро из зла?
(Воспоминания и размышления о последних советских и первых послесоветских годах)
With a foreword by Peter Reddaway
ISBN 978-3-8382-0302-7

112 **Андрей А. Ковалёв**
Свидетельство из-за кулис российской политики II
Угроза для себя и окружающих
(Наблюдения и предостережения относительно происходящего после 2000 г.)
ISBN 978-3-8382-0303-4

113 **Bernd Kappenberg**
Zeichen setzen für Europa
Der Gebrauch europäischer lateinischer Sonderzeichen in der deutschen Öffentlichkeit
Mit einem Vorwort von Peter Schlobinski
ISBN 978-3-89821-749-1

114 **Ivo Mijnssen**
The Quest for an Ideal Youth in Putin's Russia I
Back to Our Future! History, Modernity, and Patriotism according to *Nashi*, 2005-2013
With a foreword by Jeronim Perović
Second, Revised and Expanded Edition
ISBN 978-3-8382-0368-3

115 **Jussi Lassila**
The Quest for an Ideal Youth in Putin's Russia II
The Search for Distinctive Conformism in the Political Communication of *Nashi,* 2005-2009
With a foreword by Kirill Postoutenko
Second, Revised and Expanded Edition
ISBN 978-3-8382-0415-4

116 **Valerio Trabandt**
Neue Nachbarn, gute Nachbarschaft?
Die EU als internationaler Akteur am Beispiel ihrer Demokratieförderung in Belarus und der Ukraine 2004-2009
Mit einem Vorwort von Jutta Joachim
ISBN 978-3-8382-0437-6

117　Fabian Pfeiffer
　　　Estlands Außen- und Sicherheitspolitik I
　　　Der estnische Atlantizismus nach der
　　　wiedererlangten Unabhängigkeit 1991-2004
　　　Mit einem Vorwort von Helmut Hubel
　　　ISBN 978-3-8382-0127-6

118　Jana Podßuweit
　　　Estlands Außen- und Sicherheitspolitik II
　　　Handlungsoptionen eines Kleinstaates im
　　　Rahmen seiner EU-Mitgliedschaft (2004-2008)
　　　Mit einem Vorwort von Helmut Hubel
　　　ISBN 978-3-8382-0440-6

119　Karin Pointner
　　　Estlands Außen- und Sicherheitspolitik III
　　　Eine gedächtnispolitische Analyse estnischer
　　　Entwicklungskooperation 2006-2010
　　　Mit einem Vorwort von Karin Liebhart
　　　ISBN 978-3-8382-0435-2

120　Ruslana Vovk
　　　Die Offenheit der ukrainischen
　　　Verfassung für das Völkerrecht und
　　　die europäische Integration
　　　Mit einem Vorwort von Alexander
　　　Blankenagel
　　　ISBN 978-3-8382-0481-9

121　Mykhaylo Banakh
　　　Die Relevanz der Zivilgesellschaft
　　　bei den postkommunistischen
　　　Transformationsprozessen in mittel-
　　　und osteuropäischen Ländern
　　　Das Beispiel der spät- und postsowjetischen
　　　Ukraine 1986-2009
　　　Mit einem Vorwort von Gerhard Simon
　　　ISBN 978-3-8382-0499-4

122　Michael Moser
　　　Language Policy and the Discourse on
　　　Languages in Ukraine under President
　　　Viktor Yanukovych (25 February
　　　2010–28 October 2012)
　　　ISBN 978-3-8382-0497-0 (Paperback edition)
　　　ISBN 978-3-8382-0507-6 (Hardcover edition)

123　Nicole Krome
　　　Russischer Netzwerkkapitalismus
　　　Restrukturierungsprozesse in der
　　　Russischen Föderation am Beispiel des
　　　Luftfahrtunternehmens "Aviastar"
　　　Mit einem Vorwort von Petra Stykow
　　　ISBN 978-3-8382-0534-2

124　David R. Marples
　　　'Our Glorious Past'
　　　Lukashenka's Belarus and
　　　the Great Patriotic War
　　　ISBN 978-3-8382-0574-8 (Paperback edition)
　　　ISBN 978-3-8382-0675-2 (Hardcover edition)

125　Ulf Walther
　　　Russlands "neuer Adel"
　　　Die Macht des Geheimdienstes von
　　　Gorbatschow bis Putin
　　　Mit einem Vorwort von Hans-Georg Wieck
　　　ISBN 978-3-8382-0584-7

126　Simon Geissbühler (Hrsg.)
　　　Kiew – Revolution 3.0
　　　Der Euromaidan 2013/14 und die
　　　Zukunftsperspektiven der Ukraine
　　　ISBN 978-3-8382-0581-6 (Paperback edition)
　　　ISBN 978-3-8382-0681-3 (Hardcover edition)

127　Andrey Makarychev
　　　Russia and the EU
　　　in a Multipolar World
　　　Discourses, Identities, Norms
　　　With a foreword by Klaus Segbers
　　　ISBN 978-3-8382-0629-5

128　Roland Scharff
　　　Kasachstan als postsowjetischer
　　　Wohlfahrtsstaat
　　　Die Transformation des sozialen
　　　Schutzsystems
　　　Mit einem Vorwort von Joachim Ahrens
　　　ISBN 978-3-8382-0622-6

129　Katja Grupp
　　　Bild Lücke Deutschland
　　　Kaliningrader Studierende sprechen über
　　　Deutschland
　　　Mit einem Vorwort von Martin Schulz
　　　ISBN 978-3-8382-0552-6

130　Konstantin Sheiko, Stephen Brown
　　　History as Therapy
　　　Alternative History and Nationalist
　　　Imaginings in Russia, 1991-2014
　　　ISBN 978-3-8382-0665-3

131 Elisa Kriza
Alexander Solzhenitsyn: Cold War Icon, Gulag Author, Russian Nationalist?
A Study of the Western Reception of his Literary Writings, Historical Interpretations, and Political Ideas
With a foreword by Andrei Rogatchevski
ISBN 978-3-8382-0589-2 (Paperback edition)
ISBN 978-3-8382-0690-5 (Hardcover edition)

132 Serghei Golunov
The Elephant in the Room
Corruption and Cheating in Russian Universities
ISBN 978-3-8382-0570-0

133 Manja Hussner, Rainer Arnold (Hgg.)
Verfassungsgerichtsbarkeit in Zentralasien I
Sammlung von Verfassungstexten
ISBN 978-3-8382-0595-3

134 Nikolay Mitrokhin
Die "Russische Partei"
Die Bewegung der russischen Nationalisten in der UdSSR 1953-1985
Aus dem Russischen übertragen von einem Übersetzerteam unter der Leitung von Larisa Schippel
ISBN 978-3-8382-0024-8

135 Manja Hussner, Rainer Arnold (Hgg.)
Verfassungsgerichtsbarkeit in Zentralasien II
Sammlung von Verfassungstexten
ISBN 978-3-8382-0597-7

136 Manfred Zeller
Das sowjetische Fieber
Fußballfans im poststalinistischen Vielvölkerreich
Mit einem Vorwort von Nikolaus Katzer
ISBN 978-3-8382-0757-5

137 Kristin Schreiter
Stellung und Entwicklungspotential zivilgesellschaftlicher Gruppen in Russland
Menschenrechtsorganisationen im Vergleich
ISBN 978-3-8382-0673-8

138 David R. Marples, Frederick V. Mills (eds.)
Ukraine's Euromaidan
Analyses of a Civil Revolution
ISBN 978-3-8382-0660-8

139 Bernd Kappenberg
Setting Signs for Europe
Why Diacritics Matter for European Integration
With a foreword by Peter Schlobinski
ISBN 978-3-8382-0663-9

140 René Lenz
Internationalisierung, Kooperation und Transfer
Externe bildungspolitische Akteure in der Russischen Föderation
Mit einem Vorwort von Frank Ettrich
ISBN 978-3-8382-0751-3

141 Juri Plusnin, Yana Zausaeva, Natalia Zhidkevich, Artemy Pozanenko
Wandering Workers
Mores, Behavior, Way of Life, and Political Status of Domestic Russian Labor Migrants
Translated by Julia Kazantseva
ISBN 978-3-8382-0653-0

142 Matthew Kott, David J. Smith (eds.)
Latvia – A Work in Progress?
100 Years of State- and Nation-building
ISBN 978-3-8382-0648-6

143 Инна Чувычкина (ред.)
Экспортные нефте- и газопроводы на постсоветском пространстве
Анализ трубопроводной политики в свете теории международных отношений
ISBN 978-3-8382-0822-0

144 Johann Zajaczkowski
Russland – eine pragmatische Großmacht?
Eine rollentheoretische Untersuchung russischer Außenpolitik am Beispiel der Zusammenarbeit mit den USA nach 9/11 und des Georgienkrieges von 2008
Mit einem Vorwort von Siegfried Schieder
ISBN 978-3-8382-0837-4

145 Boris Popivanov
Changing Images of the Left in Bulgaria
The Challenge of Post-Communism in the Early 21st Century
ISBN 978-3-8382-0667-7

146 Lenka Krátká
     A History of the Czechoslovak Ocean
     Shipping Company 1948-1989
     How a Small, Landlocked Country Ran
     Maritime Business During the Cold War
     ISBN 978-3-8382-0666-0

147 Alexander Sergunin
     Explaining Russian Foreign Policy
     Behavior
     Theory and Practice
     ISBN 978-3-8382-0752-0

148 Darya Malyutina
     Migrant Friendships in
     a Super-Diverse City
     Russian-Speakers and their Social
     Relationships in London in the 21st Century
     With a foreword by Claire Dwyer
     ISBN 978-3-8382-0652-3

149 Alexander Sergunin, Valery Konyshev
     Russia in the Arctic
     Hard or Soft Power?
     ISBN 978-3-8382-0753-7

150 John J. Maresca
     Helsinki Revisited
     A Key U.S. Negotiator's Memoirs
     on the Development of the CSCE into the
     OSCE
     With a foreword by Hafiz Pashayev
     ISBN 978-3-8382-0852-7

151 Jardar Østbø
     The New Third Rome
     Readings of a Russian Nationalist Myth
     With a foreword by Pål Kolstø
     ISBN 978-3-8382-0870-1

152 Simon Kordonsky
     Socio-Economic Foundations of the
     Russian Post-Soviet Regime
     The Resource-Based Economy and Estate-
     Based Social Structure of Contemporary
     Russia
     With a foreword by Svetlana Barsukova
     ISBN 978-3-8382-0775-9

153 Duncan Leitch
     Assisting Reform in Post-Communist
     Ukraine 2000–2012
     The Illusions of Donors and the Disillusion of
     Beneficiaries
     With a foreword by Kataryna Wolczuk
     ISBN 978-3-8382-0844-2

154 Abel Polese
     Limits of a Post-Soviet State
     How Informality Replaces, Renegotiates, and
     Reshapes Governance in Contemporary
     Ukraine
     With a foreword by Colin Williams
     ISBN 978-3-8382-0845-9

155 Mikhail Suslov (ed.)
     Digital Orthodoxy in the Post-Soviet
     World
     The Russian Orthodox Church and Web 2.0
     ISBN 978-3-8382-0871-8

156 Leonid Luks
     "Zwei Sonderwege"? Russisch-
     deutsche Parallelen und Kontraste
     (1917-2014)
     Vergleichende Essays
     ISBN 978-3-8382-0823-7

157 Vladimir V. Karacharovskiy, Ovsey I.
     Shkaratan, Gordey A. Yastrebov
     Towards a New Russian Work Culture
     Can Western Companies and Expatriates
     Change Russian Society?
     With a foreword by Elena N. Danilova
     Translated by Julia Kazantseva
     ISBN 978-3-8382-0902-9

***ibidem*-**Verlag

Melchiorstr. 15

D-70439 Stuttgart

info@ibidem-verlag.de

www.ibidem-verlag.de
www.ibidem.eu
www.edition-noema.de
www.autorenbetreuung.de